HARPER FORUM BOOKS

General Editor Martin E. Marty

HARPER FORUM BOOKS
Martin E. Marty, *General Editor*

Published:

Personality and Religion

The Role of Religion in Personality Development

edited by

William A. Sadler, Jr.

1817

HARPER & ROW, PUBLISHERS

New York and Evanston

The reader will notice that the authors represented in this volume sometimes vary in their spellings and systems of reference. This is because the extracts are taken from previously published works, and we have not attempted to impose a consistency which could conceivably be distasteful to an individual author or publisher.

FIRST UNITED STATES EDITION

Published as a Harper Forum Book, 1970,
by Harper & Row, Publishers, Inc., New York and Evanston.

LIBRARY OF CONGRESS CATALOG CARD NUMBER: 74-109076

CONTENTS

Contents

HARPER FORUM BOOKS

Often dismissed with a shrug or accepted with thoughtless piety in the past, religion today belongs in the forum of study and discussion. In our society, this is particularly evident in both public and private colleges and universities. Scholars are exploring the claims of theology, the religious roots of culture, and the relation between beliefs and the various areas or disciplines of life. Students have not until now had a series of books which could serve as reliable resources for class or private study in a time when inquiry into religion is undertaken with new freedom and a sense of urgency. *Harper Forum Books* are intended for these purposes. Eminent scholars have selected and introduced the readings. Respectful of the spirit of religion as they are, they do not shun controversy. With these books a new generation can confront religion through exposure to significant minds in theology and related humanistic fields.

MARTIN E. MARTY, GENERAL EDITOR
The Divinity School
The University of Chicago

ACKNOWLEDGMENTS

In addition to authors and publishers who have kindly granted me permission to include material here, I am grateful to the editor of this series and to several contributors for their thoughtful assistance; to Professor George Fetter, who has been extraordinarily helpful to me while preparing this volume; and to my students, who have so often taught me more than I had hoped to teach them.

I

THE SCIENTIFIC STUDY OF RELIGION AND PERSONALITY

William A. Sadler, Jr.

PREFACE

SOME ISSUES in the forum of discussion about religion are new; the relationship between science and religion is an example. Debate about the relationship between personality and religion, however, reaches back long before either concept had begun to receive careful definition.[1] The relationship between personality and religion has received much attention particularly within the Judaeo-Christian tradition, where there has been intense preoccupation with man's inner life and disciplined examination of effects religion has been thought to produce.[2] It has been widely believed that religion has had some marked effect upon the life-style of individuals. Some have claimed that only religion can produce the virtues of saintliness; others, particularly prophets and skeptics, have maintained that there is nothing quite like religion to produce the special vice of hypocrisy. Some have asserted that nothing nourishes the life of the human spirit so effectively as religion does; others have testified that religion stifles man's spirit by dulling his senses and intelligence, warping his personal development, corrupting his natural virtues, and injuring his interpersonal relationships. Those interested in reaching some trustworthy insights into the relationship between religion and personality will find the new kind of investigation represented in this volume of special interest. Scientific examination in this area can lead to an informed, intelligent understanding of religion in some of its aspects; and it also throws light upon significant areas of personality and how these are open to the influence of religion.

Religious studies have rather recently begun to learn from research into personality. Unfortunately the personality sciences often exclude entirely from their scope the role religion still plays in shaping interests, attitudes, values, goals, behavior, and relationships. That it is difficult to measure the impact of religion upon personality formation cannot be denied; but it is perhaps no more difficult than trying to assess the impact of television upon human development and relationships. And knowledge of the former is at least as important as the latter. Whatever view one may hold about the origin and end of religion, it should be recognized that personality and religion have the same roots; discovering obscure aspects of one will lead to greater insight into the other. Our understanding of both personality and religion will be enhanced by the study of their relationship.

At the outset it should be made clear that the material in this volume does not represent theology. Except for one chapter written by a hospital chaplain, the selections were drawn entirely from the writings of eminent social scientists who have in one way or another considered the relationship between personality and religion. However, their viewpoints, methods, and findings differ; so do the kinds of religion they have studied. One assumption underlying this volume is that we need to use an interdisciplinary approach in the social sciences if we are to attain a fair understanding of religion as well as of personality. In addition to various kinds of psychology, I have chosen material which represents at least some types of sociology, anthropology, and history. I also feel that the focus in this field of inquiry has been too narrowly concentrated upon Western forms of Christianity. The varieties of religion considered here include some forms of religion found among Indians, Chinese, and primitive societies in addition to various forms, both past and present, of Pentecostalism, Protestantism, Catholicism, and Judaism. As different as their objects of study and their methods may be, the social scientists included here seem to share a common attitude: they are ambivalent toward religion, though this ambivalence ranges from the preponderantly negative position of Freud to the very positive view of Menninger. Ambivalence indicates a subjective bias on the part of investigators which has influenced their methods and findings; yet along with ambivalence there has been a strong element of doubt and uncertainty which also is an essential element in legitimate scientific inquiry. Because these scientists questioned traditional assumptions and have probed into areas that are regarded to be highly private and personal, we are now much better informed about many of the complex and mysterious dynamics that constitute the special relationship between personality and religion.

In planning this book I had at first thought that the most logical kind of introduction would be to present in broad outline some historical highlights and major topics pertinent to the scientific study of religion and personality. However, in giving this book a dry run in a seminar of bright college students, I discovered that my logic was irrelevant. Giving attention to general points did not greatly help the students see clearly the advantages and the limitations of this particular form of inquiry. There are often urgent theological questions as well as historical and textual ones which this approach cannot answer. Furthermore, students come to this study with so many differing and discordant views of religion, to say nothing of the equally numerous theories of personality, that the task of examining assumptions, clarifying definitions, and setting guidelines becomes unwieldy. Consequently to establish the framework for the study of religion as set by the personality sciences I found it most helpful to be more concrete and to focus upon one great work by the man who did more than anyone else to lay the foundations for this type of approach. This is one reason why I have devoted so much time and space to an examination of William James's *The Varieties of Religious Experience*. There are, however, other reasons which are equally important.

In addition to being the most significant founder of this particular discipline, James deserves to be given careful consideration because much of what he contributed is still relevant. I believe that many of his insights into the relationship between personality and religion are basically sound; many of the later studies as represented in this book merely refine some of his points. Furthermore, I think that if this scientific branch of inquiry is to advance, it needs to retain James's focus, although it will be necessary to alter his models and his methods. Finally, in his study of religion James made a challenge to the personality sciences, which is as valid as ever. He maintained that no psychology can claim to have achieved a whole picture of personality unless it consider religion and those personal phenomena which often play an important role in it. Because many leading personality scientists today have reached conclusions very similar to those reached by James nearly seventy years ago, we shall do well to re-examine some of his basic contributions. In some ways his insights are more relevant today than ever. Also it is possible to learn much from his omissions and limitations, so that in trying to advance we shall not be long detained by making similar mistakes. In the following pages I place James's psychological study of religion within the context of his own interests and development of thought; from there I move on to criticize him where I believe he was deficient and to appreciate him where he continues to make a valuable contribution to our understanding of personality and religion. In this way it is hoped that we may see more clearly how and why this particular study has developed since his day and what constitutes the nature of the dialogue that is part of it now.

SOME CONTRIBUTIONS OF WILLIAM JAMES

When James delivered his Gifford Lectures in 1901–1902 he was recognized, in Europe especially, as one of the world's most eminent psychologists. His now classic *The Principles of Psychology*[3] is even today being given increasingly wide attention for its significant psychological insights. His approach was unusual in his own time and in some ways it still is. The major focus of James's psychology was the phenomenon of consciousness. Though he paid great attention to physiology, he refused to reduce conscious phenomena to processes in the brain or nervous system; yet at the same time he was devastatingly critical of rationalistic theories which separated consciousness from bodily functions. As a recent book has made clear, James constantly confronted the psychophysical problem though without successfully solving it.[4] When reacting to overly intellectualistic interpretations of consciousness he moved in the direction of behavioristic psychology. Yet he could never bring himself to deny the distinctively human aspects of experience which a physicalist view is inclined to do. In spite of its ambiguities and contradictions, his psychology brought into focus the dynamic life of consciousness, what James referred to as "the stream of consciousness". In his psychology he concentrated not merely upon rational phenomena such as thinking, language, and conceptualization but also upon vital elements of consciousness such as instincts, feelings, emotions, and the will. Furthermore, he attempted to elucidate structures of experience in terms of relationships between consciousness and its field of objects, reflection and the body, psychic continuity and sensation, thinking and feeling, etc. It was a significant accomplishment, and it terminated one aspect of his scientific endeavor; but it did not signify the end of his own development of psychology.

James was a restless, adventurous, creative individual who was constantly pushing toward new insights and methods, often before he had articulated or perfected old ones. In the years immediately preceding his Gifford Lectures he began to formulate a more practical type of psychology that was influenced by his emerging views about the philosophy of pragmatism. Anyone familiar with his *Principles* is bound to notice that many of the concerns and categories found there and in other contemporary psychologies with which James was highly familiar are simply not included in his psychology of religion. Years later in a speech given to the American Philosophical Association he advocated a new, intensified examination of the limits of human powers in every conceivable direction. It was to be "a program of concrete individual psychology ... replete with interesting facts, and [which] points to practical issues superior in importance to anything we know".[5] Such a concrete, individual psychology concentrating upon existential limits was in fact underway in his Gifford Lectures. There is no doubt that *The Varieties of Religious Experience* was a significant pioneering venture not only in the study of religion but also in terms of research into the nature of the self. In the *Principles* he had raised the question: How does a human mind function? In the *Varieties* he asked another question: How does a human being achieve his highest potentialities? One requirement is to become aware of them. More recently another eminent American psychologist commented: "Most of the potentialities of man are never realized, and until we understand them better than we do, they will not be called forth."[6] James would have applauded that statement. In his *Varieties* he was attempting to bring into clear view some of the highest possibilities of human existence. Though he once referred to it as a "study of morbid psychology", his psychology of religion was more than that; it was what his subtitle stated, *A Study in Human Nature*. One of the objectives of his psychology of religion was to achieve a better understanding of selfhood and the potentialities of human existence.

In working out this psychology James came to the conclusion that he had two other goals to work for. In a letter to a friend he wrote:

The problem I have set myself is a hard one: *first* to defend ... "experience" against "philosophy" as being the real backbone of the world's religious life ... and *second* to make the hearer or reader believe, what I myself invincibly do believe, that, although all the special manifestations of religion may have been absurd (I mean its creeds and theories), yet the life of it as a whole is mankind's most important function.[7]

His defence of experience against philosophy, or rather certain types of it, was a central concern of his in the last decades of his life; and it has special relevance to the study of religion. Earlier in his famous essay "The Will to Believe" he had attacked the all too frequent method of imposing habitual categories of interpretation upon strange and unusual phenomena in order to dismiss or discredit them. He argued that the avenue to truth was to be found by returning to experience rather than by resorting merely to words and logic; and this principle obtained whether one was in philosophy or science. A dogmatic attitude was abhorrent to James, no matter whether it existed in religion or in science. In order to overcome the arrogance of dogmatic intellectualism, James sought to demonstrate that even the most precise logical categories emerge in conjunction with man's desires, wishes, and interests. Our non-intellectual nature inevitably influences our most intellectual convictions and concepts, even our interest in truth. As he wrote:

> Our belief in truth itself, for instance, that there is a truth and that our minds and it are made for each other – what is it but a passionate affirmation of desire, in which our social system backs us up? We want to have a truth; we want to believe that our experiments and studies and discussions must put us in a continually better and better position towards it; and on this line we agree to fight out our thinking lives.[8]

His argument here was in agreement with Pascal's affirmation that "all our reasoning reduces itself to feeling";[9] and it was at first not much more popular.[10]

James was attempting to do more than humble intellectual absolutism. His position was also a challenge to habitual, unquestioned skeptical attitudes toward feelings and intuition, which play a crucial role in religious phenomena. There are areas in life, he wrote, "where a fact cannot come at all unless a preliminary faith exists in its coming". Not only in religion but also in interpersonal relationships, and even in science, "the desire for a certain kind of truth . . . brings about that special truth's existence".[11] It is essential, then, that one exercise one's right to believe, not first of all in a god, but in one's own experiences, especially in one's feelings, intuition, and personal insights. Only in this way can an individual reach a fuller understanding of the potentialities of his own self and discover life's mysteries that are usually ignored in the humdrum of ordinary routine. James was calling for a reorientation toward experience in general so as to uncover the existential truth that lies concealed in deeply personal regions such as religious experience.[12]

Because he was so deeply convinced that truth is to be found by

first returning to experience, he was vehemently critical of inter-
preters of religion who centered their intellectual analyses and her-
meneutics upon creeds and theological statements. In the following
passage, so characteristic of James at his ebullient best, we note that
he could be extremely severe in castigating theological intellectualism:

> When I was a boy, I used to think that a closet-naturalist must be the vilest
> type of wretch under the sun. But surely the systematic theologians are the closet-
> naturalists of the deity. . . . What is their deduction of metaphysical attributes
> but a shuffling and matching of pedantic dictionary-adjectives, aloof from morals,
> aloof from human needs, something that might be worked out from the mere
> word "God" by one of those logical machines of wood and brass which recent
> ingenuity has contrived as well as by a man of flesh and blood. They have the
> trail of the serpent over them. One feels that in the theologians' hands, they are
> only a set of titles obtained by a mechanical manipulation of synonyms; verbality
> has stepped into the place of vision, professionalism into that of life. Instead of
> bread we have a stone; instead of a fish, a serpent. Did such conglomeration of
> abstract terms give really the gist of our knowledge of the deity, schools of
> theology might indeed continue to flourish, but religion, vital religion, would
> have taken its flight from this world. What keeps religion going is something else
> than abstract definitions and systems of concatenated adjectives, and something
> different from faculties of theology and their professors. All these things are after-
> effects, secondary accretions upon those phenomena of vital conversation with
> the unseen divine, of which I have shown you so many instances, renewing them-
> selves *in saecula saeculorum* in the lives of humble private men.[13]

Perhaps this rhetorical outburst is unfair to theology as a whole; yet
his argument has the special merit of setting the study of religion into
a new context – the living context of experience rather than a
linguistic context of definitions and assertions. To focus only upon
words is to ignore the most important aspects of both religion and
life. As he put it:

> Philosophy lives in words, but truth and fact well up into our lives in ways
> that exceed verbal formulation. There is in the living act of perception always
> something that glimmers and twinkles and will not be caught, and for which
> reflection comes too late. . . . In the religious sphere, in particular, belief that
> formulas are true can never wholly take the place of personal experience.[14]

Unlike so many of his contemporaries, both those who wanted to
defend religion and those who sought to debunk it, and who took
religious words at face value, James endeavored *to go behind the
words to recover the experiences* from which religious confessions,
myths, and theological statements emerged as secondary manifestations. That he was not completely successful and needed a different model to approach experience I shall discuss later.

It is clear that James's own version of the study of religion and
personality was closely aligned with some of those other interests

that we associate with his writings. It was part of his attack upon narrowly conceived philosophical options such as rationalism and physicalism; and it marked a significant development in his plans to establish a concrete psychology and pragmatic philosophy which turns first of all to experience. In addition it should be recognized that James was also attempting to establish a new science, what he called a "critical Science of Religions". He hoped that the latter might eventually command a general public adherence similar to that commanded by the natural sciences, and he made the following proposal for its formation:

> The science of religion would depend for its original material on facts of personal experience, and would have to square itself with personal experience through all its critical reconstructions. It could never get away from concrete life, or work in a conceptual vacuum. It would forever have to confess, as every science confesses, that the subtlety of nature flies beyond it, and that its formulas are but approximations.[15]

James did not live to see his plan for such a science materialize fully; in fact, for the next several decades there was a rise in the philosophy of religion which to some extent shared James's concern with experience but which did not employ the radical empirical method he had advocated. Only recently has the scientific study of religion come into its own and begun to gain both scientific and academic respectability. Many of the authors included in this volume have played a significant role in the development of this new branch of scientific inquiry. Those who have achieved the most profound insights have been those who, perhaps unwittingly, have attempted to let the data square themselves "with personal experience".[16]

It is also obvious that James went beyond the limitations of science in making a defense of religion; and it is worthwhile considering why he did so. He himself had no formal allegiance to any particular religion and apparently did not have the intense experiences of conversion and regeneration which he defended. His view of organized religion tended to be negative, and these sentiments are shared by many contributors in this volume. When he did upon occasion attend formal religious services he often returned home feeling bored, outraged, frustrated, or depressed. He had grown up in a home that was marked by a very liberal spirit. Though his father had experienced something like a religious conversion and had become caught up with the views of Swedenborg, no appurtenance to any institutional religion was expected or demanded. To some extent James's apologetics for religion were a tribute paid to the memory of his father.[17] But there was more to it.

Though James consistently affirmed a robust, vigorous brand of individualism that to many might seem to contrast with religion, he was also extremely concerned with what he believed to be genuine religious values. Furthermore, he was very sympathetic toward the religious experiences of others and highly appreciative of what he deemed were the distinctive strengths and fine qualities of those experiences. Though he dwelt at length upon the morbid features of some religious experiences, yet he felt that in some cases "a man's religion is the deepest and wisest thing in his life".[18] He was aware that to express such a conviction was to go against the stream of thought in much of the intellectual community of his time; in fact among many of his peers it was an outlandish view. The enlightened studies of religion in his era, as represented by the works of Tylor and Frazer, had attempted to show that religion originated in primitive man's crude endeavors to explain strange and fascinating natural phenomena and to assuage his fears in the presence of them by inventing supernatural categories. Thus organized religion was considered to be largely a survival of primitivism or infantilism; it should be discarded as men come of age in the modern world of science and technology. Others, like Nietzsche, felt that organized religion, and the Judaeo-Christian tradition in particular, originated from the bitter resentment of weaklings toward superior heroic figures who were thereby systematically repressed by a demonic "sacred" institution and constantly tortured by feelings of false guilt. From this perspective, religion should not only be discarded, it should be stamped out. For many in the intellectual community, even if they did not go this far, religion was believed to obstruct progress; and for the sake of truth, freedom, and well-being it should be set aside, except for those too weak and lacking in intelligence to live independently of it. In the face of such critical views, James insisted that religion was neither simply an anachronism in the modern world nor inevitably a hindrance to personal development. He accused the wholesale rejection of religion of being shallow, because it ignored the great function religion has in man's personal experience.

In particular James argued that personal religion, which he segregated from institutional religion, confronts us with the reality of our own individual destinies. While other approaches to truth call our attention to the past or present, religion also beckons us to look to our own future and to raise "particular questions connected with our individual destinies". Personal religion leads us to perceive with deep seriousness the dark, mysterious aspects of our own existence that other disciplines leave out of account and to raise questions about the deepest dimensions of human life. It is only by acknowledging such existential questions, by giving our concern to them, and by "living in the sphere of thought which they open up, that we become profound". And in James's view, "to live thus is to be religious". Thus, he continued, "I unhesitatingly repudiate the survival-theory of religion, as being founded on an egregious mistake."[19] That mistake included an unshakable prejudice that the world is so constructed that such events as genuine religious experiences, including communication with some greater, higher, living reality, simply cannot occur. Since James wrote, the deterministic models so important to nineteenth-century mentalities have been drastically shaken and relativized, so that it is again respectable to give consideration to this appeal to existential concern that James made in behalf of religion and to acknowledge the relevant function of religion respective to personality development in so far as it raises questions about individual human destinies.

Yet here we can see that the science of religion begins to evaluate the object of its study; instead of criticizing the apparent lack of neutrality, we should at this point examine the motives appropriate to this particular science. What does one hope to learn from it and for what purposes? James himself did not give the full answer in explicit form. With respect to his own psychopathological study of religion he wrote that it answers to our "irrepressible curiosity". Furthermore, it meets a desire to understand more precisely what the merits of religion might be by "learning at the same time to what particular dangers of corruption it may also be exposed".[20] Yet there is another reason which has to do with James's pragmatic conception of truth, and which in turn is relevant to his own religious search.

In elucidating the pragmatist's understanding of truth James was moving away from a propositional notion that conceived truth to be in the agreement between thoughts and things. Instead he defined truth in terms of a process in which we verify concepts through experience. Notions are deemed to be true because in experience they have been proven to work for us; true ideas are practical and relevant. There are many different ways, however, that ideas can "work". A philosophical or religious idea can be said to work and thus prove itself if it enables an individual to adapt to "reality's whole setting", and if it leads him in a worthwhile way.[21] In attempting to get at the truth of religion through his new concrete psychology he was more than attempting to enlarge and improve the general understanding of religion; he was also searching for some religious truth which could be true for him and which he could practice. It is better to live the truth than just to know about it. As he remarked at the conclusion of his study:

If religion be a function by which either God's cause or man's cause is to be really advanced, then he who lives the life of it, however narrowly, is a better servant than he who merely knows about it, however much. Knowledge about life is one thing; effective occupation of a place in life, with its dynamic currents passing through your being, is another.[22]

People who are interested in religion but unable to find participation in existing religious institutions palatable or positively meaningful will find James's search for a personal religion especially relevant. He was using the most advanced knowledge of his day and experimenting with new disciplines to assist him in his pursuit of a genuine and workable faith. The truth he discovered about religion did not apply specifically to a god, at least not in a Western sense. Though he had some sense of a living ideal that was greater than himself, he admitted that he did not believe in the kind of personal God which many religions talk about. What he later said of Pragmatism applies also to his scientific study of religion; it is an attempt to widen and enliven "the field of search for God".[23] The primary fact about religion, as he saw it, was not some divine being but a changed attitude toward life and a new appreciation of it: "Not God, but life, more life, a larger, richer, more satisfying life is, in the last analysis, the end of religion. The love of life, at any and every level of development, is the religious impulse."[24] From this perspective, what matters most in religion is not theological content or a prescribed course of action, but what effects a religion has upon an individual personality. He encouraged individuals to search for the religion which was best for them and then to be true to it: "The religion he stands by must be the one which he finds best for *him*, even though there were better individuals, and their religion better for them."[25]

A final reason, then, which James had for developing his new science of religion was not to defend religion as it has been traditionally believed and practiced but to investigate the possibility for individuals to discover more honest and appropriate forms of religious existence than they had been taught. The kind of religion James envisaged for individuals was not to be measured in terms of creeds, codes, rituals, or hierarchies; to him religion was a live option only if it sharpened, not dulled, one's critical abilities, whetted one's appetite for life, led one to discover and to appropriate the highest values of which he was aware, and enabled one to integrate his impulses and his interests with integrity. He insisted that we examine rigorously the dangerous corruptions which some forms of religion inflict upon existence; but it is equally important to remain open to the possibility of an authentic personal religious faith as an individual's way to discover and to actualize life's highest potentialities. The study of religion as formulated by James challenges any view of man to examine religious phenomena before attempting to formulate a picture of the whole personality. At least in certain instances, religion constitutes, as he put it, "one fundamental form of human experience".[26] Some of the authors included in this volume have responded to this kind of challenge and have made significant contributions to our understanding of both religion and personality.

As provocative as James's argument is, one is inevitably dissatisfied because one is never exactly sure just what James meant when he discussed and defended religion. His precise meaning of the term is like a slow moving cloud, omnipresent no matter in which direction you turn, yet constantly changing shape and out of reach. His definition of religion is nearly as classical as his study itself:

Religion, . . . as I now ask you arbitrarily to take it, shall mean for us *the feelings, acts, and experiences of individual men in their solitude, so far as they apprehend themselves to stand in relation to whatever they may consider the divine.*[27]

This definition has proven to be egregiously inadequate, as I shall illustrate later; but in fairness to James it should be pointed out that he himself did not restrict himself to it or refer to it when attempting to redefine religion in the conclusion of his study. He deliberately ignored the institutional aspects of religion, perhaps because in part he disliked religious formalities; unfortunately for his studies, he consequently missed the significance of these institutions which play a large role in most individuals' personal religion. Unlike his colleagues at Harvard such as Henry Adams and George Santayana he also overlooked the esthetic aspect of individual religion, thus omitting from consideration a highly significant factor.[28] Yet in spite of vagueness and important omissions, James did point out what he believed to be a distinct and irreducible structure of religious experience.[29]

In what amounts to a crude phenomenology of religious experience James made the point that religion is essentially distinct from ethics and cannot be reduced to moral awareness and behavior. He illustrated the difference between ethics and religion by characterizing the distinct attitudes of each. The moralist, he said, advises us to keep our belts tight, to be strenuous in pursuit of what ought to be. The man of faith, however, is first of all aware of a Presence which releases him from the tension and compulsion of straining toward an

Absolute Ought. The unique character of the religious message is that it encourages "passivity, not activity; relaxation, not intentness".[30] There is a different kind of awareness to be found in each. In the moral experience there is a sense of *oughtness*, whereas in a genuine religious experience there is a sense of *isness*. The Absolute manifests itself as a Presence which gives man a sense of release from overbearing demands of conscience. Men in a state of faith, he wrote, "know, . . . they have actually *felt* the higher powers, in giving up the tension of their personal will".[31] The issue here has to do with what James believed to be the unique function of religion within the economy of a personality system. In particular what he meant here was the liberating effect that some forms of radical religious experience produce. One way of putting it, said James elsewhere, is to realize that the self occasionally needs to take a moral holiday;[32] a profound religious experience justifies such a holiday. Psychologically speaking, then, religion's unique function is to give "your little private convulsive self a rest". Socially minded religious people, particularly those who think of the prophetic role of religion, will rightly object that James here ignores the vital function that faith has performed in arousing the conscience and giving men the incentive for vigorous moral and social action. Yet even the prophet knows moments of release and peace; it was to such moments in man's personal history that James called special attention.

By differentiating religion from ethics James was suggesting that in religious experience persons can discover a dimension of existence and a mode of perception that are otherwise or usually hidden from view. To say that religion adds to the enchantment of life is another way of calling attention to potentialities that lie dormant in us. Ethics calls attention to the will and its role in personality formation; but in addition to the phenomena of conscience and the will, religion also points to human transcendence, to ecstasy, and the possibility of discovering a larger self. The ethical man may be heroic in facing ugly necessities and even the tedium of everyday life; but the religious man in the state of faith will refuse to absolutize any routine and will find richly meaningful existence in rare moments of ecstasy. The ethical man may rightly accuse the religious man of escaping from responsibilities if he restricts meaningful existence to ecstatic experiences; but the religious man can countercharge that if ethics ignores ecstasy, it does so to the peril of the highest possibilities of personal fulfillment. The issue that James has raised is still very much alive, and it calls into question both the Durkheimian attempt to reduce religion to ethics and the Freudian accusation that religion is essentially a perpetuation of infantile dependency. The unique character of religious experience is re-examined, particularly in the chapter by Maslow, but also at several points in the section dealing with existential crises. James's study is still important because it calls attention to the liberating and creative aspects that can be found in some forms of religious experience. As he indicated, there are types of religious experiences that can make slaves of men; there are others, however, which can set them free. Our task is to learn to tell one from the other.

In arguing for the distinctive function of religion it becomes apparent that James was hedging on his pluralistic view wherein he endorsed a wide diversity of types of religious experience. As noted earlier, he maintained that an individual should find the religion best for him; and to the questions as to whether all men ideally should have proportionately the same amount of religion or if there should be a universal religion he answered:

> To these questions I answer "No" emphatically. And my reason is that I do not see how it is possible that creatures in such different positions and with such different powers as human individuals are should have exactly the same functions and the same duties.[33]

He began his study by distinguishing personality types. One type he characterized as "healthy-minded", referring to people who consistently view the present optimistically. Though he counted many such people as his friends, he could not bring himself to accept their type of religion as normative. As he wrote to one such friend:

> I don't see how it [healthy-mindedness] can be a *universal* solution, when the world is the seat of so much unhappiness really incurable in ordinary ways, but *cured* (in many individuals) by their religious experience. One can neither ignore the unhappy individuals nor the peculiar form of their relief, as facts of human history; and I, surveying human history objectively, couldn't help seeing *there* its possibly most characteristic manifestation.[34]

As open-minded as he tried to be toward various types of religious faith, at the end of his study James nevertheless came to the conclusion that *authentic personal religion is a solution to an existential condition,* in which we sense that "there is *something wrong about us*".[35] Thus healthy-minded religion was not what he considered to be one fundamental form of human experience. To him healthy-mindedness was neither healthy nor honest; it was a superficial view of life perpetuating a bad memory and fostering a dishonest form of perception that excluded the terrifying facts of evil.[36] Here again we note that James was implicitly suggesting a criterion by which to evaluate types of religion; a religion can be said to be true if it opens an individual to the most fundamental dimensions and possibilities of his personality and enables him to integrate them creatively and harmoniously into his personal world.

There is no question that in developing his scientific study of religion and personality James was led by a bias. He favored one type of religion and one type of personality. Most of his examination is devoted to what he called the "sick soul", whom he classified religiously as the twice-born. These are people who are possessed by an "absolute disenchantment with ordinary life", and whose basic religious utterance is a cry for "Help!"[37] Though he illuminated many unfortunate forms of religious assistance, James also detected in many cases positive effects in terms of personality change. Often these seemed to have resulted from experiences of conversion, regeneration, and mystical ecstasy. One may be inclined to write off James's study because of this bias, to see it as an expression of his individualistic temperament which honored radicals more highly than conformists. But this would overlook the immense significance his approach has had for the study of religion and personality and ignore the special relevance his findings have for important issues of our own day.

James's concern for the religion of the "sick soul" was correlative to his psychological interests; he was simply more concerned with the dynamics of personality than with its structures. The outcome of this interest has been to set an example for later studies in the area of personality and religion which is perhaps most noticeable in clinical psychology; the chapters by Pruyser and Boisen are examples of later work that is indebted to the kind of concern expressed in James's studies. Furthermore, James's illumination of diverse dynamic factors operative in motivational processes has been recognized to complement the subsequent attention given to unconscious forces by psychoanalysts; hence in addition to examination of lust, guilt, and repression modern psychology has received from James the incentive to study psychological facts such as fear, terror, doubt, loneliness, and also tenderness, hope, joy, and love. James's special interest in abnormal personalities has influenced decades of investigation into the pathology of religious existence. Such work has provided much useful insight; but often it has been one-sided, failing to appreciate positive results of religious experience. Several contributors to this volume have shared James's awareness of positive effects upon personality systems and have in turn advanced knowledge and understanding in this area.

A final contribution from James's study has to do with his view of the potential meaning of severe personal crises. He has suggested that personal maturation, if it is to develop toward the highest potentialities, will not usually be a smooth or even process, but that it is likely to entail drastic upheavals which threaten an individual's safety, security, and identity. He met resistance to these views in his day, but they are in line with contemporary theories which look positively upon conflict. Even moments of disintegration have been recognized as potential opportunities for personal growth and creativity.[38] James suggested that a personal religion in such a context can function to bring an individual through crisis to a higher stage of self-realization. In this, as in other areas previously mentioned, James has made extremely valuable contributions, not only by providing special insights but also by calling attention to functions of religion and areas of personality which might otherwise too easily be overlooked.

LATER DEVELOPMENTS IN THE SCIENTIFIC STUDY OF RELIGION AND PERSONALITY

Though James's investigations, insights, and suggestions are relevant and valuable with respect to current studies in the area of religion and personality, many of his views as well as his frame of reference need altering and in some places drastic overhaul. His attempt to get at the deeply personal aspect of religion remains sound, and the aim of this book is to explore this area further. However, James's restriction of religion to the individual's private feelings, acts, and experiences was arbitrary. Consequently he ignored what subsequently have been recognized as universal features of religion such as systems of symbols, myths, and rituals, a code of conduct, and a system of social relationships. These institutional features have a great impact upon personality; in particular they relate to what Malinowski called the social dimension of existence. By failing to consider them James overlooked crucial aspects of both religion and personality. Since then many of the gaps have been filled by subsequent work in this field, so that knowledge of religion's effects upon personality has been increased.

From the viewpoint of many social scientists today, man's distinctive human nature is constituted more by the fact that he is a bearer and a shaper of culture than by any unique physical characteristics. Human culture is man's second nature. It is composed not merely of artifacts but also – and primarily – of symbols which express men's interests, attitudes, values, fears, aspirations, and which form systems of interpretation and communication. These systems of symbols set the boundaries of a group's frame of reference within which individual members interpret their experiences and make sense of them. They convey the inherited meanings of experience and thus assist individuals to relate significantly to their environing world and to their society in particular. They also are the tools men use to communicate with each other and to develop a corporate sense of history and tradition. Symbols also convey men's ultimate concern and expectations of their future. Perhaps more than anyone, Émile Durkheim was responsible for pointing out the significant role religion has played in the formation and transmission of basic symbols. He pointed out that the primary symbols in tribal societies, such as their totems, not only convey a group's interpretation of what they consider to be sacred power, but also function to integrate individuals into their society and to provide recognizable forms of social classification and cohesion. Growing up in a culture includes a personal process of symbolic integration whereby individuals develop a particular perspective that is characteristic of their group; by internalizing conventional symbols they form basic categories of thought which lead them to interpret phenomena in a way that distinguishes them from members of foreign groups. Social psychology has also worked with anthropology and sociology in the investigation of the way symbols are believed to channel energy in certain established directions by shaping interests and attitudes. This extremely significant dimension of existence was ignored in James's study, which is a serious omission; it receives special consideration in this volume.

The discovery of a truly social self has opened up new insights into the relationship between religion and personality. The anthropological study by Dorothy Lee included in this volume suggests how religion can function with respect to shaping a total life perspective as well as specific patterns of perception by which things and activities are interpreted. Equally important is the way religion influences the way persons actively relate to their world and themselves. David McClelland's study indicates how religious ideas have affected motivation and thereby both social and individual action; he gives special attention to the high need for achievement in Western culture which in turn is closely related to the development of capitalism. Robert Bellah's study shows how different systems of religious symbols can affect the perception of others and influence both the formation of different types of interpersonal relationships as well as the emergence of new personal needs and strengths. Thomas O'Dea's chapter indicates how religious symbols can function in times of radical social change, giving to individuals a sense of security and identity by providing them with an ideology designed to help an individual cope with a serious existential crisis. James set a pattern for the study of religion in terms of effects upon personality; subsequent investigations as represented here have enlarged his insights to include the social dimension of personal existence, but they have also indirectly substantiated the value of his endeavor.

Related to the discovery of the importance of symbolization and social process in both personality and religion has been a deeper insight into the meaning of myths. Armchair scientists of the past who collected various kinds of myths often perpetuated the opinion that myths were essentially like fairy-tales. Malinowski was one of the first to correct this notion by studying the context in which myths were used in various tribal societies. He discovered that within the living context of ritual myths were highly significant forms of expression that functioned to confirm traditions, to interpret crucial events, to give reassurance to both individuals and groups in times of great stress, and to provide a horizon of meaning within which a group's patterns of social action made sense. Since then other students of religion have suggested that myths have powerful existential significance; for example, they may provide a sense of meaning and value to life by establishing exemplary models for behavior.[39] More relevant to the concern of this book, however, has been the work of psychologists such as Henry Murray and Jerome Bruner; they have seen the importance of studying myths so as to get at hidden motivating factors in individual behavior. Bruner, for example, has suggested that myths can be understood psychologically as one way for an individual to externalize his awareness of strong impulses and thereby attempt to give them a place within his particular perspective.[40] The impact of myths and symbols upon impulses emerging from close interpersonal relationships is given special consideration in the chapters by David Bakan and Robert Bellah. Probably the most influential psychologist to suggest the deep significance symbol and myth have in terms of personality formation was Carl Gustav Jung. Particularly with respect to the processes of integration and individuation, he stressed the need for a self-symbol and also the dangers inherent in the assimilation of an inadequate one. Another approach to the role of religion in the process of self-realization is provided by Erich Fromm's chapter. The chapters by Freud and Pruyser indicate how some mythological thinking can reinforce abnormal thought processes; this material complements Jung's approach by elucidating styles of thought often found in religious personalities which interfere with perception and appropriate responses.

Many investigators formerly paid too much attention to the content of myths, apparently thinking of religion mainly as a system of ideas. As we saw, James's study was significant in its attempt to get behind ideas to experience; but in so doing he overlooked what holds the attention of many studies today, namely action. Religion is better considered primarily as something done rather than essentially as something believed. One particular form of action that lies at the heart of religion is ritual. In most older societies that we know of, myth and ritual were regarded as a unit; and this unit was looked upon with utmost seriousness, and sometimes considered to be as essential to well-being as the elements of nature. As Arthur Nock wrote:

> To the ancients the essence of religion was the rite, which was thought of as a process for securing and maintaining correct relations with the world of unchartered forces around man, and the myth, which gave the traditional reason for the rite and the traditional (but changing) view of those forces.[41]

In many religions what is most important is the act; myths are significant because they guide and interpret the action, in much the same way that a script serves in the production of a play. The significance of ritual, like myth, is diverse; it can be a way of escaping from routine or releasing suppressed energy and repressed instincts, but it can also play a creative function in the lives of individuals. Ritual can be a form of play, an artistic production, and a way of enhancing the significance of an important stage or event in human development.[42] However, some ritualistic action has been noticed to resemble abnormal or neurotic behavior, as the article by Freud demonstrates. Though some of his metapsychological interpretations may be farfetched, yet in his clinical approach, as represented in this chapter, he detected the inappropriate ways some people deal with guilt feelings in terms of their religious practice. Some ritual signifies not so much creative enhancement of life but a deliberate way of avoiding challenge and insight by repeating conventional but irrelevant behavior patterns.[43] If religious ritual does play a positive role in the formation of personalities, then there is a special need for studies to verify this empirically. Unless one accepts Freud's conclusion that participants in ritual are acting out their obsessive compulsive neurosis, we need to know why so many people who otherwise evince few neurotic symptoms regularly endure the repetition of ritual actions which consciously appear to them to be meaningless; and we should want to know what effect this ritual has upon perception, awareness, attitudes, character, relationships, and total orientation. Pruyser's clinical study indicates that the impact of religion as a whole upon certain persons cannot be regarded as healthy. Maslow's essay suggests the creative aspect of spontaneous worship; it does not really explore ritual.

Freud's study suggests another serious omission that resulted from James's highly individualistic conception of religion. As Freud discovered, some of life's most agonizing problems emerge not from an individual's constitution but from unsuccessful relationships with others who are important to oneself; thus he brought into focus such interpersonal feelings as guilt, lust, and hate. More recently, studies have concentrated upon hostility that has become widespread in our world and which is particularly manifested in prejudice. Certainly one of the crucial issues we face today is the fact of prejudice; and a significant contribution to that fact is made by religion. Scientists have recently demonstrated that some of the most exaggerated forms of prejudice are to be found in people who are actively religious. In fact it often seems that the more exposure one has to religion, the more likely one is to be prejudiced against other religious, racial, and ethnic groups. For the sake of the world as well as individual well-being it is imperative that we gain better insight into the structures and dynamics of prejudice so that we might understand more clearly how it originates, what sustains it, and how it might be curbed. Highly illuminating studies have been made recently which have specifically explored the interrelationship between religion and the formation of prejudice; two of the most significant were done by Gordon Allport and Milton Rokeach. Their respective contributions in this volume represent later articles in which they reflected upon the meanings of their previous findings as well as those of others. They have found the interrelationship between personality and religion to be extremely complex and even paradoxical. While involvement in organized religion seems to engender prejudice, yet some leaders of religious organizations have discovered their religion to be an effective agent in combatting their own prejudice. Today we are witnessing the increasing conflict between some clergy who are actively engaged in fighting prejudice in society and many of their most loyal lay members who feel that in so doing these clergymen are stepping out of character and going against religion.

Investigation of prejudice clearly illustrates how important it is to examine religion in relation to social, economic, political, and historical forces even when considering its impact upon personality.

One of the most eminent social scientists who called attention to the complexity of these interrelationships and who went far in providing methods and models by which intelligent analysis could explore them was Max Weber. His hypothesis that a cultural modification of the Puritan ethic played a decisive role in the formation of capitalism is now famous;[44] it is also widely misunderstood. A more precise and detailed examination of how religious ideas have affected the mentality of Western men was more recently made by David McClelland; he concentrated upon the increased motivation toward high achievement which in turn is associated with a growing number of capitalistic entrepreneurs. I have included a few portions from his large book which are most relevant to the consideration of the impact of religion upon motivation.

Some years after writing his famous essay Weber developed a systematic sociology of religion, paying special attention to the religious systems of China, India, and Israel. One feature of his analyses is particularly important to our concern. This is the prophet, whose role has been to instigate social change in the name of religion; this change not only sometimes has drastic effects upon other personalities, it also signifies a different kind of religious function within his own personality. As indicated above, one of the paradoxes of religion today is the conflict between members of the same tradition. One reason for this is that some religious leaders have begun to identify with a certain kind of prophetic religion, which entails a different concept of religious existence than that maintained by a pietistic and otherworldly orientation. In fact, the kind of religion defended by James seems to be what prophets have often called into question. James thought of religion primarily in mystical terms. As he put it, prayer in the sense of "inward communion or conversation with the power recognized as divine . . . is the very soul and essence of religion".[45] The practice that operates on the assumption that "prayer is real religion" may produce feelings of tranquillity, tenderness, and inner harmony; but it may also produce persons whose religion makes them act like ostriches with respect to serious social issues and radical cultural change. One of the problems posed by this volume is how to develop a religion of personal integrity that includes at its core some form of ecstasy, or what Maslow has termed a peak-experience, and that is also productively relevant to social change and urgent world-problems. In searching for a concept of personal religion that is at all adequate, the focus of James's approach must be considered in relationship to insights such as provided by Weber. That these two approaches may complement each other has been demonstrated by careful studies such as Erikson's well-known book about Martin Luther. For society the most important aspect of a prophet's religion may be the radical kind of social action his teachings or his life have stimulated. Yet the prophets have also known moments of transcendence in which they experienced the effects so well described by James.

One reason for calling attention to James in the introduction is my conviction that his *Varieties* is more than a classic. It still has a contribution to make to contemporary research, reflection, and dialogue. Though nearly every item in this volume makes evident how unwarranted and restricted a pietistic or mystical notion of religion is, yet James's special focus upon the inner quality of personal religion remains important. Without it religious subjects investigated in large numbers seem to become mechanical objects, and the motivating force which they derived from their religion becomes unintelligible; but his focus can be altered and enlarged.

A New Focus for the Scientific Study of Religion and Personality

The authors represented in this volume have not by and large sought to provide a universal definition of religion. Many of them seem to work with the general notion that religion signifies more than feelings and experiences which a person considers to relate him to a divine being. For social scientists the term religion usually signifies a social system of beliefs, practices, and a moral code which unite into a community those who adopt them. This conceptual model does not, however, indicate very much about what religion can mean to an individual. When using an empirically oriented interdisciplinary approach, it becomes readily apparent that general definitions of religion are inadequate. Even very broad definitions will leave out some varieties and apply to some aspects of religion and not others. Rather than argue about the most universal definition, what we need are numerous, *ad hoc* working definitions of religion which serve in a particular context and for specific purposes. Several possible definitions of religion will emerge from reading the selections here, and one interesting task for discussion groups will be to sort them out and attempt to evaluate them.

The primary task of this book, however, is to examine the personal aspect of different types of religion. The attempt to explore and elucidate personal religion has frequently followed James's appeal to the category of religious experience; however, the latter turns out to be a much more ambiguous, misleading, and artificial term than one might at first suspect. Advocates of this approach have also suggested that religion originates in certain kinds of experiences; supposedly seeing where it originates enables one to see more clearly its essence. Yet the studies of James and later those by Otto indicate that the religious experiences they describe are more often results than causes. They describe a product more than the essence of a religious process. Furthermore, in view of the wide spectrum of religions, the numinous experiences they point to seem to be rare and infrequent. Trying to account for religion using a model that seeks to trace it to some unique experience constitutes often as much a hindrance as a help in research; it is comparable to the attempt to interpret the meaning of art when bound to a definition that is restricted to the works of fine art produced by a few old masters. The trouble stems not so much from the model of religious experience but from the term experience itself.

Difficulty arises as soon as one asks persistently what experience means. The appeal to return to experience at first sounds refreshing and sincere. Yet we understand the word in at least two basic senses. There is a difference between experience as a continuous life process and *having an experience*. Sometimes James talked in terms of the former, but often when referring to religion he seems to have had the latter in mind. To have an experience suggests bringing a process to fruition. If religion means to an individual a total way of life, as James suggested, then it is confusing to speak of personal religion in terms of having experiences, which is what he and others have done. The language brings more confusion than light. In addition to the vagueness in the above use of the term, James tended to conceive of experience too much in passive terms. He defined experience as an influence upon the mind as when something "*foreign* [is] *supposed to impress us*".[46] However, this view overlooks the full dynamic structure of experience. As John Dewey later pointed out, there is a dual element in experience; there is not merely reaction but also action. Experience is not merely something which a man *undergoes*, it is also something which he *does*.[47] Looking at this dual aspect leads to a further insight that experience is essentially a process of interaction; and it is also a creative process whereby all that a man meets is transformed by the way he receives it and acts upon it. This interaction is not just an exchange of give and take; it is a process whereby both the self and environing world are transformed. In the primary datum of experience we need to recognize this ongoing process of interaction which in turn is structured by a system of relationships that itself is shaped by human interest and concern. As de Saint-Exupéry put it: "Man is a network of relationships, and these alone matter to him."[48] Recognizing the passive, interior, and individualistic connotations which the term experience conveys in our culture as well as all that it should express, it is no surprise that social scientists have tended to avoid using it as a model to guide research and reflection.[49]

I suggest that one fruitful way to develop James's special focus, and which will take into consideration the complex system of interaction elucidated by Dewey and others, is to consider personality in terms of *the formation of a personal world*. Admittedly the discussions and controversies about the meaning of personality are as far ranging as those pertaining to religion and experience.[50] Yet there is a fair amount of agreement that personality is not merely an entity but is also a process. In the past more attention was given to enduring quantitative elements that could be sorted out and analyzed with considerable precision; today both psychologists and sociologists tend to focus more upon personality as a process. Gardner Murphy was perhaps representative in suggesting that Gordon Allport's notion of *becoming* is especially important not only because it calls attention to the dynamic process of organization but also to the unfinished and open character of today's personality systems.[51] Yet even the term becoming does not adequately suggest the full context of the process of interaction that constitutes the primordial datum of personality. What is needed is a conceptual model that will serve the purposes of this particular study. One alternative is to use the model of personality system, in light of current reflection that recognizes personality as a dynamic system of relationships. Another is to use the concept of *personal world*, which has the advantage that it connotes both the process of historical becoming and the total context in which an individual organizes his experiences into a network of relationships. World, then, is to be understood along the lines of what phenomenologists have termed the lived-world rather than as a predetermined stage in which man acts out his life.[52]

There are many ways to find the collection of studies in this volume meaningful, but I suggest that readers consider focusing upon the personal world. The object of this investigation is not to look at effects such as emotions or feelings which religion might produce, but to explore the way an individual's religion works in the formation of his personal world. One aspect of the formation of a personal world which is of crucial importance is the phenomenon of perception. Our personalities take on their distinctive shapes as we develop interests and attitudes which channel our energies in such a way that we develop a particular frame of reference within which our activities and encounters make sense. Our personal world is the world as we shape it first of all by our particular mode of perception; it is the world as it looks, smells, feels, and sounds to us. It is possible to consider religion as discussed in this volume in terms of its operation in the perceptual process and then to discover its influence in setting boundaries and directions for the field of perception, in shaping patterns of thought and of motivation, in developing certain kinds of relationships, and attempting to solve problems and crises in a particular way. Within this perspective it is possible to discover some of the meanings religion has with respect to personality in such a way that serves well the purposes of intelligent discussion and further reflection and investigation.

Another value of this particular approach has to do with the contributions it can make to a greater understanding of personality. David McClelland has suggested that more important than personality theorizing is the need to collect "systematic factual knowledge about personality".[53] Too many investigations of personality systems seem almost systematically to avoid knowledge about personality in relationship to religion. James was aware of a similar situation in his day and spoke critically of academic psychology that concentrated largely on "the A-region of personality", by which he meant "the level of full sunlit consciousness". He suggested that there is another, larger part, the B-region of personality, which is "the abode of everything that is latent and the reservoir of everything that passes unrecorded or unobserved". James argued that this larger, depth dimension of personality is the area which feeds personal religion; and, what is particularly pertinent here, "in persons deep in the religious life . . . the door into this region seems unusually wide open".[54] Religion is a legitimate and important area of research in the study of personality because in some of its manifestations we become more clearly aware of otherwise obscure dimensions of it; for James these dimensions included what later came to be called the unconscious and also phenomena such as personal feelings and intuition. In seeking to understand phenomena which are of decisive importance in our day such as alienation, prejudice, anomie, identity crisis, needs for ecstasy, achievement and trust, anxiety, and the death impulse, the scientists represented in this volume have found it helpful to look carefully into religious phenomena so as to account for many of the dynamics of modern life. Religion can and should be studied by the personality sciences, for it contains a reservoir of facts which are sources of revelation; the revelation referred to here is not of supernatural reality but of man's personal world.

Finally the study of religion in terms of the formation of the personal world signifies both a challenge and a contribution to the development of the personality sciences, particularly as they seek to establish criteria for estimating mature existence. While religion can function like a deadly disease in an individual's endeavor to create a healthy and mature world, James pointed out possible admirable effects resulting from some conversion and mystical experiences such as the following:

1. a sense of peace, harmony, and fulfillment
2. a new, keener awareness of one's world and of one's self
3. an insight into one's particular potentialities combined with an eager incentive to actualize them by making them a primary interest
4. a rediscovery of spontaneity and a sense of individual freedom
5. a deeper sense of individual continuity and personal integration
6. a more affirmative attitude toward life and a sense of zest and joy
7. a more open communication with one's environment
8. a deeper feeling of tenderness and a higher regard for one's fellow men.

James argued that religion not only produces a larger, expansive self – that was his challenge – he also pointed out that in an examination of genuinely mature religious personalities we discover some of the highest potentialities of human existence. That is a particular contribution the new science of religion can make to the personality sciences in their search for a measurement of maturity. This problem is given special attention by Maslow and Fromm, but it also figures significantly in the chapters by Allport, Bakan, Bellah, Jung, Menninger, and Rokeach. It would be a valuable project for discussion groups to elaborate what they consider to be the most important criteria for estimating personal maturity and then compare these with the effects that they estimate are likely to issue from different types of religion.

I have tried to make this volume representative of the current scientific study of religion in terms of its role in personality formation. Yet there are many important authors not included; and there are numerous areas of concern which have been left out. In exploring more aspects of the possible interrelationship between religion and personality one might well consider important areas such as: parapsychological phenomena and their significance for religion; the emergence of new and different types of religion as in Black and Hippie cultures and their effects upon personality formation; the effects upon personality, particularly in terms of perception and emergent patterns of relationships, from the religious use of drugs and the exploration of occult phenomena in rising new cults; and the nature of the relationship between established religion and those actively engaged in supporting other established public institutions such as government, business, the military, and education. All of these areas and more have been receiving special attention from social scientists who are dedicated in the search for more systematic factual knowledge and greater understanding of personality. This volume is not intended to be encyclopedic; rather, it is meant to serve as a kind of introduction to those who are engaged or interested in becoming engaged in the scientific study of religion as it lives and works in the personal world. However much has been left out, there is enough material to increase our understanding and lead to a re-evaluation of both personality and religious systems. Of one thing I am sure; discussions focusing upon the latter can be heated, but they can also be extremely worthwhile.

NOTES

1. The concept of personality is known to be modern; it is not widely recognized that the concept of religion implying a system of symbols, beliefs, liturgical actions, and a moral code which refer to some reality deemed to be of ultimate significance and which unite into a community those who adopt them is also relatively recent. Wilfred C. Smith has carefully demonstrated that our modern conception of religion is a distinct entity that can be objectively described and defined is peculiarly Western; it connotes a convenient abstraction rather than the living reality of believers. See his book *The Meaning and End of Religion* (New York: The Macmillan Co., 1963). Though Smith's approach represents the comparative study of religion, his concern is similar to that found in this book, at least in so far as he attempts to understand religious existence in terms of a particular mode of perception that is highly dynamic, motivating an individual personality in the direction of meaning and value.

2. In his study of tragedy Richard Sewall has remarked how Christians were more concerned with man's soul than were the Greeks. Though Greek tragedians opened dimensions of inwardness, "the tragic heroes knew no inner torment like Job's and nothing to compare with the Christian's. If it has been said with some justice that Socrates 'discovered' the soul his discovery hardly brought about that great shift in the individual consciousness that came with Christianity." *The Vision of Tragedy* (New Haven: Yale University Press, 1967), p. 51. Charles N. Cochrane also maintained that Christianity discovered a depth in personality which classical culture had not envisaged: *Christianity and Classical Culture* (New York: Oxford University Press, 1957).

3. William James, *The Principles of Psychology*, 2 Vols (New York: Dover Publications [authorized, unabridged edition], 1950). First published in 1890.

4. Hans Linschoten, *On the Way toward a Phenomenological Psychology: The Psychology of William James* (Pittsburgh: Duquesne University Press, 1968).

5. Quoted in Ralph B. Perry, *The Thought and Character of William James* (Briefer Version) (New York: Harper and Row, 1964), p. 199.

6. Gordon Allport, *Pattern and Growth in Personality* (New York: Holt, Rinehart and Winston, 1963), p. xii.

7. Quoted in Perry, *op. cit.*, p. 257.

8. William James, *Essays in Pragmatism* (New York: Hafner Publishing Co., 1949), p. 94.

9. Blaise Pascal, *Pensées* (London: J. M. Dent & Sons and New York: Peter Pauper Press, 1948), No. 274.

10. Subsequent reflection by scientists and philosophers, especially phenomenologists, has indicated the fundamental role which affections and feelings play in the operation of intelligence. James here is more a contemporary of our times than his own. A few notable works which make a similar point are: Martin Heidegger, *Being and Time* (New York: Harper and Row and Oxford: Basil Blackwell, 1964); Maurice Merleau-Ponty, *Phenomenology of Perception* (London: Routledge & Kegan Paul and New York: Humanities Press, 1962); Michael Polanyi, *Personal Knowledge* (Chicago: University of Chicago Press and London: Routledge & Kegan Paul, 1958); Harry Stack Sullivan, *The Interpersonal Theory of Psychiatry* (New York: W. W. Norton, 1953). I have explored this issue in some detail, particularly in chs. 1–4 and 14 in W. A. Sadler, Jr., *Existence and Love: A New Approach in Existential Phenomenology* (New York: Charles Scribner's Sons, 1969).

11. James, *Essays in Pragmatism*, pp. 104–105.

12. Cf. James's discussion of this whole new approach to experience in the *Essays in Pragmatism*, pp. 101–107 and in his *Essays in Radical Empiricism* (London and New York: Longmans, Green & Co., 1912) and *A Pluralistic Universe* (London and New York: Longmans, Green & Co., 1909).

13. William James, *The Varieties of Religious Experience* (New York: The Modern Library, Random House, n.d.), pp. 436–437 (first published in 1914 by Longmans, Green & Co., London and New York). Since James wrote, some systematic theologians, such as Paul Tillich, and most of the existential theologians have come to hold essentially a similar view, maintaining that religious words are secondary to the primary datum of religious experience. There were also a number of liberal theologians in James's day who had more in common with his views than he apparently realized.

14. *Ibid.*, p. 447.

15. *Ibid.*, p. 446.

16. Though James's work has some important unique features, his scientific investigation into religion and personality was not the first. He was indebted to his former student, Edwin D. Starbuck, and wrote the preface for the latter's *The Psychology of Religion: An Empirical Study of the Growth of Religious Consciousness* (London: 1900). Similarly, he made use of articles by James H. Leuba, who later wrote two significant books: *A Psychological Study of Religion* (New York: The Macmillan Co., 1912) and *The Psychology of Religious Mysticism* (New York: Harcourt, Brace & Co. and London: Kegan Paul & Co., 1925). Within fifteen years after the *Varieties* the anthropologist Bronislaw Malinowski and the sociologist Émil Durkheim published highly significant works that in

effect followed James's suggestion to focus upon religious experience but which went beyond his narrow individualistic framework. Unfortunately restrictions of size have made it impossible to include selections from their works in this volume. However, paperback editions do exist. See especially Malinowski's *Magic, Science and Religion* (New York: Doubleday & Co., 1955) and Durkheim's *The Elementary Forms of the Religious Life* (New York: The Free Press, 1965). Another valuable source book containing relevant material to this study is: William Lessa and Evon Vogt, eds., *Reader in Comparative Religion: An Anthropological Approach* (New York: Harper and Row, 1962). For more recent studies one will want to consult the *Journal for the Scientific Study of Religion*.

17. Cf. Perry, *op. cit.*, p. 252. Perry also points out that James apparently did have mystical experiences occasionally, particularly in the last years of his life. But these were after he had completed the *Varieties* and do not explain his ardent defense of religion there.

18. Quoted in Perry, *op. cit.*, p. 258.

19. James, *The Varieties . . .*, p. 490.

20. *Ibid.*, p. 23.

21. James, *Essays in Pragmatism*, pp. 159–171.

22. James, *The Varieties . . .*, p. 479.

23. James, *Essays in Pragmatism*, p. 157.

24. James, *The Varieties . . .*, p. 497. It is interesting to note that while not ruling out the possibility of supernatural reality, as did many of his colleagues, James refused to absolutize any set of conceptualizations about it, thus anticipating some of the most significant directions to be found in contemporary theology.

25. James, in a letter to a friend, quoted by Perry, *op. cit.*, p. 263.

26. James, *The Varieties . . .*, p. 108.

27. *Ibid.*, pp. 31–32. His emphasis.

28. The late Dutch phenomenologist and theologian Gerardus van der Leeuw has made a detailed study of the esthetic dimension of religion. He has argued that religion is intimately related to artistic expression, and that to understand either religion or art one needs to develop an appreciation of their interaction and mutual influence. See his *Sacred and Profane Beauty: The Holy in Art* (New York: Holt, Rinehart and Winston and London: Weidenfeld & Nicolson, 1963).

29. Though in many points James's views of religion were similar to those of Rudolf Otto (see his *The Idea of the Holy* [London: Oxford University Press, 1952]. First published in German, 1917), for the record it should be pointed out that his were worked out at least fifteen years before the classic work by Otto.

30. James, *The Varieties . . .*, p. 108.

31. *Ibid.*, p. 109.

32. James, *Essays in Pragmatism*, pp. 155–157.

33. James, *The Varieties . . .*, p. 477.

34. Quoted in Perry, *op. cit.*, p. 262.

35. James, *The Varieties . . .*, p. 498. His emphasis.

36. *Ibid.*, p. 160. James's critique of the religion of healthy-mindedness is similar to the charge made more recently by the sociologist Peter Berger against the dishonest mode of perception fostered by contemporary Christianity in America. See his *The Precarious Vision* and *The Noise of Solemn Assemblies*, both published by Doubleday & Co. (Garden City), 1961.

37. James, *The Varieties . . .*, pp. 137, 153–159.

38. In addition to the chapter by Boisen readers will profit from consideration

of the study by Erik Erikson, *Young Man Luther* (New York: W. W. Norton & Co., 1958 and London: Faber & Faber, 1959). See also the view of Kazimierz Dabrowski, *Personality Shaping through Positive Disintegration* (Boston: Little Brown & Co., 1967 and London: Churchill Publishers, 1968).

39. See the works by Mircea Eliade, such as: *Myth and Reality* (New York: Harper and Row, 1963 and London: Allen & Unwin, 1964); *The Myth of the Eternal Return* (New York: Pantheon Books, 1954 and London: Routledge & Kegan Paul, 1955); *The Sacred and the Profane* (New York: Harper and Row, 1961).

40. Jerome S. Bruner, "Myth and Identity", *Myth and Myth Making*, ed. H. A. Murray (New York: George Braziller, 1960).

41. Arthur Darby Nock, *Conversion* (Oxford: Oxford University Press, 1952), p. 161.

42. See the previously cited works by Eliade, Malinowski, and van der Leeuw for amplification; and also the study by Roger Caillois, *Man and the Sacred* (New York: The Free Press, 1959).

43. This charge has been made against much institutional religion in America by Peter Berger, *The Noise of Solemn Assemblies.*

44. Max Weber, *The Protestant Ethic and the Spirit of Capitalism* (New York: Charles Scribner's Sons, 1958. First published in German, 1904–1905).

45. James, *The Varieties . . .*, p. 454.

46. James, *The Principles of Psychology*, Vol. II, pp. 619–628. His emphasis.

47. Dewey stressed that our deficient understanding of experience is related to a long held notion that conceives of the organism as separate from his environing world. He argued that we need to recover a sense of the dual element of experience and to recognize that the essential nature of experience is one of *interaction*. As he put it: "Experience is a matter of the interaction of organism with its environment, an environment that is human as well as physical, that includes the materials of tradition and institutions as well as local surroundings. The organism brings with it through its own structure, native and acquired, forces that play a part in the interaction. The self acts as well as undergoes, and its undergoings are not impressions stamped upon an inert wax but depend upon the way the organism reacts and responds. There is no experience in which the human contribution is not a factor in determining what actually happens." See his *Art as Experience* (New York: G. P. Putnam's Sons [Capricorn Books], 1958), p. 246.

48. Quoted in Merleau-Ponty, *op. cit.*, p. 456.

49. Further difficulties with the term were illustrated by Harry Stack Sullivan, who illuminated radically different types of experience. There is a rudimentary form of experience whereby one picks up through prehension or feeling the signs of one's immediate context. Because certain signs arouse considerable anxiety there is another kind of experience where one is highly active in security operations designed to protect the self from the onslaught of anxiety. In this case one does not learn from experience but fails to profit from it. There is a third, mature form of experience where one becomes open to others and engages in active communication and sharing. Yet even with this enlightening breakdown of distinct types, Sullivan maintained that the most important task of human existence is not having certain types of experience but the formation of friendly, productive interpersonal relationships. The term experience, then, is not something one works back to but which one may work with in order to get at what is fundamentally more important. See his *The Interpersonal Theory of Psychiatry*.

50. Some general works reflecting the diversity of personality theories are:

H. P. David and H. von Bracken, eds., *Perspectives in Personality Theory* (New York: Basic Books and London: Tavistock Publications, 1957); C. S. Hall and G. Lindzey, *Theories of Personality* (New York: John Wiley and London: Chapman & Hall, 1957); Richard Lazarus, *Personality and Adjustment* (Englewood Cliffs: Prentice-Hall, 1963).

51. Gardner Murphy, "Determinants of Personality", *Conflict and Creativity*, eds. S. M. Farber and R. Wilson (New York: McGraw-Hill, 1963), pp. 27–41; Gordon Allport, *Becoming: Basic Considerations for a Psychology of Personality* (New Haven: Yale University Press and Oxford: Oxford University Press, 1955). See a similar view expressed by Carl Rogers, *On Becoming a Person* (Boston: Houghton Mifflin Co., 1961 and London: Constable & Co., 1962).

52. I have examined the concept of *personal world* in some detail, especially in Part Two of *Existence and Love*.

53. David C. McClelland, "Toward a Science of Personality Psychology" *Perspectives in Personality Theory*, pp. 355–381.

54. James, *The Varieties . . .*, p. 473.

2

THE RELIGIOUS DIMENSION
OF HUMAN EXPERIENCE*

Dorothy Lee

*Many observers have looked upon religion as an entity separate from
ordinary, secular life and have examined beliefs, ceremonies, and other
activities and experiences thought to be part of a particular individual or
group's religion. In studying the way of life in primitive societies the
anthropologist Dorothy Lee discovered that religion does not primarily
consist of special experiences or forms of behavior; rather, it signifies a
total way of life, not just a part of it. Not all religion functions in the
way described here; yet in attempting to understand how religion lives
and works within a personal world, it is important to consider what it
means in some cultures. A guiding question to bear in mind here and
throughout this book is: What contribution does religion make to the
process of becoming, to the formation of a personal world? Lee has
been especially concerned to explore the lived world of these people,
and she is remarkably effective in revealing how they see their world
and how they relate to their environment, their traditions, and their
future.*

* Used by permission from Dorothy Lee, *Freedom and Culture* (Englewood
Cliffs, New Jersey: Prentice-Hall, Inc., 1959), pp. 162–174; adapted from her
"Anthropology", in *Religious Perspectives in College Teaching*, eds. Hoxie N.
Fairchild and others (New York: The Ronald Press Co., 1962).

Some questions for consideration and discussion: In what way is religion a dimension of experience for these people? How does religion affect their perception? What effects does it have upon individuals in their search for meaning and their attempts to solve problems, develop skills, perform tasks, and identify with their culture? How do the effects of religion in primitive societies compare with those suggested by William James? What important dimensions of personality formation might this type of religion tend to inhibit? For further reading about some American Indians which gives special attention to the function of religion with respect to individuals and groups see: Clyde Kluckhohn and Dorothea Leighton, The Navaho *(Cambridge: Harvard University Press, 1947; a revised edition exists as a Doubleday Anchor Book, 1962).*

IN PRIMITIVE societies, we do not always find the worship of God or a god nor the idea of the supernatural. Yet religion is always present in man's view of his place in the universe, in his relatedness to man and nonhuman nature, to reality and circumstance. His universe may include the divine or may itself be divine. And his patterned behavior often has a religious dimension, so that we find religion permeating daily life – agriculture and hunting, health measures, arts and crafts.

We do find societies where a Supreme Being is recognized; but this Being is frequently so far removed from mundane affairs that it is not present in the consciousness of the people except on the specific occasions of ceremonial or prayer. But in these same societies, we find communion with the unperceivable and unknowable in nature, with an ultimate reality, whether spirit, or power, or intensified being, or personal worth, which evokes humility, respect, courtesy, or sometimes fear on man's part. This relationship to the ultimate reality is so pervasive that it may determine, for example, which hand a man will use in adjusting his loin cloth, or how much water he will drink at a time, or which way his head will point when he sleeps, or how he will butcher and utilize the carcass of a caribou. What anthropologists label "material culture", therefore, is never purely material. Often we would be at least as justified to call the operation involved religious.

All economic activities, such as hunting, gathering fuel, cultivating the land, storing food, assume a relatedness to the encompassing universe, and with many cultures, this is a religious relationship. In such cultures, men recognize a certain spiritual worth and dignity in the universe. They do not set out to control, or master, or exploit.

Their ceremonials are often periods of intensified communion, even social affairs, in a broad sense, if the term may be extended to include the forces of the universe. They are not placating or bribing or even thanking; they are rather a formal period of concentrated, enjoyable association. In their relationships with nature, the people may see themselves as the offspring of a cherishing mother, or the guests of a generous hostess, or as members of a democratic society which proceeds on the principle of consent. So, when the Baiga in India were urged to change over to the use of an iron plow, they replied with horror that they could not tear the flesh of their mother with knives. And American Indians have hunted many animals with the consent of the generic essence of these – of which the particular animal was the carnal manifestation – only after establishing a relationship or reciprocity; with man furnishing the ceremonial, and Buffalo or Salmon or Caribou making a gift of the countless manifestations of his flesh.

The great care with which so many of the Indian groups utilized every portion of the carcass of a hunted animal was an expression, not of economic thrift, but of courtesy and respect; in fact, an aspect of the religious relationship to the slain. The Wintu Indians of California, who lived on land so wooded that it was difficult to find clear land for putting up a group of houses, nevertheless used only dead wood for fuel, out of respect for nature. An old Wintu woman, speaking in prophetic vein, expressed this: "The White people never cared for land or deer or bear. When we Indians kill meat, we eat it all up. When we dig roots we make little holes. When we build houses, we make little holes. When we burn grass for grasshoppers, we don't ruin things. We shake down acorns and pinenuts. We don't chop down the trees. We only use dead wood. But the White people plow up the ground, pull up the trees, kill everything. The tree says, 'Don't. I am sore. Don't hurt me.' But they chop it down and cut it up. The spirit of the land hates them. They blast out trees and stir it up to its depths. They saw up the trees. That hurts them. The Indians never hurt anything, but the white people destroy all. They blast rocks and scatter them on the ground. The rock says, 'Don't! You are hurting me.' But the White people pay no attention. When the Indians use rocks, they take little round ones for their cooking . . . How can the spirit of the earth like the White man? . . . Everywhere the White man has touched it, it is sore."

Here we find people who do not so much *seek* communion with environing nature as *find themselves* in communion with it. In many of these societies, not even mysticism is to be found, in our sense of the word. For us, mysticism presupposes a prior separation of man from nature; and communion is achieved through loss of self and subsequent merging with that which is beyond; but for many other cultures, there is no such distinct separation between self and other, which must be overcome. Here, man is *in* nature already, and we cannot speak properly of man *and* nature.

Take the Kaingang, for example, who chops out a wild bee hive. He explains his act to the bees, as he would to a person whom he considered his coordinate. "Bee, produce! I chopped you out to make beer of you! Yukui's wife died, and I am making beer of you so that I can cut his hair." Or he may go up to a hive and say simply, "Bee, it is I." And the Arapesh of New Guinea, going to his yam garden, will first introduce to the spirit of the land the brother-in-law whom he has brought along to help him with the gardening. This is not achieved communication, brought about for definite ends. It implies an already present relatedness with the ultimate reality, with that which is accepted in faith, and which exists irrespective of man's cognition or perception or logic. If we were to abstract, out of this situation, merely the food getting or the operational techniques, we would be misrepresenting the reality.

The same present relatedness is to be found in some societies where the deity is more specifically defined. The Tikopia, in the Solomon Islands Protectorate, sit and eat their meals with their dead under the floor, and hand food and drink to them; the dead are all somewhat divine, progressively so as they come nearer to the original, fully divine ancestor of the clan. Whatever their degree of divinity, the Tikopia is at home with them; he is aware of their vague presence, though he requires the services of a medium whenever he wants to make this presence definite.

Firth describes an occasion when a chief, having instructed a medium to invite his dead nephew to come and chew betel with him, found himself occupied with something else when the dead arrived, and so asked the medium to tell the spirit – a minor deity – to chew betel by himself. At another time, during an important ceremonial, when this chief was receiving on his forehead the vertical stripe which was the symbol that he was now the incarnation of the highest god, he jokingly jerked his head aside, so that the stripe, the insignium of the presence of the god, went crooked. These are the acts of a man who feels accepted by his gods, and is at one with them. And, in fact, the Tikopia appear to live in a continuum which includes nature and the divine without defining bounds; where communion is present, not achieved; where merging is a matter of being, not of becoming.

In these societies where religion is an everpresent dimension of experience, it is doubtful that religion as such is given a name; Kluckhohn reports that the Navaho have no such word, but most ethnographers never thought to inquire. Many of these cultures, however, recognized and named the spiritual ingredient or attribute, the special quality of the wonderful, the very, the beyondness, in nature. This was sometimes considered personal, sometimes not. We have from the American Indians terms such as *manitou*, or *wakan*, or *yapaitu*, often translated as power; and we have the well-known Melanesian *mana*. But this is what they reach through faith, the other end of the relationship; the relationship itself is unnamed. Apparently, to behave and think religiously is to behave and think. To describe a way of life in its totality is to describe a religious way of life.

When we speak of agricultural taboos and rites, therefore, we often introduce an analytical factor which violates the fact. For example, when preparing seed for planting, one of the several things a Navaho traditionally does is to mix ground "mirage stone" with the seed. And in the process of storing corn, a double-eared stalk is laid at the bottom of the storage pit. In actual life, these acts are a continuous part of a total activity.

The distinction between the religious and the secular elements may even separate an act from the manner of performance, a verb from its adverb. The direction in which a man is facing when performing a secular act, or the number of times he shakes his hand when spattering water, often have their religious implications. When the Navaho planted his corn sunwise, his act reflected a total world-view, and it would be nonsense for us to separate the planting itself from the direction of the planting.

Those of us who present religion as separate from "everyday" living reflect moreover the distinctions of a culture which will identify six days with the secular in life and only the seventh with religion. In many primitive societies, religion is rarely absent from the details of everyday living, and the ceremonials represent a formalization and intensification of an everpresent attitude. We have societies such as that of the Hopi of Arizona, where ceremonials, and the preparation for them, cover most of the year. Some years ago, Crow-wing, a Hopi, kept a journal for the period of a year, putting down all events of ceremonial import. Day after day, there are entries containing some casual reference to a religious activity, or describing a ritual, or the preparation for a ceremonial. After a few weeks of such entries, we come to a sequence of four days' entries which are devoted to a description of a ball game played by two opposing groups of children and enjoyed by a large number of spectators. But, in the end, this also turns out to have been ceremonial in nature, helping the corn to grow.

Among many groups, agriculture is an expression of man's religious relatedness to the universe. As Robert Redfield and W. Lloyd Warner have written: "The agriculture of the Maya Indians of southeastern Yucatan is not simply a way of securing food. It is also a way of worshipping the gods. Before a man plants, he builds an altar in the field and prays there. He must not speak boisterously in the cornfield; it is a sort of temple. The cornfield is planted as an incident in a perpetual sacred contract between supernatural beings and men. By this agreement, the supernaturals yield part of what is theirs – the riches of the natural environment – to men. In exchange, men are pious and perform the traditional ceremonies in which offerings are made to the supernaturals. . . . The world is seen as inhabited by the supernaturals; each has his appropriate place in the woods, the sky, or the wells from which the water is drawn. The village is seen as a reflection of the quadrilateral pattern of the cosmos; the cornfield too is oriented, laid out east, west, north, and south, with reference to the supernaturals that watch over the cardinal points; and the table altars erected for the ceremonies again remind the individual of this pattern. The stories that are told at the time when men wait to perform the ceremony before the planting of the corn or that children hear as they grow up are largely stories which explain and further sanction the traditional way of life."

Art also is often so permeated with religion that sometimes, as among the Navaho, what we classify as art is actually religion. To understand the rhythm of their chants, the "plot" of their tales, the making of their sand-paintings, we have to understand Navaho religion: the concept of harmony between man and the universe as basic to health and well-being, the concept of continuity, the religious significance of the groups of four, the door of contact opened through the fifth repetition, the need to have no completely enclosing frame around any of their works so that continuity can be maintained and the evil inside can have an opening through which to leave.

The sand-paintings are no more art than they are ritual, myth, medical practice, or religious belief. They are created as an integral aspect of a ceremonial which brings into harmony with the universal order one who finds himself in discord with it; or which intensifies and ensures the continuation of a harmony which is already present. Every line and shape and color, every interrelationship of form, is the visible manifestation of myth, ritual, and religious belief. The making of the painting is accompanied with a series of sacred songs sung over a sick person, or over someone who, though healed of sickness by emergency measures, has yet to be brought back into the universal harmony; or in enhancing and giving emphasis to the present harmony. What we would call purely medical practices may or may not be part of all this. When the ceremonial is over, the painting is over too; it is destroyed; it has fulfilled its function.

This is true also of the art of the neighboring Hopi, where the outstanding form of art is the drama. In this we find wonderfully humorous clowning, involving careful planning and preparation, creation of magnificent masks and costumes, rehearsals, organization. Everyone comes to see and responds with uproarious hilarity. But this is not mere art. It is an important way of helping nature in her work of growing the corn. Even the laughter of the audience helps in this.

More than dramatic rehearsal and creation of costumes has gone into the preparation. The actors have prepared themselves as whole persons. They have refrained from sexual activity, and from anything involving conflict. They have had good thoughts only. They have refrained from anger, worry, and grief. Their preparation as well as their performance have had a religious dimension. Their drama is one act in the great process of the cyclical growing of corn, a divinity indispensable to man's well-being, and to whose well-being man is indispensable. Corn wants to grow, but cannot do so without the cooperation of the rest of nature and of man's acts and thoughts and will. And, to be happy, corn must be danced by man and participate in his ceremonials. To leave the religious dimension out of all this, and to speak of Hopi drama as merely a form of art, would be to present a fallacious picture. Art and agriculture and religion are part of the same totality for the Hopi.

In our own culture, an activity is considered to be economic when it deals with effective utilization or exploitation of resources. But this definition cannot be used when speaking of Hopi economics. To begin with, it assumes an aggressive attitude toward the environment. It describes the situation of the homesteader in Alaska, for example, who works against tremendous odds clearing land for a dairy farm, against the inexorable pressure of time, against hostile elements. By his sweat, and through ingenuity and know-how and the use of brutally effective tools, he tames nature; he subjugates the land and exploits its resources to the utmost.

The Hopi Talayesua, however, describing his work on the land, does not see himself in opposition to it. He works *with* the elements, not *against* them. He helps the corn to grow; he cooperates with the thunderstorm and the pollen and the sun. He is in harmony with the

elements, not in conflict; and he does not set out to conquer an opponent. He depends on the corn, but this is part of a mutual inter-
dependence; it is not exploitation. The corn depends on him too. It
cannot grow without his help; it finds life dull and lonely without his
company and his ceremonials. So it gives its body for his food gladly,
and enjoys living with him in his granary. The Hopi has a personal
relationship with it. He treats it with respect, and houses it with the
care and courtesy accorded to an honored guest. Is this economics?

In a work on Hopi economics we are given an account of the Hopi
Salt Journey, under the heading, "Secondary Economic Activities".
This expedition is also described in a Hopi autobiography, and here
we discover that only those men who have achieved a certain degree
of experience in the Hopi way can go on this journey; and then, only
if their minds are pure and they are in a state of harmony with the
universe. There is a period of religious preparation, followed by the
long and perilous journey which is attended by a number of rituals
along the way. Old men, lowering themselves from the overhanging
ledge onto the salt deposits, tremble with fear, knowing that they may
be unable to make the ascent. The occasion is solemnly religious. This
is no utilization of resources, in the eyes of the Hopi who makes the
journey. He goes to help the growing corn; the Salt Journey brings
needed rain. Twelve adult men will spend days and court dangers to
procure salt which they can buy for two dollars from an itinerant
peddler. By our own economic standards, this is not an efficient use
of human resources. But Hopi ends transcend our economic categories and our standards of efficiency are irrelevant to them.

In many societies, land tenure, or the transference of land, operations involved in hunting and agriculture, are often a part of a
religious way of life. In our own culture, man conceives of his relationship to his physical environment, and even sometimes his
human environment, as mechanistic and manipulative; in other cultures, we often find what Ruth Benedict has called the animistic attitude toward nature and man, underlying practices which are often
classified miscellaneously together in ethnographies, under the heading of superstitions or taboos. The courteous speech to the bear about
to be killed, the offering to the deer world before the hunter sets out,
the introduction of the brother-in-law to the garden spirit, or the
sacrifice to the rice field about to be sold, the refraining from intercourse, or from the eating of meat or from touching food with the
hand, are expressive of such an attitude. They are the practices we
find in a democratic society where there is consideration for the rights
of everyone as opposed to the brutal efficiency of the dictator who

feels free to exploit, considering the rights of none. They reflect the attitude of people who believe in conference and consent, not in coercion; of people who generally find personality or mana in nature and man, sometimes more, sometimes less. In this framework, taboo and superstitious act mean that man acts and refrains from acting in the name of a wider democracy which includes nature and the divine.

With such a conception of man's place in nature, what is for us land tenure, or ownership, or rights of use and disposal, is for other societies an intimate belongingness. So the Arapesh conceive of themselves as belonging to the land, in the way that flora and fauna belong to it. They cultivate the land by the grace of the immanent spirits, but they cannot dispose of it and cannot conceive of doing so.

This feeling of affinity between society and land is widespread and appears in various forms and varying degrees of intensity, and it is not found only among sedentary peoples. We have Australian tribes where the very spirit of the men is believed to reside in the land, where a bush or a rock or a peculiar formation is the present incarnation of myth and contains security and religious value; where a social class, a structured group of relatives, will contain, in addition to human beings, an animal and a feature of the landscape. Here, when a man moves away from the land of his group, he leaves the vital part of himself behind. When a magistrate put people from such societies in jail in a distant city, he had no idea of the terrifying severity of the punishment he was meting; he was cutting the tribesman off from the very source of his life and of his self, from the past, and the future which were incorporated and present in his land.

In the technology of such societies we are again dealing with material where the religious and secular are not distinct from each other. We have, for example, the description which Raymond Firth gives of the replacing of a worn-out wash-strake on a canoe among the Tikopia. This operation is expertly and coherently carried out, with secular and religious acts performed without distinction in continuous succession or concurrently. A tree is cut down for the new wash-strake, a libation is poured out to the deities of the canoe to announce this new timber, and a kava rite is performed to persuade the deities to step out of the canoe and on to a piece of bark cloth, where they can live undisturbed, while the canoe is being tampered with. Then comes the unlashing of the old wash-strake, the expert examination of the body of the canoe in search of lurking defects, the discovery of signs indicating the work of a borer, the cutting of the body of the canoe with a swift stroke to discover whether the borer is there, accompanied by an appeal to the deities of the canoe by the expert to witness what he is doing and the necessity for doing it.

Now a kinsman of the original builder of the canoe, now dead and a tutelary deity, spontaneously drops his head on to the side of the canoe and wails over the wounding of the body of the canoe. The borer is discovered, in the meantime, to be still there; but only a specially consecrated adze can deal with him successfully. The adze is sent for, dedicated anew to the deity, invoked, and finally wielded with success by the expert.

All this is performed with remarkable expedition and economy of motion yet the Tikopia workers are not interested in saving time; they are concerned neither with time limits nor with speed in itself. Their concern is with the dispossessed deities whose home must be made ready against their return; and the speed of their work is incidental to this religious concern. The end result is efficiency; but unlike our own efficiency, this is not rooted in the effort to utilize and exploit material and time resources to the utmost; it is rooted in that profound religious feeling which also gives rise to the time-consuming rites and the wailing procedures which, from the purely economic point of view, are wasteful and interfering.

The world-view of a particular society includes that society's conception of man's own relation to the universe, human and non-human, organic and inorganic, secular and divine, to use our own dualisms. It expresses man's view of his own role in the maintenance of life, and of the forces of nature. His attitude toward responsibility and initiative is inextricable from his conception of nature as deity-controlled, man-controlled, regulated through a balanced cooperation between god and man, or perhaps maintained through some eternal homeostasis, independent of man and perhaps of any deity. The way a man acts, his feeling of guilt and achievement, and his very personality, are affected by the way he envisions his place within the universe.

For example, there are the Tiv of Southern Nigeria who, as described by one of them in the thirties, people the universe with potentially hostile and harmful powers, *the akombo*. Man's function in the maintenance of his own life and the moderate well-being of the land and of his social unit, is to prevent the manifestation of *akombo* evil, through performing rites and observing taboos. So his rites render safe through preventing, through expulsion and purging. His role is negative, defending the normal course against the interference. Vis-à-vis the universe, his acts arise out of negative motives. Thus what corresponds to a gift of first-fruits to a deity in other cultures is phrased as a rite for preventing the deities from making a man's food go bad or diminish too quickly; fertility rites for a field are actually rites preventing the evil-intentioned from robbing the fields of their normal fertility.

In the writings of R. F. Barton, who studied the Ifugao of Luzon in the early part of this century, these people also appear to see deities as ready to interfere and to bring evil; but their conception of man's role within the structure of the universe is a different one from that of the Tiv. In Barton's descriptive accounts, the Ifugao either accept what comes as deity-given, or act without being themselves the agents; they believe that no act can come to a conclusive end without the agency of a specific deity. They have a specific deity often for every step within an operation and for every part of the implement to be used. R. F. Barton recorded the names of 1,240 deities and believed that even so he had not exhausted the list.

The Ifugao associate a deity with every structured performance and at least a large number of their deliberate acts. They cannot go hunting, for example, without enlisting the aid of the deity of each step of the chase, to render each effective, or to nullify any lurking dangers. There is a deity for the level spot where "the hunter stands watching and listening to the dogs"; one for when the dogs "are sicced on the game", one for when "the hunter leans on his spear transfixing the quarry"; twelve are listed as the deities of specific ways of rendering harmless to the hunter's feet the snags and fangs of snakes which he encounters. If he is to be successful in the hunt, a man does not ask the blessing of a deity. He pays all the particular deities of every specific spot and act, getting them to transitivize each act individually.

Even so, in most cases an Ifugao remains non-agentive, since the function of many of the deities is to save man from encounter, rather than to give him success in his dealing with it. For example, in the area of interpersonal relations, we have Tupya who is invoked so that "the creditor comes for dun for what is owed, but on the way he forgets and goes about other business"; and Dulaiya, who is invoked so that "the enemies just don't think about us, so they don't attack". His tools, also, are ineffective of themselves so that, when setting a deadfall, he invokes and bribes such deities as that for the Flat Stone of the Deadfall, the Main Posts of the Deadfall, the Fall of the Deadfall, the Trigger of the Deadfall. Most of the Ifugao economy is involved in providing sacrifices to the deities, big or little according to the magnitude of the operation and the importance of the deities. There is no warmth in the sacrifices; no expression of gratitude or appeal or belongingness. As the Ifugaos see it, the sacrifice is a bribe.

With such bribes, they buy the miraculous intervention and transitivization which are essential for achievement, health, and good personal relations.

The Ifugao show no humility in the face of this ineffective role in the universe; they merely accept it as the state of things. They accept their own failures, the frequent deaths, the sudden and disastrous flaring up of tempers, as things that are bound to happen irrespective of their own desires and efforts. But they are neither passive nor helpless. They carry on great undertakings and, even now, they go on forbidden head-hunts. They know when and how and whom to bribe so as to perfect their defective acts. When, however, a deity states a decision, they accept it as immutable. A Catholic priest tells a story about the neighboring Iloko which illustrates this acceptance. A Christian Iloko was on his deathbed, and the priest, trying to persuade him to repent of his sin, painted to him vividly the horrors of hell; but the dying man merely answered, "If God wants me to go to hell, I am perfectly willing."

Among the Wintu Indians of California we find that man sees himself as effective but in a clearly limited way. An examination of the myths of the Wintu shows that the individual was conceived as having a limited agentive role, shaping, using, intervening, actualizing, and temporalizing the given, but never creating; that man was viewed as needing skill for his operations, but that specific skill was useless without "luck" which a man received through communion and pleading with some universal power.

It is to this limited role of man, geared to the working of the universe, that I referred when I spoke earlier of Hopi drama and agriculture. Without an understanding of this role, no Hopi activity or attitude or relationship can be understood. The Hopi have developed the idea of man's limited effectiveness in their own fashion, and have elaborated it systematically in what they call the "Hopi Way". Laura Thompson says of the Hopi: "All phenomena relevant to the life of the tribe – including man, the animals, and plants, the earth, sun, moon, clouds, the ancestors, and the spirits – are believed to be interdependent. . . . In this system each individual – human and nonhuman – is believed to have . . . a definite role in the universal order." Traditionally, fulfillment of the law of nature – the growth of corn, the movements of the sun – can come only with man's participation, only with man's performance of the established ceremonials. Here man was effective, but only in cooperation with the rest of the phenomena of nature.

The Indians of the Plains, such as the Crow and the Sioux, have given a somewhat different form to this conception of man's circumscribed agency. The aggressive behavior for which they have been known, their great personal autonomy, their self-assurance and assertiveness, and, in recent years, their great dependence and apathy, have been explained as an expression of this conception. These societies envisioned the universe as pervaded by an undifferentiated religious force on which they were dependent for success in their undertakings and in life generally. The specific formulation differed in the different tribes, but, essentially, in all it was believed that each individual and particularly each man must tap this universal force if his undertakings were to be successful. Without this "power" a man could not achieve success in any of the valued activities, whether warfare or the hunt; and no leadership was possible without this power. This was a force enhancing and intensifying the being of the man who acted; it was not, as with the Ifugao, an effectiveness applied to specific details of activities. The individual himself prepared himself in the hardihood, self-control, skills, and areas of knowledge necessary. Little boys of five or seven took pride in their ability to withstand pain, physical hardship, and the terrors of running errands alone in the night. The Sioux did not appeal for divine intervention; he did not want the enemy to forget to come. Yet neither was he fearless. He appealed for divine strength to overcome his own fears as well as the external enemy.

The relationship with the divine, in this case, is personal and intense. The Plains Indian Sioux did not, like the Hopi, inherit a specific relatedness when he was born in a specific clan. Each man, each preadolescent boy, had to achieve the relationship for himself. He had to go out into the wilderness and spend days and nights without food or drink, in the cold, among wild beasts, afraid and hungry and anxious, humbling himself and supplicating, sometimes inflicting excruciating pain upon himself, until some particular manifestation of the universal force took pity upon him and came to him to become his life-long guardian and power. The appeals to the universal force were made sometimes in a group, through the institution of the Sun Dance. But here also they were individual in nature. The relationship with the divine was an inner experience; and when the Dakota Black Elk recounted his autobiography, he spoke mainly of these intense, personal religious experiences. Within this range of variation in form and concept and world-view, we find expressed by all the same immediate relatedness to the divine.

REFERENCES

Barton, R. F., "The Religion of the Ifugao", *American Anthropologica Association Memoirs*, No. 65 (1946).

Black Elk Speaks. Being the Life Story of a Holy Man of the Oglala Sioux, as told to John G. Neihardt (Flaming Rainbow) (New York: William Morrow & Company, 1932).

Brown, Joseph Epes, *The Sacred Pipe, Black Elk's Account of the Seven Rites of the Oglala Sioux*. Recorded and edited by Joseph Epes Brown (Norman: University of Oklahoma Press, 1953).

Firth, Raymond, *The Work of the Gods in Tikopia* (London: Lund, Humphries & Company, Ltd., 1940).

Firth, Raymond, *Primitive Polynesian Economy* (New York: Humanities Press, 1950).

Henry, Jules, *Jungle People* (New York: J. J. Augustin, Inc., 1941).

Redfield, Robert and Warner, W. Lloyd, "Cultural Anthropology and Modern Agriculture", *Farmers in a Changing World, 1940 Yearbook of Agriculture* (Washington, D.C.: United States Government Printing Office).

Thompson, Laura, *The Hopi Crisis*: Report to Administrators (Mimeograph) (1946).

Vanoverbergh, Morice, *The Isneg Life Cycle* (Publication of the Catholic Anthropological Conference, 3, No. 2, 1936).

3

OBSESSIVE ACTIONS AND RELIGIOUS PRACTICES*

Sigmund Freud

Though some religion can be appreciated for its positive effects in providing individuals with meaning, identity, and security, yet in our culture religion has also been seen as a form of reinforcement of fears, guilt feelings, and strong dependency needs. Sigmund Freud has been enormously influential in bringing about a re-examination of religion in terms of its impact upon personality formation. Freud did not consider religion to be a productive element in the formation of perception; he suggested that religion interferes with perception by fostering a mental projection of fears, repressed wishes, and guilt feelings upon phenomena which are in no way responsible for them. From his psychoanalytic approach religion could, at least in some individuals, be understood as part of an elaborate system of defense designed to keep the personality secure at the expense of honesty and creative development. Anthropologists generally have not found much merit in Freud's theories about primitive people and their religions, such as worked out in his Totem and Taboo *(Collected Works, Vol. 13, which also exists as a paperback published by W. W. Norton Co. of New York and Routledge & Kegan Paul of London); yet in his clinical papers, as indicated in the following selection, he illuminated some significant aspects of religion as it functions in the lives of some people, in particular those whom Freud had*

* From *The Standard Edition of the Complete Psychological Works of Sigmund Freud*, Vol. IX, pp. 117–127. Trans. James Strachey. © 1959 by the Hogarth Press, Ltd., London. Acknowledgment is made for permission to use this material to Sigmund Freud Copyrights Limited, the Institute of Psycho-Analysis, the Hogarth Press, and Basic Books, Inc., New York, which holds the American copyright to the edition by Ernest Jones of *The Collected Papers of Sigmund Freud*, Vol. II, in which this chapter appears in a slightly different translation.

observed as his patients. This chapter also shows how the study of religious phenomena can help to clarify some aspects of abnormal personality formation, in this case obsessive compulsive behavior.

Some questions for consideration and discussion are: Since both Freud and James think of religion arising from a feeling of helplessness, what accounts for their different views? What role does Freud see religion playing in personal conflict? What exactly is the relationship between fear, guilt feelings, repression, and religious ritual? How does Freud's conception of the function of religious beliefs compare with those manifest in subsequent chapters? If deficient in some respects, in what ways do his suggestions apply to religion as you know it? For a brief, later, more generalized interpretation of religion see his The Future of an Illusion (*Collected Works, Vol. 21, which also exists as a Doubleday Anchor Book*). *For a number of more recent case studies elucidating religion in the development of some American abnormal personalities see Margaretta K. Bowers,* Conflicts of the Clergy (*New York: Thomas Nelson and Sons, 1963*).

I AM certainly not the first person to have been struck by the resemblance between what are called obsessive actions in sufferers from nervous affections and the observances by means of which believers give expression to their piety. The term "ceremonial", which has been applied to some of these obsessive actions, is evidence of this. The resemblance, however, seems to me to be more than a superficial one, so that an insight into the origin of neurotic ceremonial may embolden us to draw inferences by analogy about the psychological processes of religious life.

People who carry out obsessive actions or ceremonials belong to the same class as those who suffer from obsessive thinking, obsessive ideas, obsessive impulses, and the like. Taken together, these form a particular clinical entity, to which the name of "obsessional neurosis" ["*Zwangsneurose*"] is customarily applied.[1] But one should not attempt to deduce the character of the illness from its name; for, strictly speaking, other kinds of morbid mental phenomena have an equal claim to possessing what are spoken of as "obsessional" characteristics. In place of a definition we must for the time being be content with obtaining a detailed knowledge of these states, since we have not yet been able to arrive at a criterion of obsessional neuroses; it probably lies very deep, although we seem to sense its presence everywhere in the manifestations of the illness.

Neurotic ceremonials consist in making small adjustments to particular everyday actions, small additions or restrictions or arrangements, which have always to be carried out in the same, or in a methodically varied, manner. These activities give the impression of being mere formalities, and they seem quite meaningless to us. Nor do they appear otherwise to the patient himself; yet he is incapable of giving them up, for any deviation from the ceremonial is visited by intolerable anxiety, which obliges him at once to make his omission good. Just as trivial as the ceremonial actions themselves are the occasions and activities which are embellished, encumbered, and in any case prolonged by the ceremonial – for instance, dressing and undressing, going to bed or satisfying bodily needs. The performance of a ceremonial can be described by replacing it, as it were, by a series of unwritten laws. For instance, to take the case of the bed ceremonial: the chair must stand in a particular place beside the bed; the clothes must lie upon it folded in a particular order; the blanket must be tucked in at the bottom and the sheet smoothed out; the pillows must be arranged in such and such a manner, and the subject's own body must lie in a precisely defined position. Only after all this may he go to sleep. Thus in slight cases the ceremonial seems to be no more than an exaggeration of an orderly procedure that is customary and justifiable; but the special conscientiousness with which it is carried out and the anxiety which follows upon its neglect stamp the ceremonial as a "sacred act". Any interruption of it is for the most part badly tolerated, and the presence of other people during its performance is almost always ruled out.

Any activities whatever may become obsessive actions in the wider sense of the term if they are elaborated by small additions or given a rhythmic character by means of pauses and repetitions. We shall not expect to find a sharp distinction between "ceremonials" and "obsessive actions". As a rule obsessive actions have grown out of ceremonials. Besides these two, prohibitions and hindrances (abulias) make up the content of the disorder; these, in fact, only continue the work of the obsessive actions, inasmuch as some things are completely forbidden to the patient and others only allowed subject to his following a prescribed ceremonial.

It is remarkable that both compulsions and prohibitions (having to do something and having *not* to do something) apply in the first instance only to the subject's solitary activities and for a long time leave his social behaviour unaffected. Sufferers from this illness are consequently able to treat their affliction as a private matter and keep it concealed for many years. And, indeed, many more people suffer from these forms of obsessional neurosis than doctors hear of. For many sufferers, too, concealment is made easier from the fact that they are quite well able to fulfil their social duties during a part of the day, once they have devoted a number of hours to their secret goings, hidden from view like Mélusine.[2]

It is easy to see where the resemblances lie between neurotic ceremonials and the sacred acts of religious ritual: in the qualms of conscience brought on by their neglect, in their complete isolation from all other actions (shown in the prohibition against interruption), and in the conscientiousness with which they are carried out in every detail. But the differences are equally obvious, and a few of them are so glaring that they make the comparison a sacrilege: the greater individual variability of [neurotic] ceremonial actions in contrast to the stereotyped character of rituals (prayer, turning to the East, etc.), their private nature as opposed to the public and communal character of religious observances, above all, however, the fact that, while the minutiae of religious ceremonial are full of significance and have a symbolic meaning, those of neurotics seem foolish and senseless. In this respect an obsessional neurosis presents a travesty, half comic and half tragic, of a private religion. But it is precisely this sharpest difference between neurotic and religious ceremonial which disappears when, with the help of the psychoanalytic technique of investigation, one penetrates to the true meaning of obsessive actions.[3] In the course of such an investigation the appearance which obsessive actions afford of being foolish and senseless is completely effaced, and the reason for their having that appearance is explained. It is found that the obsessive actions are perfectly significant in every detail, that they serve important interests of the personality, and that they give expression to experiences that are still operative and to thoughts that are cathected with affect. They do this in two ways, either by direct or by symbolic representation; and they are consequently to be interpreted either historically or symbolically.

I must give a few examples to illustrate my point. Those who are familiar with the findings of psychoanalytic investigation into the psychoneuroses will not be surprised to learn that what is being represented in obsessive actions or in ceremonials is derived from the most intimate, and for the most part from the sexual, experiences of the patient.

(a) A girl whom I was able to observe was under a compulsion to rinse round her wash-basin several times after washing. The significance of this ceremonial action lay in the proverbial saying: "Don't throw away dirty water till you have clean." Her action was intended to give a warning to her sister, of whom she was very fond, and to restrain her from getting divorced from her unsatisfactory husband until she had established a relationship with a better man.

(*b*) A woman who was living apart from her husband was subject to a compulsion, whenever she ate anything, to leave what was the best of it behind: for example, she would only take the outside of a piece of roast meat. This renunciation was explained by the date of its origin. It appeared on the day after she had refused marital relations with her husband – that is to say, after she had given up what was the best.

(*c*) The same patient could only sit on one particular chair and could only get up from it with difficulty. In regard to certain details of her married life, the chair symbolized her husband, to whom she remained faithful. She found an explanation of her compulsion in this sentence: "It is so hard to part from anything (a husband, a chair) upon which one has once settled."

(*d*) Over a period of time she used to repeat an especially noticeable and senseless obsessive action. She would run out of her room into another room in the middle of which there was a table. She would straighten the table-cloth on it in a particular manner and ring for the housemaid. The latter had to come up to the table, and the patient would then dismiss her on some indifferent errand. In the attempts to explain this compulsion, it occurred to her that at one place on the table-cloth there was a stain, and that she always arranged the cloth in such a way that the housemaid was bound to see the stain. The whole scene proved to be a reproduction of an experience in her married life which had later on given her thoughts a problem to solve. On the wedding-night her husband had met with a not unusual mishap. He found himself impotent, and "many times in the course of the night he came hurrying from his room into hers" to try once more whether he could succeed. In the morning he said he would feel ashamed in front of the hotel housemaid who made the beds, and he took a bottle of red ink and poured its contents over the sheet; but he did it so clumsily that the red stain came in a place that was very unsuitable for his purpose. With her obsessive action, therefore, she was representing the wedding-night. "Bed and board"[4] between them make up marriage.

(*e*) Another compulsion which she started – of writing down the number of every bank-note before parting with it – had also to be interpreted historically. At a time when she was still intending to leave her husband if she could find another more trustworthy man, she allowed herself to receive advances from a man whom she met at a watering-place, but she was in doubt as to whether his intentions were serious. One day, being short of small change, she asked him to change a five-kronen[5] piece for her. He did so, pocketed the large coin, and declared with a gallant air that he would never part with it, since it had passed through her hands. At their later meetings she was frequently tempted to challenge him to show her the five-kronen piece, as though she wanted to convince herself that she could believe in his intentions. But she refrained, for the good reason that it is impossible to distinguish between coins of the same value. Thus her doubt remained unresolved; and it left her with the compulsion to write down the number of each bank-note, by which it *can* be distinguished from all others of the same value.[6]

These few examples, selected from the great number I have met with, are merely intended to illustrate my assertion that in obsessive actions everything has its meaning and can be interpreted. The same is true of ceremonials in the strict sense, only that the evidence for this would require a more circumstantial presentation. I am quite aware of how far our explanations of obsessive actions are apparently taking us from the sphere of religious thought.

It is one of the conditions of the illness that the person who is obeying a compulsion carries it out without understanding its meaning – or at any rate its chief meaning. It is only thanks to the efforts of psychoanalytic treatment that he becomes conscious of the meaning of his obsessive action and, with it, of the motives that are impelling him to it. We express this important fact by saying that the obsessive action serves to express *unconscious* motives and ideas. In this, we seem to find a further departure from religious practices; but we must remember that as a rule the ordinary pious individual, too, performs a ceremonial without concerning himself with its significance, although priests and scientific investigators may be familiar with the – mostly symbolic – meaning of the ritual. In all believers, however, the motives which impel them to religious practices are unknown to them or are represented in consciousness by others which are advanced in their place.

Analysis of obsessive actions has already given us some sort of an insight into their causes and into the chain of motives which bring them into effect. We may say that the sufferer from compulsions and prohibitions behaves as if he were dominated by a sense of guilt, of which, however, he knows nothing, so that we must call it an unconscious sense of guilt, in spite of the apparent contradiction in terms.[7] This sense of guilt has its source in certain early mental events, but it is constantly being revived by renewed temptations which arise whenever there is a contemporary provocation. Moreover, it occasions a lurking sense of expectant anxiety, an expectation of misfortune, which is linked, through the idea of punishment, with the internal perception of the temptation. When the ceremonial is first being constructed, the patient is still conscious that he must do this or that lest some ill should befall, and as a rule the nature of the ill that is to be expected is still known to his consciousness. But what is already hidden from him is the connection – which is always demonstrable – between the occasion on which this expectant anxiety arises and the danger which it conjures up. Thus a ceremonial starts as an *action for defense* or *insurance*, a *protective measure*.

The sense of guilt of obsessional neurotics finds its counterpart in the protestations of pious people that they know that at heart they are miserable sinners; and the pious observances (such as prayers, invocations, etc.) with which such people preface every daily act, and in especial every unusual undertaking, seem to have the value of defensive or protective measures.

A deeper insight into the mechanism of obsessional neurosis is gained if we take into account the primary fact which lies at the bottom of it. This is always *the repression of an instinctual impulse*[8] (a component of the sexual instinct) which was present in the subject's constitution and which was allowed to find expression for a while during his childhood but later succumbed to suppression. In the course of the repression of this instinct a special *conscientiousness* is created which is directed against the instinct's aims; but this psychical reaction-formation feels insecure and constantly threatened by the instinct which is lurking in the unconscious. The influence of the repressed instinct is felt as a temptation, and during the process of repression itself anxiety is generated, which gains control over the future in the form of *expectant* anxiety. The process of repression which leads to obsessional neurosis must be considered as one which is only partly successful and which increasingly threatens to fail. It may thus be compared to an unending conflict; fresh psychical efforts are continually required to counterbalance the forward pressure of the instinct.[9] Thus the ceremonial and obsessive actions arise partly as a defense against the temptation and partly as a protection against the ill which is expected. Against the temptation the protective measures seem soon to become inadequate; then the prohibitions come into play, with the purpose of keeping at a distance situations that give rise to temptation. Prohibitions take the place of obsessive actions, it will be seen, just as a phobia is designed to avert a hysterical attack. Again, a ceremonial represents the sum of the conditions subject to which something that is not yet absolutely forbidden is permitted, just as the Church's marriage ceremony signifies for the believer a sanctioning of sexual enjoyment which would otherwise be sinful. A further characteristic of obsessional neurosis, as of all similar affections, is that its manifestations (its symptoms, including the obsessive actions) fulfil the condition of being a compromise between the warring forces of the mind. They thus always reproduce something of the pleasure which they are designed to prevent; they serve the repressed instinct no less than the agencies which are repressing it. As the illness progresses, indeed, actions which were originally mostly concerned with maintaining the defense come to approximate more and more to the proscribed actions through which the instinct was able to find expression in childhood.

Some features of this state of affairs may be seen in the sphere religious life as well. The formation of a religion, too, seems to be based on the suppression, the renunciation, of certain instinctual impulses. These impulses, however, are not, as in the neuroses, exclusively components of the sexual instinct; they are self-seeking, socially harmful instincts, though, even so, they are usually not without a sexual component. A sense of guilt following upon continual temptation and an expectant anxiety in the form of fear of divine punishment have, after all, been familiar to us in the field of religion longer than in that of neurosis. Perhaps because of the admixture of sexual components, perhaps because of some general characteristics of the instincts, the suppression of instinct proves to be an inadequate and interminable process in religious life also. Indeed, complete backslidings into sin are more common among pious people than among neurotics and these give rise to a new form of religious activity, namely acts of penance, which have their counterpart in obsessional neurosis.

We have noted as a curious and derogatory characteristic of obsessional neurosis that its ceremonials are concerned with the small actions of daily life and are expressed in foolish regulations and restrictions in connection with them. We cannot understand this remarkable feature of the clinical picture until we have realized that the mechanism of psychical *displacement*, which was first discovered by me in the construction of dreams,[10] dominates the mental processes of obsessional neurosis. It is already clear from the few examples of obsessive actions given above that their symbolism and the detail of their execution are brought about by a displacement from the actual, important thing on to a small one which takes its place – for instance, from a husband on to a chair.[11] It is this tendency to displacement which progressively changes the clinical picture and eventually succeeds in turning what is apparently the most trivial matter into something of the utmost importance and urgency. It cannot be denied that in the religious field as well there is a similar tendency to a displacement of psychical values, and in the same direction, so that the petty ceremonials of religious practice gradually become the essential thing and push aside the underlying thoughts. That is why religions are subject to reforms which work retroactively and aim at a re-establishment of the original balance of values.

The character of compromise which obsessive actions possess in their capacity as neurotic symptoms is the character least easily detected in corresponding religious observances. Yet here, too, one is reminded of this feature of neuroses when one remembers how commonly all the acts which religion forbids – the expressions of the instincts it has suppressed – are committed precisely in the name of, and ostensibly for the sake of, religion.

In view of these similarities and analogies one might venture to regard obsessional neurosis as a pathological counterpart of the formation of a religion, and to describe that neurosis as an individual religiosity and religion as a universal obsessional neurosis. The most essential similarity would reside in the underlying renunciation of the activation of instincts that are constitutionally present; and the chief difference would lie in the nature of those instincts, which in the neurosis are exclusively sexual in their origin, while in religion they spring from egoistic sources.

A progressive renunciation of constitutional instincts, whose activation might afford the ego primary pleasure, appears to be one of the foundations of the development of human civilization.[12] Some part of this instinctual repression is effected by its religions, in that they require the individual to sacrifice his instinctual pleasure to the Deity: "Vengeance is mine, saith the Lord." In the development of the ancient religions one seems to discern that many things which mankind had renounced as "iniquities" had been surrendered to the Deity and were still permitted in his name, so that the handing over to him of bad and socially harmful instincts was the means by which man freed himself from their domination. For this reason, it is surely no accident that all the attributes of man, along with the misdeeds that follow from them, were to an unlimited amount ascribed to the ancient gods. Nor is it a contradiction of this that nevertheless man was not permitted to justify his own iniquities by appealing to divine example.

Vienna, February 1907

NOTES

1. See Löwenfeld (1904). According to that author (*ibid.*, p. 8) the term *"Zwangsvorstellung"* ("obsessional idea" or simply "obsession") was introduced by Krafft-Ebing in 1867. The concept (and the term) "obsessional neurosis" originated (on the same authority, *ibid.*, pp. 296 and 487) from Freud himself. His first published use of it was in his first paper on anxiety neurosis (1895*b*).

2. A beautiful woman in mediaeval legend, who led a secret existence as a water-nymph.

3. See the collection of my shorter papers on the theory of the neuroses published in 1906 [*Standard Ed.*, 3].

4. In German *"Tisch und Bett"* ("table and bed"). Cf. a paper on fairy-tales in dreams (1913*d*), *Standard Ed.*, 12, p. 282, footnote 3.

5. Equivalent at that time to four shillings or a dollar.

6. Freud discussed this case again at considerable length in Lecture XVII of his *Introductory Lectures* (1916–1917).

7. The German word used here for "sense of guilt" is *"Schuldbewusstsein"*, literally "consciousness of guilt". – This seems to be the earliest explicit appearance of the "unconscious sense of guilt" which was to play such an important part in Freud's later writings – e.g. at the beginning of the last chapter of *The Ego and the Id* (1923*b*). The way had been prepared for the notion, however, very much earlier, in Section II of the first paper on "The Neuro-Psychoses of Defence" (1894*a*).

8. *Triebregung*. This appears to be Freud's first published use of what was to be one of his most used terms.

9. This passage foreshadows the concept of "anticathexis", which is developed at length in Section IV of the paper on "The Unconscious" (1915*e*), *Standard Ed.*, 14, pp. 180 ff.

10. See *The Interpretation of Dreams* (1900*a*), Chapter VI, Section B (*Standard Ed.*, 4, pp. 305 ff.).

11. Freud had already described this mechanism in his book on jokes (1905*c*), near the end of Section 11 of Chapter II. He often recurred to the point – for instance, in the "Rat Man" analysis (1909*d*), *Standard Ed.*, 10, p. 241, and in the metapsychological paper on repression (1915*d*), *ibid.*, 14, p. 157.

12. This idea was expanded by Freud in the paper on sexual ethics written about a year later (1908*d*), pp. 186 ff. below.

4

THOUGHT ORGANIZATION
IN RELIGION*

Paul Pruyser

Religious people frequently manifest ambivalent attitudes toward their own perception. In some situations they may be open to what is given; yet in others they may distrust their encounter, admit into consciousness certain aspects while selecting out others, and set new material within conceptual molds that may impose irrelevant meanings upon it. To explore more fully how religion can influence the processes of perception and conceptualization it is helpful to examine how religious people think about their world; one way of doing this is to investigate their patterns of thought, in contrast to comparing contents of beliefs in different religious systems. Paul Pruyser is a clinical psychologist who has given special attention to religion; the following study which concentrates upon thought organization reveals significant phenomena which come to light using a clinical approach. Instead of investigating manifest beliefs and religious experiences, he, too, has looked at religion as a formative element in the shaping of a personality system. In preparing the following material he has asked himself if religious people have thoughts for which non-religious people have little use. Does religion enliven or stifle perception? Does it tend to produce distinctive thought patterns? How are these thought patterns called into operation in the encounter with certain types of situations? Though he does not suggest that his findings apply to all religious persons, nevertheless his empirical method is one way of discovering the meaning some types of religion have for some people.

* An edited version, used by permission of both the author and the publisher, of a much longer chapter from Paul Pruyser, *A Dynamic Psychology of Religion* (New York: Harper and Row, 1968), pp. 74–101.

Questions for discussion: What types of thought patterns in religious people may be detected by use of the sorting test? To what extent are such patterns typical of religious people that you know of? What other significant ways might religious persons use to organize their thoughts? How do the analyses by Freud and Pruyser compare with Dorothy Lee's views respective to religion's role in perception? If the patterns of religious thought pointed out by Freud and Pruyser pertain to abnormal personalities, what kind of thought patterns would you expect to find in healthy, mature religious personalities?

IN THE Thematic Apperception Test, widely used by clinicians for diagnostic studies, a person is presented with a series of pictures most of which depict life situations involving one or more persons. They are somewhat ambiguous so that each picture can be interpreted in many different ways. The assigned task is to narrate a little story for each picture, possibly developing a plot that the picture portrays. One of the pictures is a black surface of about six by six inches, within the left half of which is a sharp cutout in white suggesting a window opening in which a human figure stands leaning with one arm against the window jamb. The entire picture is a silhouette in stark black and white.

From seven clergymen, all with advanced theological training beyond the Bachelor of Divinity level, I obtained . . . stories to fit this picture, . . . [and received] seven views of one scene. Some of the stories are rich in detail and imaginative; others are very meager. Some are global and diffuse; others are articulate. Some are poetic or almost mystical; others are pedestrian and commonplace. In some the thought process is highly organized from the start; in others it glides along fairly loosely, *ad hoc*, from thought to thought. Some are quite symbolic; others are factual or operational.

These considerations bring up an important problem which the psychology of religion cannot avoid: the organization of thought in the religious pursuit. In *The Future of an Illusion*, Freud noted sharply what others before him and after him had observed: that the status of religious assertions, creedal formulations, doctrines, and dogmas is cognitively somewhat odd in that they carry an authoritativeness that seems indefensible on the ground of reason. One cannot justify or check the validity of this authority by extraneous criteria. It is an inherent part of the system of thought, and it is taught along with the texts of the formulations. A stock-in-trade example is the various proofs that have been advanced for the existence of God; [but] one can raise all kinds of questions about such proofs. . . .

Before these questions can be answered or even approached, it would behoove us to sketch in broad outlines the major dimensions of thought organization with which clinicians are confronted when they have to make an appraisal of a person's mode or style of thought. I will essay to do this with the help of a model that has given rise to an immensely useful clinical test: the sorting test.[1] The materials of this test consist of about thirty items, all very trite and simple, such as eating utensils, a few household tools such as a screwdriver, a pair of pliers, nails, smoking articles such as a cigarette, cigar, and pipe, a few cardboard forms such as a square, a circle, and a file-card, a lock and key, a rubber sinkstopper, a ball, a bicycle bell, etc. A few of these items are duplicated in toy version such as a tiny fork, knife, and spoon, some toy tools from a toddler's carpentry set, and an imitation cigar and cigarette. The articles are made of various materials: metal, wood, paper, rubber, etc. The articles have different colors and sizes. The task is twofold. First, the articles are spread out in random order in front of the subject, who is asked to pick up one article and place it away from the "heap" in a clear section of his table. He is then asked to "put with that everything that belongs with it". When the subject has made his sorting, i.e. when he has established some class or category by practically putting some things together, he is asked why these things belong together. In other words, he must verbalize or give a rationale for the sorting that he has made. In a second part of the test he is presented with some groupings of objects arranged by the examiner, who asks why all these belong together. He is again to verbalize, but this time he must search for a concept which encompasses exactly all the items of the selection in front of him.

Obviously such a test (which can be endlessly varied) allows one to see how a person "chops up" his universe (or at least a sample of it) and by what criteria he establishes groups of belongingness, likeness, relevance, internal consistency, identity, etc. Something about the scope and manner of his thought organization becomes explicit, together with his verbal justification of what he is doing. Moreover, he categorizes actively by "doing" as well as passively by searching for a principle of coherence in selections offered to him. . . .

DISPARATE CONCEPT FORMATIONS

During the administration of a sorting test it happens occasionally that a person produces a clear and cohesive group of objects, but defines it in ways that are not commensurate with his sorting. The formulation may sound articulate and conceptual enough, but it does not pertain to the actual assortment of objects. For instance, a person may say, "These are all toys" for a sorting consisting of a paper disk, a filecard, and a cardboard cutout. "Toys" is a good concept, and so is "paper articles". But the two do not match; there is a disparity between the actual sorting (i.e. the way in which the person chops up his universe) and his verbal grasp or designation of it.

Such disparate conceptions, in which two realms are brought together, one practically and the other verbally, occur at times in religious thought. A rather trite example of it is the idea of the "Christian gentleman", which suggests a practical sorting (gentleman) that divides the nice, good, or well-behaved people from dishonorable persons and then borrows, from an entirely different realm of discourse, a term (Christian) which makes an essentially different grouping. Christian ideology and literature have much to say about men and women, but are oblivious of the British civil idea of the gentleman. Civil codes and mores may have much to say about polite behavior and desirable manners, but they are oblivious of the ideas of sin and salvation that adhere to the idea of the Christian man. Disparities of this sort between a verbalized thought and a practical referent are seen very frequently in political discourses. They are encountered quite regularly among white American middle-class Protestants who assume that their way of life can be described as the Christian way. Members of such groups will describe their life goals, mores, or preferences with practical references to their friends or business associates, hinting at their playing golf together and voting for the same political party, giving vent to their support of the PTA or their admiration for the FBI, and then formulate all these references as the "Christian way of life", unaware of their having slipped from one category to another. . . .

After noting . . . instances of disparate concept formations the question remains why they occur so frequently in religious thinking. Is religious thought conspicuously sloppy? Does it lack logical discipline? Is it anti-intellectual? Certainly, it sometimes shows all of these. But many of its more articulate spokesmen are highly aware of these dangers and have worked hard on perfecting the instrument of thought through courses in logic and epistemology, much as scientists venerate their courses in method and statistics. The reasons must lie deeper. Two thoughts are suggested. One is that religious conceptions do not stand in cognitive isolation but occur in the fabric of religious activities such as worship, prayer, or mystical experiences. In thinking and talking about one's objects of worship a certain amount of exaltation and a sense of plenitude will rub off on the concepts themselves and give the thoughts a great deal of acuteness and pertinence. Moreover, if religion stems from an awareness of one's contingency upon nature or the universe, any explanation of that contingency will have to deal with the idea of the noncontingent, which, however it be called, is more absolute, more ultimate, and more original. And as soon as one arrives at that point it is easy to slip from a playful assumption or a serious hypothesis into an ontology, in which the object of worship is declared to be the really real, on which all else hinges. In this way, religious conceptions tend to absorb other conceptual domains, and to be impatient with the viability and autonomy of different perspectives. They tend to subdue other points of view or relegate them to a less serious status.

The other thought is Freud's. "The matured stock of religious ideas"[2] which culture transmits (i.e. dogmas) have an aura of authority that transcends the degree of certainty with which one draws inferences from one's own experiences. They claim belief and posit themselves with inherent strength. Where does such extravagant strength come from? The answer is that religious dogmas are illusions, i.e. "fulfillments of the oldest, strongest and most insistent wishes of mankind; the secret of their strength is the strength of these wishes".

FUNCTIONAL DEFINITIONS

When on the sorting test a person selects from the "heap" a pair of pliers, a toy hammer, and a screwdriver and formulates this grouping as "tools", he puts in a generic term the essential common content of these three articles. This is an advanced form of abstraction which requires some perceptual and motor detachment from the objects so that pure cognition may occur which sorts out the essential from the accidental features of the objects and brings their essence under one common denominator. But not all conceptual thinking is so pure and detached. Some thinking is much closer to the motor system, entwined with movements and actions. It is a "thinking with the fingertips", a "thinking while doing" which is characteristic of young children. When it occurs in adults it shows the predominance of impulse over reflection. In our example, the abstract formulation "tools" then gives way to a functional definition such as "you can do carpenter's work with them" or "they are all used in repairing things".

Since life requires much action, functional concepts abound in everyday language, and one may say that a good deal of our daily world is organized along functional lines. Also, it is often much easier to say what something is for, or what its use is, than what it is in essence. This is conspicuously true for tools, gadgets, and practical things; moderately true for things to eat and drink; less so for family rules, and still less for art. Yet children repeatedly ask why they should be home at dark and what such rules "are good for", and artists who aim at pure art are perpetually plagued by people who want to know what paintings and sculptures are for, what use they have, and what one can do with them.

Functional conceptualization is no stranger to religious thought. An abundance of books and tracts beleaguers people in all walks of life with the idea that praying is very useful and always good for something. There is even a book on the power of praying over plants, which sets out to demonstrate that plants grow more vigorously when one prays hard for them. Keyrings and amulets with short prayers can be found in any dime store, for those anxious moments when one will have need of them. Placards on taxis admonish us to go to the church of our choice on Sunday mornings, with the implication that it is good for something. From time to time, juvenile court judges find it useful to sentence a youthful offender to attendance at Sunday School. Biblical movies have proven to be very useful to the film industry. Indeed, one can move mountains if one has only a shred of faith. These examples are trite, but they are a telling demonstration of functional thinking in regard to religion, which permeates the whole culture.

And why not? Gods have always been used. That is their *raison d'être*, from the human point of view. And long before religion became a contemplative exercise, it was a useful activity in the service of man's immediate needs for food, shelter, safety, fertility, and social security. The original stress was on activities-with-accompanying-thoughts such as praying, offering, and warding off danger by dancing and drumbeating rather than on pondering essences in pure thought. The primordial gods themselves, moreover, were far from contemplative. They were always busy doing things, upsetting the order if things became static, and keeping the cycles of the seasons moving. They worked and bred and feasted and traveled; they rarely slept. And if they brooded from time to time, they always came up with something new to demonstrate their activism. Mana is energy and power, and so is the original *numen*. Only gradually does the power become a discerning power and an ethical force.

With such clues from the deities themselves and with so much original emphasis on ritualistic doings, the religious life can hardly ever be divorced from actions and impulses, no matter how quietly sophisticated and pensive it may become in the course of time. And as long as there is functional activity, even conceptual thought in religion is prone to retain a functional orientation. This is not functionalism as a school of thought or a point of view about religion; it is merely that concept formation in religion tends to be of several types, including functional definitions. People use their gods. They use grace and guilt and shame. They use worship and prayer. They use covenants and promises. They use visions of the unseen. They use intimations of the life hereafter. And so their thoughts about all these things will include these uses or focus on them. . . .

The fact that organized religion is always a mixture of creed, cult, and custom entails a constant pressure against purely abstract conceptual thought. It forces many people, perpetually or only at times, to organize their thinking through what they do, and to engage in a type of concept formation that is based on functional definitions. The triadic relations between creed, cult, and custom both demand and provide opportunities for a flexible use of various types of thought organization. All kinds of patterns may be expected; no type is entirely alien to anyone who reflects about his religious experience.

CONCRETISM

Abstraction is an achievement. What the world presents to the senses may vary from a buzzing, blooming confusion to a patterned scene of sun, sky, green trees, and lakeshore, but what it presents is situationally concrete. It is a specific "this" and "that" of light, colors, forms, tones, hardness, etc. Abstraction rises above the concreteness of situations to the larger units of classes, groups, or families of things; it transforms sense impressions into ideas; it establishes relations of similarity, difference, distance, cause, and effect; it can playfully assume an "as if" attitude. I once knew a patient who, under the impact of an expanding brain tumor, had a disastrous loss of abstraction capacity. Before his illness he was an intelligent man, moderately well-situated, who had been a foreman in a shoe factory. Slowly, as he began to fail, he sank to ever simpler jobs in the plant, till he ended up in the shipping department, where his last job consisted of wrapping several boxes of shoes into large sheets of wrapping paper and tying the package with rope. He had courageously continued working until hospitalization for surgery was inevitable. But great changes had taken place in his mental life. He had gradually lost the capacity to think abstractedly; he had even lost the idea of space dimensions, losing his sense for left and right, "in front of" and "behind". He packed his shoeboxes through long-accustomed motor movements of his arms and hands, rather than by "knowing" the relations between the wrapping paper and the boxes.

With this severe disturbance in space relations, he nevertheless left home every morning to walk to work. How did he do it? He followed a written-out list of prescriptions, more or less as follows: "On closing the house door behind me, I look for the gate in the white picket fence and walk to it; at the gate I look in the distance for a telephone pole with a large transformer, and when I have arrived at that point, I cross the street. I look around for a red fire hydrant, where I cross the street again. There I will see one block away the fence of the factory, and I follow it until I reach the entrance gate." His life had become extremely concretized. Almost everything was a specific "this" or "that". Words such as "if", "supposedly", and "however" made little sense in his speech, though they were still part of his vocabulary.

Concreteness of this extreme degree is an inability to come to grips with mere possibilities, large class concepts, propositions, playful assumptions, or speculations. The world has shrunk to visible and tangible realities, specific memories, movements, one's body, and simple verbal exchanges with a down-to-earth reference. Loss of composure is imminent when wishes are denied, when situations become too complex to handle, or when changes occur that give a baffling strangeness to old and familiar arrangements. Things that are not in their place are seen as a frightening loss of order. Every change in habit or circumstance arouses anxiety, and tears come easily, especially when one is confronted with one's own incapacity to grasp and master a task or situation.

Pathological extremes may be rare, but they can have great teaching value. They can throw a glaring light on common things, hitherto shrugged off as not particularly interesting or meaningful. Enlightened by our sad case of concretization of thought under the impact of brain damage, can we begin to see concretism as a mode of thought in some religious persons or groups? I believe we can, by pointing to all beliefs which insist on a radically literal interpretation of scriptures, which refuse to admit any change whatsoever, or which depict specific and almost tangible Antichrists in popes, taverns, or sex. Such forms of belief arrive at specific dates for world disaster or predict minutely the day and way of Christ's Second Coming. They can lead to concrete repetitions of biblical scenes in the modern world, such as walking seven times around City Hall with a placard spelling doom, in the expectation that the walls will crumble down. They lead to an insistence on ancient and biblically hallowed calendar items, in which Hebraic Saturdays are exchanged for Julian Sundays, at the cost of much embarrassment and sometimes with time lost from work.

In this kind of thought organization, tradition reigns supreme. It extols strange anachronisms, proudly, defiantly, and sometimes stupidly. When buttons on coats were once a luxury and therefore possibly a tempting vanity, there was some sense in anxiously proscribing their use in favor of more humble hooks and eyes, but maintaining this rule in the modern world becomes almost the acme of vanity, since hooks and eyes are now quite a rarity or oddity. Yet, some Amish-Mennonite sectarians insist on such manifestations of piety. Since biblical women do not seem to have shortened their hair (although they did much to ornament their coiffure), some Protestant sectarians feel persuaded that short hairdos on women are sinful. Since Latin was once the common tongue in Rome, and then an international language among the educated clergy through whom it became firmly affixed to the liturgy of the Mass, some modern Americans insist that it is really the only language in which one can worship. Though Gregorian chant stands historically in the monodic plainsong tradition between the fourth and sixth centuries in Europe, it is for certain people *the* music of the church no matter how much it may be at variance with the development of musical styles and tastes. It is, to them, a specific fixture of religious expression and experience that bars experimentation with other forms.

In a broad sense, fundamentalism may be seen as concretism, even when it is defended or advocated by people who are quite capable of making abstractions in their apologetics. It makes the Bible a thing, if not an idol. Biblical phrases become concrete admonitions that require minute adherence. In the Scopes trial, the first chapter of Genesis was taken up as a cudgel against Darwinian propositions, completely misunderstanding the intent, method, and nature of scientific formulations. It insists on radical conformity, oblivious of humor and grace. . . .

Baptismal rituals have been the subject of much bitter contending within Christianity. How complete should the washing be? Total immersion, say some, insisting on a concrete enactment of cleansing procedures. Sprinkling, say others, permitting condensation and abbreviation, and insisting on the symbolic value and intent of the ritual. Shall one "gather at the river" for immersion, or shall one stand erect with babe in arms in a sanctuary with wall-to-wall carpeting for the ceremony? The answer depends on the organization of one's thoughts: abstract, functional, or concrete. The example of baptism highlights a feature of all ritual, namely, that it is always regulated to the finest minutiae, very specific and utterly concrete. It is not free action, but a chained series of motor sequences. But action will demand our attention in a later chapter; the point to be made in this chapter is that *thinking about action* can also become very concretistic, particularly when it is concerned with ritual.

Concretism in religion engenders several more characteristics which are so common that they are of diagnostic significance. One is the fear of novelty. Though the word "system" sounds somewhat high-flown for the organization of concrete thinking, it is nevertheless apparent that concreteness has all the trappings of reasoning within a closed system. Thought cannot or is not allowed to spread its wings; venture requires openness to unheard-of possibilities. Abstraction produces some freedom from bondage to the world of sensory stimuli and motor action. The concretistic thinker, however, is locked in his world of specific situations, literal formulas, and ritualistic activities, and has learned to feel comfortable within it precisely because it provides him with the structure he needs. He is not only suspicious of novelty, but afraid of it, and when conditions may force him to change he responds typically with panic and anger.

The other characteristic of concreteness is what Goldstein[3] has called the catastrophic reaction. When a brain-damaged person is confronted with tasks that supersede his slim intellectual resources, and when he becomes aware of impending failure in solving such tasks, he senses an acute loss of mastery. Thus undermined in his control, he may lose his composure and cry. He becomes hyper-emotional, and under the impact of strong negative feelings such as fear, anger, shame, or worthlessness he may for a moment resort to irrational thoughts or activities, until he has regained some modicum of self-esteem. So it is with the concretistic thinker in religion. Intellectual challenges beyond his powers can precipitate him into a catastrophic reaction which in due course may produce irrational fantasies of persecution, revenge, and world catastrophe, with the lively images of Antichrists, threatening beasts, or number magic familiar to readers of apocalyptic literature.

SYNCRETISM

Faced with the unassorted heap of objects that comprise the sorting test, a person may make a grouping, usually fairly large, which cuts across the natural categories of tools, eating utensils, paper articles, etc. In straining for a concept that unifies his group he may say: "You can find these around the house", or "They are all man-made objects", or "In some way or other they all come from the ground". These are syncretistic definitions and groupings, which try to bring under one conceptual heading a great variety of things, often unrelated things, which are members of quite distinct or discrepant classes. The subject overlooks or overrules these distinctions in favor of a more embracing idea. Usually this can only be done by moving high on the abstraction ladder, indeed too high above the range in which the more articulate and useful concepts are formed. Syncretism is a fumbling overinclusiveness which combines discordant things under flimsy constructs, with a formula which is usually too trite to be false and too meaningless to be correct.

Syncretism is nothing new in religion. . . . Theologians have used the term for specific eras in the Christian church in which dilutions of Christianity took place through mixing with Hellenistic and Gnostic ideas. To them syncretism describes the loss of authenticity which occurs when incompatible ideas are allowed to distort original and cohesive conceptions. . . .

But our concern is not so much with large historical movements as with the way individuals organize their thoughts on religious issues. . . . Syncretistic thinking seems to be an ever-present danger for the pious soul who knows by heart all the saintly phrases of his tradition and the seraphic epithets of his God, and applies them wantonly to the economy, the military, mechanics, literature, and the arts in order to explain all that is. "God made it all, and isn't everything wonderful! He wins our battles for us, he endowed Paris with the Eiffel tower, and he foresaw in his wisdom that television would spread the impact of Billy Graham crusades on his behalf. Religion is something beautiful, and art is really so religious!" Syncretism is also prevalent among professional men such as physicians, biologists, psychiatrists, or psychologists who, awestruck by the equally noble goals of their work as well as their religious tradition, make strenuous efforts to amalgamate their scientific concepts with their religious ideas so that "all will be one". An example is the direct comparison and intermingling of guilt (a legal concept), guilt feelings (a psychological concept), and sin (a theological concept) under a nebulous general idea of "wrongdoing". Another example is the life-force concept of a vitalistic biology linked up with the Creator-God of Judaism.

Even when one is indulgent toward unhappy metaphors and poetic license, a hard core of syncretism is often present in religious hymns. An example is the well-known hymn, "In the Garden". In the atmosphere it describes, the Jesus of Christianity has been alloyed with the oreads of Greek mythology and a Victorian lover in crinoline or rustling silks. A nebulous idea of romantic pleasantness is used to subordinate such conceptions as lovely roses, the Son of God, a chat with one's lover, and the orderliness of a well-kept garden. Syncretisms usually are too trite to be false, too meaningless to be correct. We may now add: so discrepant are these ideas at closer look that the suggested unity is spurious.

From the lines of this popular hymn and its frequent use in funeral services the reader may already have anticipated what is perhaps the most abundant source of syncretism in religion: notions about immortality and their relations to burial practices and funeral rites. The belief in one's personal immortality and the desire to speculate about its forms are so strong that they tend to become juxtaposed with, or even overrule, doctrinal formulations about one's professed religious beliefs. Very often, the speculations about immortality are a far departure from the tenets of corporate faith and contradict them grossly. The result is that two beliefs are held concomitantly, not in creative tension or in paradoxical richness, but abjectly in a loose arrangement. . . . According to most Christian creeds and articles of faith, Christians are assured of only one thing at the time of their death, and that is that this extraordinary event, too, is in the hand of their God, and that his arrangements can be trusted. But the natural proclivity toward denying one's own demise is so strong that even professing Christians invent various *ad hoc* theories in order to reassure themselves of some form of self-perpetuation. Faced with the issue of death, they suddenly use the concept of a detachable soul which is allowed to roam the wide open spaces; they suddenly despise the body as "mere ashes or dust"; they suddenly insist on treating the dead as if they were living and make comfortable arrangements for a quasi-sleep in satin-lined boxes. I have stressed the sudden and *ad hoc* nature of these constructions because they form a jarring note in the symphony of professed corporate beliefs. They cannot be rhymed together with the established framework of thought, and any effort to do so leads to a helpless and hapless straining toward supraordinate concepts at a very high level of abstraction, which are so all-embracing that they become inarticulate or inane.

In syncretistic thought organization, essential differences are glossed over in favor of a loose or highly contrived unity. Thus, there is a range of syncretistic possibilities. Some are due to sloppy thinking. Others derive from suspicion of natural categories or conventional concepts and present an effort at unique assertions of a hyper-intellectual sort. I am afraid that most of the syncretisms engendered by immortality fantasies amount to sloppy inconsistencies induced by the strength of irrational wishes. . . .

FABULATION

Most readers will know the word "fable" as the name of a literary form and of a story with a moral, in which animals converse with one another. The word "fabulation" in the title of this section is broader: it denotes a type of concept formation in which objects are being brought together as items in a story or narrative that unfolds. For instance, on the sorting test one might pick up a screwdriver and say: "This is the tool of a carpenter, who is at work on a project (adding a piece of wood); he also smokes (adding a cigarette), and when he hears the whistle blow he will go for lunch (adding a fork and two sugar cubes) and smoke a cigar afterward (adding the cigar)." The resultant grouping is of articles from different classes, which are thought to "belong together" because each of them is related to a central figure (the carpenter), and not because of any inherent common quality. In one sense, such fabulized concept formations are very concretistic in that they represent an extreme case of situationalism; in another sense they are very loose because of their fictitiousness.

I once knew a psychiatric patient whose admission to the hospital was occasioned by the following episode. He was a farmer, and one day, on coming home from the fields, he entered his kitchen and saw on the table three empty Coke bottles. He immediately stepped out into his den, took a gun off the wall, loaded it, and with the exclamation "Father, Son, and Holy Ghost" proceeded to shoot each of the bottles to pieces. In doing this, he used a form of thinking whose rules are: things are not what they seem to be. They may be something else, and it is up to us to let them be what we want them to be.

We have seen in the previous chapter that the imagination can be very rich and daring, and that it plays a large role in religion. In this section our concern is with concept formation and its modalities. Thought organization can take the form of fabulation which creates out of the chaos of things a unique order by permitting them to "act" within the flow of a narrative. Whether the narrative is historical or fictitious, plausible or outlandish, is an important question, but that question is for our purposes here subordinated to the structure of the thought plan, which is that a *plot* can create order and cohesiveness in the "heap" of things and experiences.

In this sense, fabulation plays a very large role in religion. The wish for immortality, which we already encountered, soon leads to the mapping out of plots in which the blessed souls will walk on golden pavements and through pearly gates, assemble in splendid halls, and get ready to join in choruses and orchestras. An October 8, 1966, newspaper release from the Associated Press reports that Bishop Tomlinson of a branch of the Church of God, to whom we referred earlier, has now indeed crowned himself "king of the world" by a plot which required that he first make many airplane trips to the world's major cities proclaiming the kingdom to come, and then a final visit to Jerusalem where his royal gesture places the whole world under God's dominion. In such cases, the order of things is not inherent in what is, but evolves from a fiction, over a stretch of time, and the "things" or "conditions" change their obvious qualities into something else.

Fabulation as a mode of thought is conspicuous in the origin of new religious movements. In 1820 and 1823 Joseph Smith, Jr., claimed that angels had visited him and that they gave him several years later a set of gold plates:

... written by way of commandment, and also by the spirit of prophecy and of revelation. Written, and sealed up, and hid unto the Lord, that they might not be destroyed; to come forth by the gift and power of God unto the interpretation thereof; sealed by the hand of Moroni, and hid up unto the Lord, to come forth in due time by the way of Gentile; the interpretation thereof by the gift of God.[4]

Translated by Smith, these plates constituted *The Book of Mormon*, which itself is a long narration of the migrations of the so-called lost tribes of Israel till they reached the shores of the New World. The origin of the movement is a story about a story, and the stories link together a great variety of dissimilar things: ethnological puzzles, polygamous desires, traditional Christianity, "a movement nurtured in the revivalist atmosphere of the 'burned-over' district of upstate New York",[5] the American frontier spirit, and one man's claims of prophecy and angelic assistance.

In order to establish authority for certain beliefs, fabulation is a favorite mode of thought. "Things that are" becomes "things that have happened" in some sequence. To establish the authority of scriptures, both Judaism and Christianity developed stories about their origins, which advanced propositions that they were written in religious ecstasy, or dictated to the writers by the divine voice, or written by some special inspiration of the Holy Spirit who used the writer as a kind of penman. Historical text research has shown that the actual composition of the four gospel texts from the oral tradition is itself a case of fabulation in that each author created his own narration, for different purposes and perhaps for different audiences, of the alleged facts about the life of Jesus and his reported sayings. . . .

The power of narration to bring discrepant things together is nowhere better illustrated than in the great religious festivals, such as the Jewish Seder celebration or the Christian Christmas observances. The mere thought "Christmas" calls up a great variety of things and events, bound together by strands of meaning which are woven in memory or in anticipation; the fiction (from the Latin, "to form, invent, or feign" – all three) creates order in the following chaotic manifold of things:

> acts of charity: donations, gifts, sacrificing time and effort
> musical pursuits, pageants, singing, bell-ringing
> receiving gratification through gifts
> aiming at parity in the exchange of presents
> snowy landscapes and the pleasures of winter
> profit-making
> display of proud home-ownership through decorations
> coziness near glowing fireplaces
> lectures about Christmas in other countries
> lectures about Christmas 100, 200, or 300 years ago
> stories about "the first Christmas"
> indulgent attitudes toward traffic and parking problems
> special foods
> special moods
> cacophonies in streets and stores
> logistics of mailing cards and parcels
> techniques of wrapping and adorning
> visiting relatives and friends
> keeping secrets
> promises for good behavior
> upsurges of parental goodwill
> learning technical innovations in toys
> festive worship
> displacement of furniture by trees
> changes in lighting

This list is not offered with tongue in cheek, but in an effort to demonstrate the enormous discrepancy of ideas, things, events, motives, and wishes which are organized in one fell swoop by the leading thought of Christmas. Fiction is a powerful ordering principle, and in the case of Christmas there is a veritable historical avalanche of stories about stories in an ever-growing progression of complexity. More and more things become absorbed by it. Without fabulation our list would be no more than a heap of discordant items; with fabulation the heap becomes a cohesive whole.

Fabulation is potentially omnivorous, but its span can be held in check by making distinctions between historical fact, fictitious elaboration, and outright fabrication. Aesthetic and other considerations can be used to bind the formative principle of fabulation into specific literary forms such as parable, allegory, metaphor, drama, myth, legend, saga, fable, commentary, and various poetic styles, each of which has its own rules and patterns.

In distinction to the other forms of thought organization which were presented in the previous sections of this chapter, fabulation imposes order by a process of unfolding. Its "truth" is not in a cross section or a "slice" of reality, but in an arrangement of events in time, related through human or divine actors. Because of religion's preoccupation with the question of origins, with genealogies and with destiny, fabulation in religion tends to be saturated with numinous qualities. It is peculiarly fitted to convey and portray the feeling of createdness, the cosmic *mysterium*, the great acts and passions that rule the events of life, the resolute power of history, and the energies that actuate man, beasts, plants, things, and ideas. In fabulation, what *is* turns into what *happens*, which presents man with the unfathomable mystery of why things happen the way they do or did, rather than otherwise.

Without stories no religion.

NOTES

1. D. Rapaport, M. Gill, and R. Schafer, *Diagnostic Psychological Testing*, 2 Vols (Chicago: Year Book Publishers, 1945).

2. S. Freud, *The Future of an Illusion* (New York: Doubleday Anchor Book, p. 40.

3. K. Goldstein, *Human Nature in the Light of Psychopathology* (Cambridge: Harvard University Press, 1940).

4. *The Book of Mormon*, tr. J. Smith, Jr. (Independence, Mo.: Board of Publication of the Reorganized Church of Jesus Christ of Latter Day Saints, 1953), p. iii.

5. W. Walker, *A History of the Christian Church*, rev. ed. (New York: Charles Scribner's Sons, 1959 and Edinburgh: T. & T. Clarke, 1960), p. 514.

5

THE RELIGIOUS CONTEXT
OF PREJUDICE*

Gordon W. Allport

In the previous two chapters some unfortunate effects of the relationship between religion and an individual's personality system were brought into view. In this chapter another unfortunate effect is brought to our attention and examined; this particular phenomenon has drastic repercussions not merely for individual histories but for society as a whole. One of the most crucial problems in the world today is prejudice; it is a powerful dynamic factor, contributing to wars, violence, persecution, aggressive conflict between diverse groups, social inequality, and cruelty of all kinds. We might hope that religion would prove itself to be an effective force combatting prejudice. However, numerous scientific studies have indicated that religion is one of the most influential factors in building up and perpetuating prejudice. One such study which has gained much respect is The Nature of Prejudice *by the psychologist Gordon Allport. [© 1954 by the Addison-Wesley Publishing Co. of Reading, Mass. An abridged edition exists as a Doubleday Anchor Book, 1958.] About ten years later he wrote an article based on further research and reflection; it is included here. Allport showed that the relationship between religion and prejudice is much more complex than some studies would indicate. While some forms of religion seem to foster prejudice, other forms seem to resist it. Earlier studies suggested that very religious people would be less prone to prejudice than*

* This chapter is from *The Person in Psychology*, © 1968 by Gordon W. Allport, published by Beacon Press, Boston and used with permission. It was originally printed in the *Journal for the Scientific Study of Religion*, V, 3 (Fall, 1966), 447–457. It is included here with the permission of this journal.

moderately religious people. Recent events have reminded us that the most religious people can also be the most prejudiced; yet very religious prejudiced people are sometimes strongly opposed by other very religious people who belong to the same tradition, church group, and social class. Allport was led to distinguish between different types of religion to explain such phenomena; this distinction was made not in terms of specific beliefs and practices but with respect to models applicable to values and personality growth.

Questions for reflection and discussion: What are the underlying factors in prejudice? How does religion meet the same needs that might be met and served by prejudice? What kind of religion seems most likely to foster prejudice? What kind most likely to combat it? What are the differences between them? How do the differences relate to patterns and growth in personality systems? How are prejudice, ignorance, and fanaticism related?

With respect to further study, the literature which treats of the relationship between religion and personality in terms of prejudice is rapidly becoming voluminous. For a study of how the religious system of Christianity has fostered anti-semitic prejudice see the book by Charles Glock and Rodney Stark, Christian Beliefs and Anti-Semitism *(New York: Harper and Row, 1966). A helpful measurement of prejudice in relationship to religious dogmatism was worked out by Milton Rokeach in his* The Open and Closed Mind *(New York: Basic Books, 1960), and also his essay in this volume. Allport's distinction between intrinsic and extrinsic religions was first worked out in an article,* "Prejudice: Is it Societal or Personal?", The Journal of Social Issues, *XVIII (1962), 120–134. An investigation testing this distinction was described by Joe R. Feagin,* "Prejudice and Religious Types: A Focused Study of Southern Fundamentalists", Journal for the Scientific Study of Religion, *IV (Fall, 1964), 3–13. Allport previously worked out a distinction between immature and mature religion which is still relevant to this area of concern; see his* The Individual and His Religion *(New York: The Macmillan Co., 1950 and London: Constable & Co., 1951).*

TWO CONTRARY sets of threads are woven into the fabric of all religion – the warp of brotherhood and the woof of bigotry. I am not speaking of religion in any ideal sense, but rather of religion-in-the-round, as it actually exists historically, culturally, and in the lives of individual men and women, the great majority of whom (in our land) profess some religious affiliation and belief. Taken in the round, there is something about religion that makes for prejudice, and something about it that unmakes prejudice. It is this paradoxical situation that I wish here to explore.

It is a well-established fact in social science that, on the average, churchgoers in our country harbor more racial, ethnic, and religious prejudice than do nonchurchgoers. Needless to say, this fact is both surprising and distressing to thoughtful religionists. This finding has been established by many public opinion surveys, as well as by intensive investigations by Adorno and his collaborators, Rokeach, Allport and Kramer, Williams, Stouffer, and others.[1] The finding is always the same: It is secularism and not religion that is interwoven with tolerance. In Stouffer's words: "More churchgoers are intolerant of ... non-conformity ... than non-churchgoers." And this relationship holds "when education, age, region, and type of community are taken into account".[2]

Although we do not know whether this correlation holds for other lands, or for past centuries, we can assume that it does. At least we know that most persecutions and inquisitions of the past, especially the vicious and shameful, have occurred within religious contexts.

One can become immediately defensive and argue that today, as in the past, many (perhaps most) battlers for civil rights, for social justice, for tolerance and equi-mindedness – in short, for brotherhood – have been religiously motivated and fortified by religious doctrine. The array of such spiritual heroes is long; it would include Christ himself and many followers: Tertullian, Pope Gelasius the First, Raymond Lully who dared oppose both the crusades and the rising inquisition, Cardinal Cusa, Sebastian Castellio, Schwenkfeld, and the Irenicists; and in this country Roger Williams, John Woolman, and modern figures such as Father John La Farge, Martin Luther King, and an expanding army of religiously motivated workers for civil rights. Gandhi, a non-Christian, was also religiously motivated. It is further possible to point to recent pronouncements from nearly every major religious body stating in golden words its stand for racial justice and brotherhood.

All this evidence is convincing, but it does not cancel the fact that members of Christian churches in this country are on the average more bigoted than nonchurchgoers. Since the evidence on both sides is incontestable, we are surely confronted with a paradoxical situation which requires careful analysis in order to unravel the contrary sets of threads.

The needed analysis can follow three lines of inspection,

corresponding to the three religious contexts which seem to me to contain the seeds of bigotry:

1. the theological context
2. the sociocultural context
3. the personal-psychological context.

WHAT IS PREJUDICE?

Before entering upon our analysis, it is well to pause for a moment to ask what we mean by prejudice. At what point do our justifiable predilections, beliefs, and convictions spill over into prejudice?

The clearest answer, I think, comes from Thomistic philosophy which defines prejudice very simply, as "thinking ill of others without sufficient warrant". Such is a definition of "prejudice against", what Spinoza calls "hate prejudice". There is of course a condition of "thinking *well* of others without sufficient warrant" (as we sometimes do concerning our own children) – Spinoza's "love prejudice".

By this definition of hate prejudice (the type that concerns us here), we identify two ingredients: a negative feeling or attitude, and a failure of rationality. A particularly ugly example is the illogic of the Ku Klux Klan rabble rouser who justified the killing of Negro children in Birmingham on the grounds that if one kills rattlesnakes one does not care whether they are old rattlers or young. Or take a person who was once cheated by a Jew and thereupon turns anti-Semite. Here also is a clear case of "insufficient warrant". Sometimes the situation is subtler, as with the rabbi who had vigorously fought against the McCarthy concept of guilt by association, but who judged Kennedy unfit to be president on the basis of a medieval papal encyclical.

Here we should recall that in many regions of human life we learn through harsh experience not to think or act without sufficient warrant. Our scientific work, our family budgets, our jobs, our health, require a measured calculation of warranted cause-and-effect relationships. But in other regions of our life there is little, if any, objective monitoring of our activities or beliefs. Religion is one such region; our view of our fellow men is another. Both of these contexts of living are particularly prone to unwarranted assumptions.

A more recent attempt to define prejudice proceeds in a different way. It takes off from certain ideal values affirmed by our democratic society. It declares that prejudice is a departure from three different sets of ideal norms. Since prejudice is ordinarily a matter of gross and unwarranted overgeneralizations, it departs from the norm of *rationality* (just as the Thomistic definition says). Since prejudice often leads to segregation, discrimination, and denial of rights, it is a departure from the norm of *justice*. And finally, since it entails contempt, rejection, or condescension, it is a departure from the norm of *human-heartedness*.[3] This threefold definition somewhat amplifies the Thomistic, but is not inconsistent with it.

I am not saying that it is always possible to ticket a given state of mind as clearly prejudiced or unprejudiced. As in all of our mental life there are borderline conditions. My argument is simply that there are attitudes that are unwarranted, unjust, and insensitive; and that these attitudes may all be, in varying degrees and for varying reasons, interlocked with their possesor's religious life.

THE THEOLOGICAL CONTEXT

Now we come to the theological context of prejudice. Although I have little competence in the field, I venture to suggest that while plentiful supports for brotherhood are found in nearly all systems of theology, these systems also contain three invitations to bigotry. In the past all three have led to prejudice, injustice, outrage, and inquisition. Even today the peril exists, although it is greatly lessened.

First, the doctrine of *revelation* has led, and can still lead, a religion to claim exclusive possession of final truth concerning the destiny of man, as well as sole authority and means for interpreting that end. Held rigidly, this position regards the teaching of other religious and philosophical formulations as a threat to human salvation. St. Augustine declared that where truth is known, men have not the right to err. Within the Protestant tradition heresy was for long a capital crime. Menno Simons, the Anabaptist, reinterpreted St. Paul's injunction to "judge nothing before the time, until the Lord shall come". It meant, he said, "None may judge unless he have the Judging Word on his side."[4]

The General Court of Massachusetts decreed in 1647 that "No Jesuit or spiritual or ecclesiastical person (as they are termed), ordained by a pope of the see of Rome, shall henceforth come into Massachusetts. Any person not freeing himself of suspicion shall be jailed, then banished. If taken a second time he shall be put to death." If the law has not been repealed, 3,200 Catholic clergy in Massachusetts are there illegally.[5]

Most theologians today, of course, take a far softer position, agreeing in effect with Bishop Leslie Newbigin, who writes, "We must claim absoluteness and finality for Christ and His finished work; but that very claim forbids us to claim absoluteness and finality for our understanding of it."[6] Firm faith in revelation is not incompatible with tentativeness and tolerance in our attempts to interpret this faith to mankind. From the practical point of view this leniency is not different from the "fallibilism" of Charles Peirce and John Dewey, who held that the best society is one that remains open and encourages all men to search with equal freedom for satisfying truths.

Whatever the reasons may be, persecutions deriving from rigid interpretations of divine revelation have largely vanished. Today's religious wars – and we still have them – between Moslem and Hindu, between Buddhist and Catholic, are largely due to traditional economic and ethnic hostilities wearing convenient religious tags.

The second theological goad to bigotry (likewise more common in the past than in the present) is the doctrine of *election*. The frenzied battlecry of the Crusades, *Deus vult*, the more recent *Gott mit uns*, the very concepts of God's chosen people, of God's country, have all conferred sanctions for persecution and cruelty. The infidel is accurst; so too the black children of Ham. In speaking to the Jews, St. Chrysostom said, "God hates you." The doctrine of election divides the ins from the outs with surgical precision. Since God is for the ins, the outs must be excluded from privileges, and in extreme cases eliminated by sword or by fire.

Such divinely sanctioned ethnocentricism is decreasing; ecumenicism, its polar opposite, is in ascendance. It seems that the principal active residue of prejudice based on the doctrine of election is the racial bigotry of South Africa and our South, where we find lingering doctrinal justification for keeping the descendants of Ham in the position of drawers of water and hewers of wood.

The third and last theological peril has by now virtually disappeared. I speak of *theocracy* – the view that a monarch rules by divine right; that the church is a legitimate guide for civil government; or that a legal code (perhaps based, as in early New England, on the Ten Commandments), being divinely ordained, is inviolable on the pain of fierce punishment or death. No theological idea has caused so much persecution and suffering in both the old world and the new as have the various versions of theocracy. By virtue of its control over civil government, ecclesiastical whims based on doctrines of revelation and election could be translated into immediate and cruel sanctions.

Theocracy, we now know, disappeared soon after this country adopted the first amendment to its Constitution, guaranteeing religious liberty and the separation of church and state. Historians have claimed that this achievement is America's principal contribution to civilization.[7]

What I have been saying is that, for all its stress on compassion, theology itself has been far from blameless. It has encouraged bigotry in thought, in word, and in deed. At the same time this particular context of prejudice, prominent in the past, has undergone marked relaxation, and may be destined to vanish.

THE SOCIOCULTURAL CONTEXT

Since the average churchgoer has only vague intimations of theology, it seems farfetched to search for the roots of his prejudices in their theological context – especially since, as we have seen, the pathogenic elements in theology are disappearing. But if theological influences in daily life are diminishing, sociocultural influences in religion are increasing. What are the sociocultural factors in religion that predispose the churchgoer to prejudice?

If we stand off and look at our contemporary social edifice we note that without doubt religion is one of its pillars, but also that a parallel pillar is built of the clichés of secular prejudice. Where would our social structure be if most people did not believe in "my country right or wrong", in the superiority of Western culture, in the prevailing social stratification and earmarks of status, in the moral superiority of people with ambition over people without ambition – which means in effect in the moral superiority of privileged over unprivileged classes, in the evils of miscegenation, in the backwardness of immigrants, and in the undesirability of deviants? Secular prejudice is a pillar of a functioning society.

Now pillars must be well matched. Religion therefore finds itself peculiarly tailored to the nationalistic, class, and ethnic cleavages and outlooks that sustain the prevailing social order. It is a conservative agent, rather than an agent of change. A striking instance is the extent to which German Catholicism capitulated to the political and cultural demands of Nazi pressure.[8]

The phenomenon is also clearly visible at the parish level. By and large every congregation is an assemblage of like-minded people, each congregation representing the ethnic, class, and racial cleavages of society, over and above denominational cleavages. Churches exclude Jews, and synagogues exclude Christians. Protestants and Catholics keep apart in their religious subcommunities. Negro churches are peculiarly isolated in tradition and in function.[9] *Sects* affirm values held by the less educated working classes; *churches* foster congenial middle-class values. The fact that many parishioners leave their group when Negroes or other deviants are admitted shows that for them ethnic and class values hold priority over religious values. Church membership for them is primarily of sociocultural significance, a matter of class and caste – a support for their own ethnocentricism.

Here we find a key to our riddle. The reason why churchgoers on the average are more prejudiced than nonchurchgoers is not because religion instills prejudice. It is rather that a large number of people, by virtue of their psychological make-up, require for their economy of living both prejudice and religion. Some, for example, are tormented by self-doubt and insecurity. Prejudice enhances their self-esteem; religion provides them a tailored security. Others are guilt-ridden; prejudice provides a scapegoat, and religion relief. Still others live in fear of failure. Prejudice provides an explanation in terms of menacing out-groups; religion promises a heavenly, if not terrestrial, reward. Thus for many individuals the functional significance of prejudice and religion is identical. One does not cause the other; rather both satisfy the same psychological needs. Multitudes of churchgoers, perhaps especially in times of social anomie and crisis, embrace both supports.

According to this line of reasoning we assume that nonchurchgoers on the whole have less psychological need for prejudice and for religion. Their philosophy of life, whatever it is, seems self-contained, requiring no direct reliance on these two common social supports.

Here then, in broadest outline, is an explanation for the troublesome correlation we find between churchgoing and bigotry. We need, however, to look much more closely at both data and theory in order to sharpen our understanding of the religious context of prejudice.

First we must remind ourselves that there are churchgoers *and* churchgoers. Today 63% of the population in the United States claims formal religious affiliation, a figure far larger than in earlier decades. Also we recall the common poll finding that as many as 96% of the American people say they believe in God. Religion seems to be neither dead nor dying.

But here we need to draw an immediate distinction between two polar types of religious affiliation, as Herberg and Lenski have done.[10] Some religious groups and many individuals stress the sociocultural factor in membership. The result is a "communal" type of affiliation. For example, many Jewish congregations and Negro Protestant groups provide an important communal service quite apart from their specifically religious functions. Herberg and Lenski both argue that Americans are turning increasingly to their religious groups for the satisfaction of their communal identification and need to belong. Paradoxically it can be said that Americans are becoming more religious while at the same time they are becoming more secular.

In *all* religious groups we find parishioners whose interests are primarily communal. Affiliation is in fashion; it provides status for some, a gossip center for others, a meeting place for the lonely, entertainment for the disengaged, and even a good way to sell insurance. One study reports that 80% of members indicate they are more concerned about a comfortable life on earth than about other-worldly considerations, and 54% admit that their religious beliefs do not have any effect on the way they conduct their daily affairs.[11]

The type opposite to "communal" is "associational", which includes those members whose involvement is primarily for purposes of religious fellowship. In comparing these types, revealing differences emerge. To give one example: Lenski finds that among Detroit Catholics whose communal involvement is high and whose associational involvement is low, 59% favor segregated schools; whereas among Catholics whose associational involvement is high and whose communal involvement is low, only 27% favor segregated schools – a difference of 32 percentage points between the religiously oriented and communally oriented churchgoers. A significant trend in the same direction is found also among Detroit Protestants.[12]

Thus we see that one type of churchgoer tends to be prejudiced; another type relatively unprejudiced. To my mind it is precisely here that we find the analytic tool we need to solve our problem. Soon I shall return to this mode of analysis and to several relevant supporting researches.

Meanwhile let me say that a sociological or historical scholar could point to many additional relationships between religion as a cultural institution and prejudice. For one thing, almost every religious group has been a target for hostility. The fierce anti-Catholicism in the United States during the nineteenth century was certainly in large part a mask for the workingman's resentments against the flood of immigration from Ireland, and later from Italy and other Catholic countries. Not only was there vague uneasiness about the curious folkways of these foreigners, there was growing fear of the power of the cities where they settled. Rural nativism focused upon ecclesiastical visibility as a target and likewise upon the Jew who was also an identifiable foreigner.

A different line of sociological interest deals with the ideological differences between Protestant, Catholic, and Jew, and sometimes between Negro and white churches. Lenski, for example, argues that the communications networks, being relatively limited to the adherents of the same faith, facilitate the development and transmission of distinctive political and economic norms and outlooks.[13] In short, religious groups favor provincialism and a compartmentalization of living. Since immigration has virtually ceased, the socioreligious community is becoming a substitute for ethnic groupings, and we must accordingly expect many of the prejudices formerly supported in ethnic terms to be sustained in socioreligious communities. The drift he sees is toward a more compartmentalized society where the heightened sense of religious group loyalty will lead to a lessened sense of responsibility toward those outside. Lenski's research establishes the fact that there are appreciable differences (independent of social class) that mark the political and social attitudes of the major religious groups and affect their images of one another. The Jews, for example, turn out to be the least critical of other groups, but at the same time to suffer the severest criticism from others.

Virtually all of the studies of religion and social conflict are focused on the demographic level. That is to say, trends are found to be true of certain groups taken as a whole. The spirit of capitalism, says Weber, is built into Protestantism and not into Catholicism. Negro religion is, by and large, a religion of protection and protest; Jews, having most to lose through violations of the first amendment, are its strongest supporters. Churches guard middle-class values, sects working-class values.[14]

All such analyses are, of course, useful as background to the study of the religious context of prejudice. And yet I feel that they fail to reach the heart of the matter. They focus upon religion as a sociocultural phenomenon, that is to say in its communal aspects, and overlook its place in the personal life. Both religion and prejudice are intensely personal states of mind. To understand their inherent relationships (whether positive or negative), we have to examine the psychological composition of individual people.

THE PERSONAL-PSYCHOLOGICAL CONTEXT

There are, as we have observed, churchgoers *and* churchgoers. Now what is the simplest possible distinction between them? Well, some attend frequently and regularly, some only on occasion or rarely. Offhand this distinction may seem to be purely demographic – the "regulars" versus the "irregulars". But in reality the process of forming the habit of regular attendance, or the state of mind that lets weather, circumstance, and mood determine attendance, clearly depends on personal motives and attitudes. True, there is a tendency for Protestants to attend less regularly than Catholics, although much more regularly than Jews. In Detroit, among self-styled Protestants 30% go to church every Sunday; 20% between one and three times a month; 30% only occasionally; and 14% never.[15] But for our purposes the important consideration is that each major religious group has its nuclear and its marginal members in terms of attendance. The outer fringe of the marginal group consists of those who attend exceedingly rarely – as someone has said, only thrice in a lifetime: once when they are hatched; again when matched; and finally when dispatched.

Now many investigations have shown that regular and frequent church attenders harbor by and large less ethnic and racial hostility than do members who are casual about their attendance. An illustrative study is one made by Streuning whose data come from nearly 900 faculty members in a large midwestern university.[16] Besides obtaining scores on a prejudice scale, he learned what their habits were regarding church attendance. Almost a third never attended church at all, and they had a low prejudice score (14·7). Many attended once a month, and for these the average prejudice score nearly doubled (25). This finding immediately confirms our earlier statement that nonchurchgoers are less prejudiced than churchgoers or at least than casual churchgoers. The prejudice scores of those attending once, twice, or three times a month were all high. For weekly attenders the score fell, and it continued to fall rapidly for those whose attendance ranged from 5 to 11 or more times a month. For the last group (11 or more times a month) the average score of 11·7 was significantly lower even than for the nonattenders. In these data we clearly perceive what is called a curvilinear relation: nonattenders and frequent attenders having low prejudice scores, intermediate attenders high.

This evidence fits well with Lenski's distinction between communal and associational religion. Frequent attendance is not required to maintain nominal membership or to derive the benefits of communal contact. On the other hand, a religiously motivated person who seeks spiritual association is drawn with greater regularity and frequency to the church's fellowship. An imposing array of studies conducted by Holtzman, Kelly, Friedrichs, Tumin, and others supports this finding and interpretation.[17]

The lives of many marginal attenders, it seems, are regulated in a fitful way by what we may call "religious tokenism". A token of churchmanship is all they need – an occasional anchorage against the gusts of fate. Tokenism while superficial may be fiercely important. Its devotees may incline to see in the Supreme Court ruling against prescribed prayers in public schools a menacing threat. Religion resides in a symbol. One Southern politician complained that while the Supreme Court ushered Negroes into the public schools it ushered God out – as though God dwells in a token.

While the data on frequency of church attendance and its relation to prejudice are revealing, they do not tell us directly about the nature of the personal religious sentiment that provides the context for prejudice, nor about the nature of the contrary sentiment that engenders tolerance, fair play, and humane regard.

To take this additional step we borrow from axiology the concept of *extrinsic* value and *intrinsic* value. The distinction helps us to separate churchgoers whose communal type of membership supports and serves other nonreligious ends from those for whom religion is an end in itself – a final, not instrumental, good.

The distinction clearly overlaps with that drawn by Father Joseph Fichter in his study of the urban Catholic parish.[18] What he calls the "marginal" and "modal" parishioner corresponds fairly well to our extrinsic type. What he calls the "nuclear" parishioner – who orients his life wholly by the full doctrine of the church – is essentially our intrinsic type. For our purposes it is important to note that Father Fichter assigns less than 10% to the intrinsic or nuclear group. Unless I am mistaken, the ratio is roughly what we would find in the average congregation of any Christian (and perhaps Jewish) parish.

Every minister knows and laments the preponderance of the extrinsic type. Some such parishioners find self-expression in managing investments, arranging flowers, running bazaars, in simply avoiding loneliness. They have no true association with the religious function of the church. Others do to varying degrees accept the spiritual ministry, but remain dabblers because their connections are determined exclusively by mood or by crisis. Many extrinsics do, of course, have religious needs, but they feel no obligation to attend church regularly nor to integrate religion into their way of life. Lenski, we have seen, regards compartmentalization as the chief mark of religion today. It is something for an occasional Sunday morning, for High Holy days, or for moments of crisis. Since its function is to serve other needs we call it an extrinsic value in the personal life.

While most extrinsics are casual and peripheral churchgoers, a few are ideological extremists. With equal fervor they embrace some political nostrum along with the tenets of some religious (usually fundamentalist) sect. In such cases religious extremism is found to be ancillary to a prejudiced philosophy of life. I am thinking here of the right-wing groups whose ardent desire is to escape from the complexities of modern life. They do not seek so much to preserve the *status quo* as to return to a former simple small-town or agrarian way of life where individual achievement and responsibility are the only virtues. God has an important role in this ideology as a dispenser of rewards for individual achievement. Modern life threatens this idyll; immigrants threaten it; Negroes, Jews, Catholics are seen as menacing. Extreme right ideology invariably harbors this sort of bigotry; and its supporting religion justifies and rationalizes the prejudice, often through the selection of congenial scriptural passages.

The same phenomenon is seen, though less often, in ideologies of the extreme left. Ralph Roy has pointed to cases of clergy who justify hatred of the wealthy, expropriation, and extreme left-wing policies by one-sided scriptural interpretations.[19]

Thus while there are several varieties of extrinsic religious orientation, we may say they all point to a type of religion that is strictly utilitarian: useful for the self in granting safety, social standing, solace, and endorsement for one's chosen way of life. As such it provides a congenial soil for all forms of prejudice, whether racial, national, political, or religious. Since extrinsic religion predominates among churchgoers we have an explanation for our riddle.

By contrast, the intrinsic form of the religious sentiment regards faith as a supreme value in its own right. It is oriented toward a unification of being, takes seriously the commandment of brotherhood, and strives to transcend all self-centered needs. Dogma is tempered with humility, and in keeping with the biblical injunction the possessor withholds judgment until the day of the harvest. A religious sentiment of this sort floods the whole life with motivation and meaning. Religion is no longer limited to single segments of self-interest.[20]

While many of the intrinsically religious are pietists and express their religion chiefly by being good neighbors, others are of a militant stripe. Were not St. Francis, John Wesley, Mahatma Gandhi – was not Christ himself – intrinsically religious; and were they not all zealous beyond the bounds of moderation? Yes, there are intrinsic as well as extrinsic zealots. We can usually distinguish between them:

The latter group having ulterior motives of personal or political advantage; the former being fired only by a conviction that the kingdom of God should be realized on earth.

AN EMPIRICAL APPROACH

Up to now we have been speaking chiefly in theoretical terms concerning the religious context of prejudice. And I have been moving the argument closer and closer toward a psychological analysis of the situation, with the claim that in the last analysis both prejudice and religion are subjective formations within the personal life. One of these formations (the extrinsic) is entirely compatible with prejudice; the other (the intrinsic) rules out enmity, contempt, and bigotry.

With the proposition stated in this way, an empiricist will ask, "Can we not test it? After all, you have simply stated a hypothesis at the speculative level. Do not all hypotheses need empirical verification before they can be accepted?"

In a series of investigations, my students and I have undertaken this very task. There is not time to describe the studies in detail. Essentially they consist of using two questionnaires with assorted groups of churchgoers. One undertakes – and I apologize for the audacity – to determine to what extent a given parishioner holds an extrinsic or an intrinsic view of his religion. As an example, a person who agrees with the following propositions would receive scores indicating an *extrinsic* orientation:

The purpose of prayer is to secure a happy and peaceful life.
The Church is most important as a place to formulate good social relationships.

A person would be credited with an *intrinsic* orientation if he subscribed to such statements as the following:

I try to carry my religion over into all my other dealings in life.
Quite often I have been keenly aware of the presence of God or the Divine Being.

There are twenty-one items in the scale which enables us to locate each subject on a continuum from consistently extrinsic to consistently intrinsic. There are also a number of subjects who are inconsistent in the sense that they endorse any and all propositions favorable to religion, even though these propositions are contradictory to one another.

A second questionnaire consists of a valid measure of prejudice.[21] It deals primarily with the extent to which the subject favors discriminatory practices and segregation.

In brief, the findings, not yet published, support the hypothesis that the extrinsic religious orientation in personality is indeed the context of prejudice. The intrinsic orientation is the matrix of tolerance. An additional interesting finding is that those subjects who are inconsistent – who grasp at any and all statements favorable to religion, regardless of their logical consistency – are the most prejudiced of all. Thus it seems that the religious context for bigotry lies in both the extrinsic and in the muddled-headed types of religious sentiment. Only the consistently intrinsic type (a small minority) escapes.

CONCLUSION

It is clear that these investigations, still in progress, tend to confirm demographic and sociological studies that we have also reviewed. Further, I believe they are compatible with our theological analysis, since it is clear that communal and extrinsic religion can draw strong support from the doctrines of revelation, election, and theocracy, which, as we have seen, provide the theological context of prejudice, so far as such exists.

We can hope that this convergence of theological, sociological, and psychological analyses will lead to a further cooperation between behavioral and religious disciplines. We can also hope that our findings, when understood by clergy and laity, may lead to a decrease in bigotry and to an enhancement of charity in modern religious life.

If I were asked what practical applications ensue from this analysis I would, of course, say that to reduce prejudice we need to enlarge the population of intrinsically religious people. There is no simple formula, for each personality is unique, and is stubbornly resistant to change. Yet precisely here lies the pastor's task, his opportunity, and his challenge.

NOTES

1. T. W. Adorno, Else Frenkel-Brunswik, D. J. Levinson, and R. N. Sanford, *The Authoritarian Personality* (New York: Harper, 1950); M. Rokeach, *The Open and Closed Mind* (New York: Basic Books, 1960); G. W. Allport and B. M. Kramer, "Some Roots of Prejudice", *Journal of Psychology*, 22 (1946), 9–39; R. M. Williams, Jr., *Strangers Next Door* (Englewood Cliffs, New Jersey: Prentice-Hall, 1964); S. A. Stouffer, *Communism, Conformity and Civil Liberties* (Garden City: Doubleday, 1955).

2. Stouffer, *op. cit.*, p. 147.

3. Cf., H. Schuman, "Sympathetic identification with the underdog", *Public Opinion Quarterly*, 27 (1963), 230–241. Additional reports in preparation.

4. Menno Simons, "A Foundation and plain instruction of the saving doctrine of Christ", *On the Ban: Questions and Answers* (1550), tr. I. D. Rupp (Lancaster: Elias Barr, 1863).

5. This and similar instances of theologically induced intolerance are presented in G. W. Allport, "Religion and prejudice", *The Crane Review*, **2** (1959), 1–10. See also G. Myers, *History of Bigotry in the United States* (New York: Random House, 1943).

6. L. Newbigin, "The quest for unity through religion", *Journal of Religion*, **35** (1955), 17–33.

7. L. Peffer, "Freedom and separation: America's contribution to civilization", *Journal of Church and State*, **2** (1960), 100–111.

8. See G. Lewy, *The Catholic Church and Nazi Germany* (New York: McGraw-Hill and London: Weidenfeld & Nicolson, 1964); also G. Zahn, *German Catholics and Hitler's Wars* (New York and London: Sheed and Ward, 1962).

9. J. R. Washington, *Black Religion* (Boston: Beacon Press, 1964).

10. W. Herberg, *Protestant – Catholic – Jew* (Garden City: Doubleday and London: Bailey Bros. & Swinfen, 1956); G. Lenski, *The Religious Factor* (Garden City: Doubleday, 1961).

11. E. Raab, ed., *Religious Conflict in America* (Garden City: Doubleday, Anchor Books, 1964), p. 15.

12. Lenski, *op. cit.*, p. 173.

13. *Ibid.*, p. 303.

14. Analyses at this demographic level are plentiful. See, e.g., R. Lee and M. E. Marty, eds., *Religion and Social Conflict* (New York: Oxford University Press, 1964).

15. Lenski, *op. cit.*, p. 35.

16. E. L. Streuning, "The dimensions, distributions and correlates of authoritarianism in a midwestern university faculty propulation" (unpublished Ph.D. dissertation, Purdue University, 1957).

17. W. H. Holtzman, "Attitudes of college men toward non-segregation in Texas schools", *Public Opinion Quarterly*, **20** (1956), 559–569; J. G. Kelly, J. E. Ferson, and W. H. Holtzman, "The measurement of attitudes toward the Negro of the South", *Journal of Social Psychology*, **48** (1958), 305–317; R. W. Friedrichs, "Christians and residential exclusion: an empirical study of a Northern dilemma", *Journal of Social Issues*, **15** (1959), 14–23; M. Tumin, *Desegregation* (Princeton: Princeton University Press, 1958); R. M. Williams, Jr., *Strangers Next Door*.

18. J. H. Fichter, S.J., *Social Relations in the Urban Parish* (Chicago: University of Chicago Press, 1954 and Cambridge: Cambridge University Press, 1955).

19. R. L. Roy, "Conflict from the communist left and the radical right", R. Lee and M. E. Marty, eds., *op. cit.*, pp. 55–68.

20. For further discussion of the extrinsic and intrinsic types see G. W. Allport, "Behavioral science, religion, and mental health", *Journal of Religion and Health*, **2** (1963), 187–197; also *Personality and Social Encounter* (Boston: Beacon Press, 1960), ch. 16; also *The Nature of Prejudice* (Reading, Mass.: Addison-Wesley, 1954), ch. 23.

21. Devised by J. Harding and H. Schuman, in preparation.

6

THE PROPHET*

Max Weber

As he considers the full impact and the extensiveness of important phenomena such as the relationship between religion and prejudice, the psychologist finds himself broadening his perspective to consider social dimensions of the personal world. He can receive much assistance from sociologists, such as Max Weber who called attention to the many factors which operate within religious individuals; in particular Weber showed how religious ideas act upon political, economic, social, and historical forces that also are at work motivating individuals and shaping their worlds. Weber also made useful and original distinctions between types of religious systems and individuals. One extremely significant type of religious individual is the prophet, who is to be contrasted with the mystic, magician, priest, and ordinary layman. While some prophets may manifest fanaticism, others have opposed fanaticism and prejudice. The prophetic type suggests itself for correlation with Allport's concept of intrinsic religion; yet it also is distinct from types of religion thus far considered. Religion influences the prophet's perception to see his world in terms of change rather than continuity, in so far as he is oriented to this world; and his view of religion challenges rather than confirms existing patterns of belief and practice. As Weber indicates, the prophet is a highly complex individual who organizes many strong interests through the assistance of an overriding religious insight.

The writings of Weber frequently make very difficult reading; this article is no exception. Though the average reader may not be able to

* Reprint by permission from Max Weber, *The Sociology of Religion*, 4th ed., tr. Ephraim Fischoff (Boston: Beacon Press, 1964 and London: Methuen & Co., 1965 [© 1922, 1956 by J. C. B. Mohr (Paul Siebeck)]), pp. 46–56.

identify numerous references to a diversity of religious and historical traditions, the following questions may help to maintain a focus upon essential features and lead into a profitable discussion. What are the characteristic features of prophets? How do they "see" their world? What significance does this insight of theirs have upon the formation of their own personal worlds? In view of Weber's distinction between different types of prophets, how would you characterize prophetic leaders you are aware of? What does a transforming adult experience indicated by a prophet's life history suggest about our modern conceptions that tend to consider personality patterns as permanently established in childhood? How would you distinguish a prophet from a demagogue or a fanatic?

For further reading, in addition to his The Protestant Ethic and the Spirit of Capitalism (*New York: Charles Scribner's Sons, 1958. First published in German, 1904–1905), one may wish to consult the relevant essays in* From Max Weber, *eds. H. H. Gerth and C. Wright Mills (New York and Oxford: Oxford University Press, 1958). Weber's trilogy,* Ancient Judaism, The Religion of India, *and* The Religion of China, *have been issued in paperback by the Free Press of New York and Collier-Macmillan of London, 1967–1968.*

WHAT IS a prophet, from the perspective of sociology?

We shall forego here any consideration of the general question regarding the "bringer of salvation" (*Heilbringer*) as raised by Breysig. Not every anthropomorphic god is a deified bringer of salvation, whether external or internal salvation. And certainly not every provider of salvation became a god or even a savior, although such phenomena were widespread.

We shall understand "prophet" to mean a purely individual bearer of charisma, who by virtue of his mission proclaims a religious doctrine or divine commandment. No radical distinction will be drawn between a "renewer of religion" who preaches an older revelation, actual or supposititious, and a "founder of religion" who claims to bring completely new deliverances. The two types merge into one another. In any case, the formation of a new religious community need not be the result of doctrinal preaching by prophets, since it may be produced by the activities of non-prophetic reformers. Nor shall we be concerned in this context with the question whether the followers of a prophet are more attracted to his person, as in the cases of Zoroaster, Jesus, and Muhammad, or to his doctrine, as in the cases of Buddha and the prophets of Israel.

For our purposes here, the personal call is the decisive element distinguishing the prophet from the priest. The latter lays claim to authority by virtue of his service in a sacred tradition, while the prophet's claim is based on personal revelation and charisma. It is no accident that almost no prophets have emerged from the priestly class. As a rule, the Indian teachers of salvation were not Brahmins, nor were the Israelite prophets priests. Zoroaster's case is exceptional in that there exists a possibility that he may have descended from the hieratic nobility. The priest, in clear contrast, dispenses salvation by virtue of his office. Even in cases in which personal charisma may be involved, it is the hierarchical office that confers legitimate authority upon the priest as a member of a corporate enterprise of salvation.

But the prophet, like the magician, exerts his power simply by virtue of his personal gifts. Unlike the magician, however, the prophet claims definite revelations, and the core of his mission is doctrine or commandment, not magic. Outwardly, at least, the distinction is fluid, for the magician is frequently a knowledgeable expert in divination, and sometimes in this alone. At this stage, revelation functions continuously as oracle or dream interpretation. Without prior consultation with the magician, no innovations in communal relations could be adopted in primitive times. To this day, in certain parts of Australia, it is the dream revelations of magicians that are set before the councils of clan heads for adoption, and it is a mark of secularization that this practice is receding.

On the other hand, it was only under very unusual circumstances that a prophet succeeded in establishing his authority without charismatic authentication, which in practice meant magic. At least the bearers of new doctrine practically always needed such validation. It must not be forgotten for an instant that the entire basis of Jesus' own legitimation, as well as his claim that he and only he knew the Father and that the way to God led through faith in him alone, was the magical charisma he felt within himself. It was doubtless this consciousness of power, more than anything else, that enabled him to traverse the road of the prophets. During the apostolic period of early Christianity and thereafter the figure of the wandering prophet was a constant phenomenon. There was always required of such prophets a proof of their possession of particular gifts of the spirit, of special magical or ecstatic abilities.

Prophets very often practiced divination as well as magical healing and counseling. This was true, for example, of the prophets (*nabi, nebim*) so frequently mentioned in the Old Testament, especially in the prophetic books and Chronicles. But what distinguishes the prophet, in the sense that we are employing the term, from the types just described is an economic factor, i.e. that his prophecy is unremunerated. Thus, Amos indignantly rejected the appellation of *nabi*. This criterion of gratuitous service also distinguishes the prophet from the priest. The typical prophet propagates ideas for their own sake and not for fees, at least in any obvious or regulated form. The provisions enjoining the nonremunerative character of prophetic propaganda have taken various forms. Thus developed the carefully cultivated postulate that the apostle, prophet, or teacher of ancient Christianity must not professionalize his religious proclamations. Also, limitations were set upon the length of the time he could enjoy the hospitality of his friends. The Christian prophet was enjoined to live by the labor of his own hands or, as among the Buddhists, only from alms which he had not specifically solicited. These injunctions were repeatedly emphasized in the Pauline epistles, and in another form, in the Buddhist monastic regulations. The dictum "whosoever will not work, shall not eat" applied to missionaries, and it constitutes one of the chief mysteries of the success of prophetic propaganda itself.

The period of the older Israelite prophecy at about the time of Elijah was an epoch of strong prophetic propaganda throughout the Near East and Greece. It is likely that prophecy in all its forms arose, especially in the Near East, in connection with the growth of great world empires in Asia, and the resumption and intensification of international commerce after a long interruption. At that time Greece was exposed to the invasion of the Thracian cult of Dionysos, as well as to the most diverse types of prophecies. In addition to the semi-prophetic social reformers, certain purely religious movements now broke into the magical and cultic lore of the Homeric priests. Emotional cults, emotional prophecy based on "speaking with tongues", and highly valued intoxicating ecstasy vied with the evolving theological rationalism (Hesiod); the incipient cosmogonic and philosophic speculation was intersected by philosophical mystery doctrines and salvation religions. The growth of these emotional cults paralleled both overseas colonization and, above all, the formation of cities and the transformation of the *polis* which resulted from the development of a citizen army.

It is not necessary to detail here these developments of the eighth and seventh centuries, so brilliantly analyzed by Rohde, some of which reached into the sixth and even the fifth century. They were contemporary with Jewish, Persian, and Hindu prophetic movements, and probably also with the achievements of Chinese ethics in the pre-Confucian period, although we have only scant knowledge of the latter. These Greek "prophets" differed widely among themselves in regard to the economic criterion of professionalism, and in regard to the possession of a "doctrine". The Greeks also made a distinction between professional teaching and unremunerated propagandizing of ideas, as we see from the example of Socrates. In Greece, furthermore, there existed a clear differentiation between the only real congregational type of religion, namely Orphism with its doctrine of salvation, and every other type of prophecy and technique of salvation, especially those of the mysteries. The basis of this distinction was the presence in Orphism of a genuine doctrine of salvation.

Our primary task is to differentiate the various types of prophets from the sundry purveyors of salvation, religious or otherwise. Even in historical times the transition from the prophet to the legislator is fluid, if one understands the latter to mean a personage who in any given case has been assigned the responsibility of codifying a law systematically or of reconstituting it, as was the case notably with the Greek *aisymnete* (e.g. Solon, Charondas, etc.). In no case did such a legislator or his labor fail to receive divine approval, at least subsequently.

A legislator is quite different from the Italian *podesta*, who is summoned from outside the group, not for the purpose of creating a new social order, but to provide a detached, impartial arbitrator, especially for cases in which the adversaries are of the same social status. On the other hand, legislators were generally, though not always, called to their office when social tensions were in evidence. This was apt to occur with special frequency in the one situation which commonly provided the earliest stimulus to a planned social policy. One of the conditions fostering the need for a new planned policy was the economic development of a warrior class as a result of growing monetary wealth and the debt enslavement of another stratum; an additional factor was the dissatisfaction arising from the unrealized political aspirations of a rising commercial class which, having acquired wealth through economic activity, was now challenging the old warrior nobility. It was the function of the *aisymnete* to resolve the conflicts between classes and to produce a new sacred law of eternal validity, for which he had to secure divine approbation.

It is very likely that Moses was a historical figure, in which case he would be classified functionally as an *aisymnete*. For the prescriptions of the oldest sacred legislation of the Hebrews presuppose a money economy and hence sharp conflicts of class interests, whether impending or already existing, within the confederacy. It was Moses' great achievement to find a compromise solution of, or prophylactic for, these class conflicts (e.g. the *seisachthie* of the year of release) and to organize the Israelite confederacy by means of an integral national god. In essence, his work stands midway between the functioning of an ancient *aisymnete* and that of Muhammad. The reception of the law formulated by Moses stimulated a period of expansion of the newly unified people in much the same way that the leveling of classes stimulated expansion in so many other cases, particularly in Athens and Rome. The scriptural dictum that "after Moses there arose not in Israel any prophet like unto him" means that the Jews never had another *aisymnete*.

Not only were none of the prophets *aisymnetes* in this sense, but in general what normally passes for prophecy does not belong to this category. To be sure, even the later prophets of Israel were concerned with social reform. They hurled their "woe be unto you" against those who oppressed and enslaved the poor, those who joined field to field, and those who deflected justice by bribes. These were the typical actions leading to class stratification everywhere in the ancient world, and were everywhere intensified by the development of the city-state (*polis*). Jerusalem too had been organized into a city-state by the time of these later prophets. A distinctive concern with social reform is characteristic of Israelite prophets. This concern is all the more notable, because such a trait is lacking in Hindu prophecy of the same period, although the conditions in India at the time of the Buddha have been described as relatively similar to those in Greece during the sixth century.

An explanation for Hebrew prophecy's unique concern for social reform is to be sought in religious grounds, which we shall set forth subsequently. But it must not be forgotten that in the motivation of the Israelite prophets these social reforms were only means to an end. Their primary concern was with foreign politics, chiefly because it constituted the theater of their god's activity. The Israelite prophets were concerned with social and other types of injustice as a violation of the Mosaic code primarily in order to explain God's wrath, and not in order to institute a program of social reform. It is noteworthy that the real theoretician of social reform, Ezekiel, was a priestly theorist who can scarcely be categorized as a prophet at all. Finally, Jesus was not at all interested in social reform as such.

Zoroaster shared with his cattle-raising people a hatred of the despoiling nomads, but the heart of his message was essentially religious. His central concerns were his faith in his own divine mission and his struggle against the magical cult of ecstasy. A similar primary focus upon religion appeared very clearly in the case of Muhammad, whose program of social action, which Umar carried through consistently, was oriented almost entirely to the goal of the psychological preparation of the faithful for battle in order to maintain a maximum number of warriors for the faith.

It is characteristic of the prophets that they do not receive their mission from any human agency, but seize it, as it were. To be sure, usurpation also characterized the assumption of power by tyrants in the Greek *polis*. These Greek tyrants remind one of the legal *aisymnetes* in their general functioning, and they frequently pursued their own characteristic religious policies, e.g. supporting the emotional cult of Dionysos, which was popular with the masses rather than with the nobility. But the aforementioned assumption of power by the prophets came about as a consequence of divine revelation, essentially for religious purposes. Furthermore, their characteristic religious message and their struggle against ecstatic cults tended to move in an opposite direction from that taken by the typical religious policy of the Greek tyrants. The religion of Muhammad, which is fundamentally political in its orientation, and his position in Medina, which was in between that of an Italian *podesta* and that of Calvin at Geneva, grew primarily out of his purely prophetic mission. A merchant, he was first a leader of pietistic conventicles in Mecca, until he realized more and more clearly that the organization of the interests of warrior clans in the acquisition of booty was the external basis provided for his missionizing.

On the other hand, there are various transitional phases linking the prophet to the teacher of ethics, especially the teacher of social ethics. Such a teacher, full of a new or recovered understanding of ancient wisdom, gathers disciples about him, counsels private individuals in personal matters and nobles in questions relating to public affairs, and purports to mold ethical ways of life, with the ultimate goal of influencing the crystallization of ethical regulations. The bond between the teacher of religious or philosophical wisdom and his disciple is uncommonly strong and is regulated in an authoritarian fashion, particularly in the sacred laws of Asia. Everywhere the disciple–master relationship is classified among those involving reverence. Generally, the doctrine of magic, like that of heroism, is so regulated that the novice is assigned to a particularly experienced master or is required to seek him out. This is comparable to the relationship in German fraternities, in which the junior member (the *Leibbursche*) is attached by a kind of personal piety to the senior member (the *Leibfuchs*), who watches over his training. All the Greek poetry of pederasty derives from such a relationship of respect, and similar phenomena are to be found among Buddhists and Confucianists, indeed in all monastic education.

The most complete expression of this disciple–master relationship is to be found in the position of the *guru* in Hindu sacred law. Every young man belonging to polite society was unconditionally required to devote himself for many years to the instruction and direction of life provided by such a Brahminic teacher. The obligation of obedience to the *guru*, who had absolute power over his charges, a relationship comparable to that of the occidental *famulus* to his *magister*, took precedence over loyalty to family, even as the position of the court Brahmin (*purohita*) was officially regulated so as to raise his position far above that of the most powerful father confessor in the Occident. Yet the *guru* is, after all, only a teacher who transmits acquired, not revealed, knowledge, and this by virtue of a commission and not on his own authority.

The philosophical ethicist and the social reformer are not prophets in our sense of the word, no matter how closely they may seem to resemble prophets. Actually, the oldest Greek sages, who like Empedocles are wreathed in legend, and other Greek sages such as Pythagoras stand closer to the prophets. They have left at least some legacy of a distinctive doctrine of salvation and conduct of life, and they laid some claim to the status of savior. Such intellectual teachers of salvation have parallels in India, but the Greek teachers fell far short of the Hindu teachers in consistently focusing both life and doctrine on salvation.

Even less can the founders and heads of actual "schools of philosophy" be regarded as prophets in our sense, no matter how closely they may approach this category in some respects. From Confucius, in whose temple even the emperor made obeisance, graded transitions lead to Plato. But both of them were simply academic teaching philosophers, who differed chiefly in that Confucius was centrally concerned and Plato only occasionally concerned to influence princes in the direction of particular social reforms.

What primarily differentiates such figures from the prophets is their lack of that vital emotional preaching which is distinctive of prophecy, regardless of whether this is disseminated by the spoken word, the pamphlet, or any other type of literary composition (e.g. the *suras* of Muhammad). The enterprise of the prophet is closer to that of the popular orator (*demagogue*) or political publicist than to that of the teacher. On the other hand, the activity of a Socrates, who also felt himself opposed to the professional teaching enterprise of the

Sophists, must be distinguished in theory from the activities of a prophet, by the absence of a directly revealed religious mission in the case of Socrates. Socrates' demon (*daimonion*) reacted only to concrete situations, and then only to dissuade and admonish. For Socrates, this was the outer limit of his ethical and strongly utilitarian rationalism, which occupied for him the position that magical divination assumed for Confucius. For this reason, Socrates' demon cannot be compared at all to the conscience of a genuine religious ethic; much less can it be regarded as the instrument of prophecy.

Such a divergence from the characteristic traits of the Hebrew prophets holds true of all philosophers and their schools as they were known in China, India, ancient Hellas, and in the medieval period among Jews, Arabs, and Christians alike. All such philosophies had the same sociological form. But philosophic teaching, as in the case of the Cynics, might take the form of an exemplary prophecy of salvation (in the sense presently to be explained) by virtue of practicing the pattern of life achieved and propagated by a particular school. These prophets and their schools might, as in the case of the Cynics, who protested against the sacramental grace of the mysteries, show certain outer and inner affinities to Hindu and Oriental ascetic sects. But the prophet, in our special sense, is never to be found where the proclamation of a religious truth of salvation through personal revelation is lacking. In our view, this qualification must be regarded as the decisive hallmark of prophecy.

Finally, the Hindu reformers of religion such as Shankara and Ramanuja and their occidental counterparts like Luther, Zwingli, Calvin, and Wesley are to be distinguished from the category of prophets by virtue of the fact that they do not claim to be offering a substantively new revelation or to be speaking in the name of a special divine injunction. This is what characterized the founder of the Mormon church, who resembled, even in matters of detail, Muhammad and above all the Jewish prophets. The prophetic type is also manifest in Montanus and Novitianus, and in such figures as Mani and Manus, whose message had a more rational doctrinal content than did that of George Fox, a prophet type with emotional nuances.

When we have separated out from the category of prophet all the aforementioned types, which sometimes abut very closely, various others still remain. The first is that of the mystagogue. He performs sacraments, i.e. magical actions that contain the boons of salvation. Throughout the entire world there have been saviors of this type whose difference from the average magician is only one of degree, the extent of which is determined by the formation of a special congregation around him. Very frequently dynasties of mystagogues developed on the basis of a sacramental charisma which was regarded as hereditary. These dynasties maintained their prestige for centuries, investing their disciples with great authority and thus developing a kind of hierarchical position. This was especially true in India, where the title of *guru* was also used to designate distributors of salvation and their plenipotentiaries. It was likewise the case in China, where the hierarch of the Taoists and the heads of certain secret sects played just such hereditary roles. Finally, one type of exemplary prophet to be discussed presently was also generally transformed into a mystagogue in the second generation.

The mystagogues were also very widely distributed throughout the Near East, and they entered Greece in the prophetic age to which reference was made earlier. Yet the far more ancient noble families, who were the hereditary incumbents of the Eleusinian mysteries, also represented at least another marginal manifestation of the simple hereditary priestly families. Ethical doctrine was lacking in the mystagogue, who distributed magical salvation, or at least doctrine played only a very subordinate role in his work. Instead, his primary gift was hereditarily transmitted magical art. Moreover, he normally made a living from his art, for which there was a great demand. Consequently we must exclude him, too, from the conception of prophet, even though he sometimes revealed new ways of salvation.

Thus, there remain only two kinds of prophets in our sense, one represented most clearly by the Buddha, the other with especial clarity by Zoroaster and Muhammad. The prophet may be primarily, as in the cases just noted, an instrument for the proclamation of a god and his will, be this a concrete command or an abstract norm. Preaching as one who has received a commission from god, he demands obedience as an ethical duty. This type we shall term the "ethical prophet". On the other hand, the prophet may be an exemplary man who, by his personal example, demonstrates to others the way to religious salvation, as in the case of the Buddha. The preaching of this type of prophet says nothing about a divine mission or an ethical duty of obedience, but rather directs itself to the self-interest of those who crave salvation, recommending to them the same path as he himself traversed. Our designation for this second type of prophecy is "exemplary".

The exemplary type is particularly characteristic of prophecy in India, although there have been a few manifestations of it in China (e.g. Lao Tzu) and the Near East. On the other hand, the ethical type is confined to the Near East, regardless of racial differences there. For neither the Vedas nor the classical books of the Chinese – the oldest portions of which in both cases consist of songs of praise and thanksgiving by sacred singers, and of magical rites and ceremonies – makes it appear at all probable that prophecy of the ethical type, such as developed in the Near East or Iran, could ever have arisen in India or China. The decisive reason for this is the absence of a personal, transcendental, and ethical god. In India this concept was found only in a sacramental and magical form, and then only in the later and popular faiths. But in the religions of those social classes within which the decisive prophetic conceptions of Mahavira and Buddha were developed, ethical prophecy appeared only intermittently and was constantly subjected to reinterpretations in the direction of pantheism. In China the notion of ethical prophecy was altogether lacking in the ethics of the class that exercised the greatest influence in the society. To what degree this may presumably be associated with the intellectual distinctiveness of such classes, which was of course determined by various social factors, will be discussed later.

As far as purely religious factors are concerned, it was decisive for both India and China that the conception of a rationally regulated world had its point of origin in the ceremonial order of sacrifices, on the unalterable sequence of which everything depended. In this regard, crucial importance was attached to the indispensable regularity of meteorological processes, which were thought of in animistic terms. What was involved here was the normal activity or inactivity of the spirits and demons. According to both classical and heterodox Chinese views, these processes were held to be insured by the ethically proper conduct of government, that followed the correct path of virtue, the Tao; without this everything would fail, even according to Vedic doctrine. Thus, in India and China, rita and Tao respectively represented similar superdivine, impersonal forces.

On the other hand, the personal, transcendental, and ethical god is a Near-Eastern concept. It corresponds so closely to that of an all-powerful mundane king with his rational bureaucratic regime that a causal connection can scarcely be overlooked. Throughout the world the magician is in the first instance a rainmaker, for the harvest depends on timely and sufficient rain, though not in excessive quantity. Until the present time the pontifical Chinese emperor has remained a rainmaker, for in northern China, at least, the uncertainty of the weather renders dubious the operation of irrigation procedures, no matter how extensive they are. Of greater significance was the construction of dams and internal canals, which became the real source of the imperial bureaucracy. The emperor sought to avert meteorological disturbances through sacrifices, public atonement, and various virtuous practices, e.g. the termination of abuses in the administration, or the organization of a raid on unpunished malefactors. For it was always assumed that the reason for the excitation of the spirits and the disturbances of the cosmic order had to be sought either in the personal derelictions of the monarch or in some manifestation of social disorganization. Again, rain was one of the rewards promised by Yahweh to his devotees, who were at that time primarily agriculturalists, as is clearly apparent in the older portions of the tradition. God promised neither too scanty rain nor yet excessive precipitation or deluge.

But throughout Mesopotamia and Arabia, however, it was not rain that was the creator of the harvest, but artificial irrigation alone. In Mesopotamia, irrigation was the sole source of the absolute power of the monarch, who derived his income by compelling his conquered subjects to build canals and cities adjoining them, just as the regulation of the Nile was the source of the Egyptian monarch's strength. In the desert and semiarid regions of the Near East this control of irrigation waters was indeed one source of the conception of a god who had created the earth and man out of nothing and not merely fashioned them, as was believed elsewhere. A riparian economy of this kind actually did produce a harvest out of nothing, from the desert sands. The monarch even created law by legislation and rationalization, a development the world experienced for the first time in Mesopotamia. It seems quite reasonable, therefore, that as a result of such experiences the ordering of the world should be conceived as the law of a freely acting, transcendental, and personal god.

Another, and negative, factor accounting for the development in the Near East of a world order that reflected the operation of a personal god was the relative absence of those distinctive classes who were the bearers of the Hindu and Chinese ethics, and who created the godless religious ethics found in those countries. But even in Egypt, where originally Pharaoh himself was a god, the attempt of Ikhnaton to produce an astral monotheism foundered because of the power of the priesthood, which had by then systematized popular animism and become invincible. In Mesopotamia the development of monotheism and demagogic prophecy was opposed by the ancient pantheon, which was politically organized and had been systematized by the priests, and was further opposed and limited by the rigid development of the state.

The kingdom of the Pharaohs and of Mesopotamia made an even more powerful impression upon the Israelites than the great Persian monarch, the *basileus kat exochen*, made upon the Greeks (the strong impact of Cyrus upon the Greeks is mirrored in the eulogistic account of him formulated in the pedagogical treatise, the *Cyropaidia*, despite the defeat of this monarch). The Israelites had gained their freedom from the "house of bondage" of the earthly Pharaoh only because a divine king had come to their assistance. Indeed, their subsequent establishment of a worldly monarchy was expressly declared to be a declension from Yahweh, the real ruler of the people. Hebrew prophecy was completely oriented to a relationship with the great political powers of the time, the great kings, who as the rods of God's wrath first destroy Israel and then, as a consequence of divine intervention, permit Israelites to return from the Exile to their own land. In the case of Zoroaster, too, it can be asserted that the range of his vision was also oriented to the views of the civilized lands of the West.

Thus, the distinctive character of the earliest prophecy, in both its dualistic and monotheistic forms, seems to have been determined decisively – aside from the operation of certain other concrete historical influences – by the pressure of relatively contiguous great centers of rigid social organization upon less developed neighboring peoples. The latter tended to see in their own continuous peril from the pitiless bellicosity of terrible nations the anger and grace of a heavenly king.

Regardless of whether a particular religious prophet is predominantly of the ethical or predominantly of the exemplary type, prophetic revelation involves for both the prophet himself and for his followers – and this is the element common to both varieties – a unified view of the world derived from a consciously integrated and meaningful attitude toward life. To the prophet, both the life of man and the world, both social and cosmic events, have a certain systematic and coherent meaning. To this meaning the conduct of mankind must be oriented if it is to bring salvation, for only in relation to this meaning does life obtain a unified and significant pattern. Now the structure of this meaning may take varied forms, and it may weld together into a unity motives that are logically quite heterogeneous. The whole conception is dominated, not by logical consistency, but by practical valuations. Yet it always denotes, regardless of any variations in scope and in measure of success, an effort to systematize all the manifestations of life; that is, to organize practical behavior into a direction of life, regardless of the form it may assume in any individual case. Moreover, it always contains the important religious conception of the world as a cosmos which is challenged to produce somehow a "meaningful", ordered totality, the particular manifestations of which are to be measured and evaluated according to this requirement.

The conflict between empirical reality and this conception of the world as a meaningful totality, which is based on a religious postulate, produces the strongest tensions in man's inner life as well as in his external relationship to the world. To be sure, this problem is by no means dealt with by prophecy alone. Both priestly wisdom and all completely nonsacerdotal philosophy, the intellectualist as well as the popular varieties, are somehow concerned with it. The ultimate question of all metaphysics has always been something like this: if the world as a whole and life in particular were to have a meaning, what might it be, and how would the world have to look in order to correspond to it? The religious problem-complex of prophets and priests is the womb from which nonsacerdotal philosophy emanated, wherever it developed. Subsequently, nonsacerdotal philosophy was bound to take issue with the antecedent thought of the religious functionaries; and the struggle between them provided one of the very important components of religious evolution.

7

FORMATION OF THE NEED
TO ACHIEVE*

David C. McClelland

*Until consideration of the prophet, our investigations have suggested
that religion often has adverse effects upon personality formation,
sometimes harmfully interfering with perception and the development
of attitudes, thought organization, and relationships. Weber in turn has
pointed out that religion can influence persons in radically different
ways; significant factors include how an individual conceives of his relationship to his god and of the way to salvation. A religion which
envisages salvation as a result of tight conformity to traditional
standards or of disengagement from worldly affairs is not likely to
motivate its adherents to change social structures or achieve worldly
results. However, a very personal religion which emphasizes that individuals must work out their salvation through disciplined worldly involvement is much more likely to motivate its members strongly in the
direction of secular achievement. On the assumption that religious ideas
affect the development of personality by establishing motives, Weber
argued in* The Protestant Ethic and the Spirit of Capitalism *that
where Calvinistic theology developed into a Puritan ethic, it played a
highly significant role in producing an attitude and frame of mind that
was highly conducive to a capitalistic system, when environmental factors were also favorable to the development of capitalism.*

*The psychologist David McClelland has developed this hypothesis
of Weber using empirical, quantitative measurements; his objective was
to illuminate some of the psychological origins of economic growth, by*

* Used with permission from David C. McClelland, *The Achieving Society* (New
York: D. Van Nostrand Co., 1961), pp. 143–148 and 367–372.

showing how social norms are reflected in the attitudes of individuals.
He points out that a strong need for achievement is necessary for
economic growth; having isolated by scientific methods this psycho-
logical factor (n Achievement) he examined numerous diverse situations
to verify the correlation between the rise in capitalistic entrepreneurs,
for example, with marked increase in the motivation for achievement.
He also tested the hypothesis that religion is a significant variable in
developing a strong need for achievement. If this hypothesis is valid, we
should expect to find behind upsurges of capitalistic growth a com-
parable increase in highly individualistic and activistic religion. Two
brief selections follow from his study. In the first he correlates the
economic growth in England during the eighteenth century with the
development of religious sects, in particular Wesleyan evangelicalism.
In the second he considers sources of n *Achievement. In addition to*
environmental factors and child rearing, he discovered that some re-
ligion has been a significant source in the development of n *Achieve-*
ment, as his examination of the special attitudes fostered by this type
of religion indicates. However, his findings indicate that the situation
is considerably more complex than we might expect if we were to rely
on Weber's hypothesis without carefully examining diverse situations.

Some questions for discussion and reflection: What characteristic
features of religion have been the most influential in forming the strong
need for achievement? How do you think religion has been able to have
such a powerful influence in the formation of a personal world? What
other needs and attitudes has religion fostered? Assuming religion has
been a significant variable with respect to the development of n *Achieve-*
ment in the past, to what extent do you think it is significant in de-
veloping this need today? If you do not think religion is the source for
n *Achievement today, what do you think is?*

For further study, one may wish to read the discussion about religion
and personality in terms of the effects concepts of salvation have upon
attitudes and life styles by Milton Yinger, Religion, Society and the
Individual (*New York: The Macmillan Co., 1957*), *pp. 73–124.*
Further reading in McClelland's book, The Achieving Society (*New*
York: D. Van Nostrand Co., 1961). *The book also exists in a paper-*
back edition published by The Free Press (New York).

IT IS extremely hazardous to draw inferences about economic life
from what happens in other spheres of human activity, yet it is perhaps worth mentioning that the first half of the eighteenth century
in England might well be described by some such term as "stag-

nation" or "consolidation" in many fields of endeavor. Politically, Walpole was primarily interested in peace and compromise, in letting sleeping dogs lie. The universities and the Royal Navy languished. Kroeber notes "a definite dip in the first half of the eighteenth century in the production of eminent men of science in England, and other eminent men as well. . . . The emphasis of the time was on 'politeness'; which, earlier developed in France than in England, and perhaps contributed to the premature ending of the great Descartes–Fermat growth. . . . That the interregnum was profound though short is indicated also by the miscellaneous origins of the participants when British science began producing again after 1750."[1] The one really outstanding achievement during this time was the firm establishment of parliamentary rule and the codification of English law, culminating in Blackstone's famous Commentaries. But evidence strongly suggests that interest in law, in codification of the traditional, is antithetical to interests in exploiting the new fields represented both by science and business. . . .

To turn now to the *n* Achievement data, there is no question but that the economic slump characterizing the first half of the eighteenth century was preceded by a fall in *n* Achievement level beginning in the period 1625–1675 and continuing through the next fifty years to 1725. The drop appears in all three forms of literary samples. The simplest statistical comparison is between the level for 1500–1625 versus the level for 1626–1725. *T* tests were computed for the comparison for each of the three types of literature separately, and their *p* values combined by the chi-square technique. The results show that the chances of the drop arising from sampling fluctuations are less than one in a hundred, i.e. the drop in *n* Achievement is marked and statistically highly significant. What produced it is really not a question for detailed examination here, but it may be noted in passing that these were years of great internal stress and civil war in Britain, of struggles between kings and Parliament as to who should rule. Apparently the generally unsettled conditions of ordinary life affected the motives and the values of the people at the time more than it did England's economy, which continued to thrive throughout the seventeenth century, a finding which may come as a surprise to some historians who look to more direct and immediate connections between political and economic developments. If our argument is correct, the political instability of the seventeenth century did affect the economy not at the time, but a generation or two later and then only indirectly by affecting the motives and aspirations of people.

Fortunately the third phase in the development of the English economy is not likely to be questioned seriously by anyone except those who are trapped by their belief that national income per capita is the best measure of economic development. A marked increase in the rate of growth began near the end of the eighteenth century and continued on through the Industrial Revolution. The coal import figures show that the gains from around 1770 to 1833 were well above average and reached a magnitude several times as great as the earlier spurt in Elizabethan times. . . . The chief agent of change was the rapid growth in technology brought about by the marriage of science and industry. The last third of the eighteenth century saw the practical application of many technological improvements which made greatly increased productivity possible – the spinning "jenny", the power loom, Watt's steam engine, new applications of chemistry to industry, improved methods of producing pig iron, and the use of iron wire rope for winding up coal.

Did a rise in n Achievement level precede this striking economic development? Once again the answer must be in the affirmative. All three types of literature showed a rise in n Achievement between 1700 and 1750. The simplest statistical comparison again is to check the low point in n Achievement from 1625–1725 with the level in the succeeding century, 1725–1825. All three measures of n Achievement show a rise from one to the other of these time periods and the probability of such increases occurring by chance is less than one in a hundred using the combined chi-square technique as in previous comparisons. . . .

THE WESLEYAN REVIVAL, n ACHIEVEMENT, AND ECONOMIC GROWTH

Once again there is an opportunity to check the connection between n Achievement and the rise of Protestantism. Was the increase in n Achievement between 1700 and 1750 accompanied by a Protestant revival? Certainly yes. It was precisely during this period beginning in 1729 at Oxford that John Wesley sparked the religious revival that culminated in the foundation of the nonconformist Methodist Church. Trevelyan notes that "the dissenting bodies of the Bunyan tradition which had been founded in the heat and zeal of the Cromwellian era" had tended to become more respectable and less enthusiastic (roughly from 1680 to 1730). The zeal of the first Methodists like John Wesley and George Whitefield "was opposed in every respect to the characteristic faults and merits of the eighteenth century attitude of mind", and put new life in the dissenting bodies. Furthermore, Methodism was influential precisely among those commercial and industrial classes that spearheaded the Industrial Revolution. History appears to have repeated itself. Once again in the first half of the eighteenth century as in the first half of the sixteenth century a strong Protestant movement coincides with a high *n* Achievement level and both are followed in a generation or so by a greatly increased rate of economic growth.

Our interpretation of Weber's hypothesis in Chapter 2 has two specific implications for developments in England at this time: (1) the higher *n* Achievement reflected in the literary samples was more heavily concentrated in the nonconformist Protestant group and (2) the nonconformist group, because of its higher *n* Achievement, was more responsible for the increased entrepreneurial activity that sparked the Industrial Revolution from around 1770 on. Direct quantitative evidence on the first hypothesis is not available yet, although it could be obtained by comparing, for example, the *n* Achievement levels in nonconformist versus Anglican sermons or in other personal documents produced by key individuals of the two religious persuasions. But indirect evidence strongly supports the hypothesis. The twin keynotes of Methodism were stress on constant personal communion with God and on Christian perfection in this life. The one promotes self-reliance in establishing and maintaining continuous contact with God and the other, high standards of excellence in judging one's own conduct. These happen also to be the key elements in the formation of *n* Achievement.

Both are nicely expressed in a verse from one of the well-known hymns of Charles Wesley:

> Heavenly Adam, Life divine
> Change my nature into thine
> Move and spread throughout my soul
> Activate and fill the whole.

The singer is, in effect, making a direct personal approach to God to help him be more perfect. And the perfection of the individual's relationship to God is "known by its fruits", by right conduct. Wesley's insistence on the importance of Christian perfection was so strong that it got him into serious trouble with the established church: "Christians are saved in this world from all sin, from all unrighteousness, that they are now in such a sense perfect, as not to commit sin." Whatever its political or theological implications, such an uncompromising stress on excellence (as the very name Methodist implies) seems almost certain to have acted to promote the development of achievement motivation in Methodist children. And the picture was similar in other nonconformist bodies in England in the eighteenth century. It is one of the ironies of history that while the religious revivalists were almost exclusively concerned with man's relationship to God, they defined it in such a way that it tended to promote a trait of character – high n Achievement – that led in turn very often to marked business success. Wesley himself was puzzled and somewhat alarmed by the fact that Methodists tended to grow rich since he also believed that it was harder for a rich man to get into heaven than for a "camel to pass through the needle's eye".

TABLE 4.7   BIRTHPLACE AND RELIGIOUS AFFILIATION OF BRITISH INNOVATORS IN THE INDUSTRIAL REVOLUTION 1725–1850 (After Hagen, 1861)

Birthplace	Population estimates (around 1800)	Number of innovators	p
England and Wales	9,187,000	55	
Scotland	1,652,000	18	
Per cent Scottish	15·2%	24·6%	<0·05
Unknown or other		9	
Religious affiliation			
Anglican	—	27	
Unknown	—	27	
Nonconformist	650,000	28	
Per cent nonconformist	6·0%	34·1%	<0·001

Evidence for the second hypothesis – that nonconformists sparked the Industrial Revolution in England – is more direct. Historians and economists have long accepted the point without much question, illustrating it with a number of striking examples like the Quakers in the iron industry, but only recently has Hagen (1961) collected the figures which permit a systematic test of the hypothesis. Relevant data are summarized in Table 4.7 which shows the origins of innovating entrepreneurs in the Industrial Revolution. Hagen took all the names of such entrepreneurs mentioned by T. S. Ashton (1948) in his book *The Industrial Revolution* and tried to track down their nationality and religious affiliation. The advantage of such a technique is that it starts with a presumably unbiased sample of industrial innovators and then attempts to see whether they are drawn in greater numbers from different segments of the population than would be expected on the basis of the proportion of that segment to the whole. The breakdown by birthplace is of interest here because the established church of Scotland was more Protestant in Weber's

Calvinistic sense than the established church of England. And it is true that the percentage of known Scotchmen among the innovating group is significantly higher than it should be based on the estimate of the per cent of Scotchmen in the total British population. However, the finding loses some of its force when it is noted that four of the eighteen Scotchmen were actually Anglicans. If they are eliminated, the difference in percentages becomes insignificant and it is doubtful that a case can be made for Calvinism being a more effective breeder of industrial entrepreneurs than other forms of Protestantism, at least so far as this comparison is concerned.

The situation is quite different so far as the nonconformist bodies are concerned. They formed at the very most around 1800 six to eight per cent of the total population of England, Wales, and Scotland, yet they produced at least a third of the innovators in the sample, a difference over the expected per cent which is highly significant statistically. Unfortunately it is not possible to compare very precisely the yield of the nonconformist and established churches in numbers of innovators because no figures are available on what proportion of the population belonged in any real sense to the Anglican Church. If one argues that everyone who was not a dissenter was an Anglican, then of course the yield of the nonconformist bodies was much greater than that of the established church, but it is doubtful if being an Anglican meant very much religiously to a considerable percentage of the population. That is, an unknown percentage of the population ought really to be considered not religious, rather than included with the Anglican population. But even if one assumes that only half of the population belonged to the Anglican faith in any real sense, it can be seen from Table 4.7 that this 50% of the population produced a significantly smaller percentage of the industrial entrepreneurs than it should have on a proportional basis. The connection of the particular form of Protestantism common to the dissenting bodies (Methodism, Quakerism, Unitarianism, etc.) with the innovating leadership of the Industrial Revolution seems firmly established. The presumptive reasons for the connection – a higher *n* Achievement level among the dissenting groups – has not been directly checked but is strongly supported by an analysis of the nature of religious revivals like Methodism in the eighteenth century and by inferences based on contemporary evidence.

In summary, Bradburn and Berlew's findings provide three separate confirmations of our basic hypothesis in the course of English economic development between 1600 and 1800. A rise or at least a high level of *n* Achievement in the sixteenth century preceded the first wave of economic growth in the early seventeenth century; a fall in n Achievement concentrated in the years 1650–1700 preceded the economic stagnation of the early eighteenth century; and a decisive rise in n Achievement beginning around the middle of the eighteenth century preceded the spectacular economic growth of the Industrial Revolution. . . . Furthermore, both the sixteenth and eighteenth-century increases in n Achievement level were accompanied by strong popular Protestant movements within the church, and the fall in n Achievement corresponds to a time when Protestantism in England was not very active but was becoming "respectable". . . .

CORE RELIGIOUS VALUES: POSITIVE MYSTICISM

Dealing in terms of the religious labels of Protestant, Catholic, and Jew has not gotten us very far in our search for the basic values associated with the development of n Achievement. It is obviously necessary to go behind the labels to elements within each of the religions which may be more closely associated with achievement training. A more promising place to begin is with the religious attitudes of sects within all religions that have been conspicuously successful in the business world.

The original impulse to the Protestant Reformation was certainly antisacerdotal and individualistic. It may have come at least in part from the Scandinavian ethic of the Vikings, . . . for the Vikings were rather defiant of supernatural powers and showed the interest in trade and travel that we have found to be characteristic of a people with high n Achievement. But both in England in Anglicanism and in Germany in Lutheranism, the impulse was curbed by the weight of Catholic tradition and produced churches that as institutions were compromises between the old and the new. They relied, at least to some extent, on tradition and on centralized church authority and ritual as the Roman Church did. The individualistic spirit persisted in purer form in some of the minor Protestant sects, like the Anabaptists on the Continent or the Quakers and later the Methodists in England, and the Unitarians in the United States. Oddly enough, it is these smaller Protestant bodies which were generally more revolutionary than the established Protestant churches and which were especially associated with business success. For example, eight out of the eighty-two industrial innovators in Hagen's list were Quakers, a much larger number than would have been predicted on the basis of the proportion that the Quakers were of all the nonconformist sects. Likewise, Quakers in Philadelphia were showing a remarkable talent for business. It may, therefore, be rewarding to look for a moment at the religious characteristics of these sects.

First, they were nearly all more strongly against traditional church authority than even the larger Protestant denominations had been. The Quakers went all the way: they were even opposed to having sacred places of worship – churches, which George Fox referred to contemptuously as "steeple houses". They discarded all outward signs of religious authority – sacraments, priestly robes, religious pictures, and sacred music – and revolted even against the notion of a special class of men whose duty it was to look after religious matters. They were strongly opposed to the "hireling ministry". On the positive side, they emphasized the mystical strains in Christianity which had stressed direct communion of the individual with God. Rufus Jones, in describing the religious character of mystics of all kinds, succeeds, as a good Quaker, in giving a vivid picture of the positive mysticism characteristic of Quakerism at its best:

> They [the mystics] had saved Christianity from being submerged under scholastic formalism and ecclesiastical systems, which were alien to man's essential nature and need. They have been spiritual leaders, they are the persons who shifted the levels of life for the race. They have been able to render these services because they felt themselves allied inwardly with a larger personal Power than themselves, and they have been aware that they were in immediate correspondence with Some One – a Holy Spirit, a Great Companion – who is working with them and through them. This *furtherance of life* by incoming energy, the heightening of power by correspondence with what *seems* to be God, is, however, by no means confined to a few chosen spirits and rare geniuses; it is a widespread fact to be reckoned with everywhere.[2]

As the quotation demonstrates, this particular type of mysticism was not world-renouncing, in the sense of the asceticism of the Catholic or Buddhist monk, nor was it confined to a few "rare spirits". Rather, everyone could get renewed energy by direct contact with the Divine. The Methodists certainly also belonged to some extent in this tradition in that they, too, stressed spiritual union with Christ for every believer, so that man's will becomes God's will through Perfect Love. Furthermore, for many of these people, mysticism implied a reverence for life which took the form of renunciation of violence, or pacifism.

The fact that these mystical religious sects happened also to be unusually successful in business might be regarded as an accident except for a curious fact. In India, where the religious traditions have been totally different and entirely outside the stream of Christianity, the picture is amazingly similar. In northern India, for example, the conspicuously successful business communities again represent small, minority religious sects – the Jains, the Vaishnava Hindus, and the Parsees. All of these religious groups, like the minor Protestant bodies in the West, are characterized by opposition to dominant traditional religious authority – in this case Hindu Brahmanism. Furthermore, both the Jains and the Vaishnavas practice *ahimsa* or "nonviolence toward living beings". . . .

It is at least an odd coincidence that an attitude of nonviolence or reverence for life should be associated with business success both in the East and in the West. The connecting link seems to be the mystical reverence for life rather than asceticism. Both the Quakers and Jains are notorious ascetics, but the Vaishnavas, if anything, are epicurean in their tastes. But "reverence for life" may not be the psychologically significant variable running through all these religions either, for the Parsees do not practice *ahimsa*. They are a remnant of Persians who fled to India centuries ago who were Zoroastrians. The key doctrine in Zoroastrianism is psychologically somewhat akin to the key notion in Calvinism: every single act that a man makes has eternal significance for his salvation as it contributes either to the forces of good or evil fighting for control of the universe and his individual soul. Thus a man's life "is, in spite of dangers and temptations, a responsible one" in which there is no "remission of sins" or divine forgiveness for very human foibles. If a man does something evil, it is never wiped out in the eternal accounting books, although it may be outweighed by corresponding good deeds. Psychologically speaking, what all of these religious viewpoints appear to mean for the individual believer is a sense of being religiously "on his toes", so to speak. He must consider the religious significance of every act, not in the ritualistic Brahman sense but in the sense of having to make a responsible decision as to whether he is showing reverence for life or contributing to his eternal salvation. In the negative sense, the picture is even somewhat clearer; these are all sects which do not hand over religious authority exclusively to experts or traditions that prescribe minutely for them how they should behave ritually. Rejection of the priestly caste was by no means as extreme in the East as it had been in the West under Quakerism, but in all three of the Indian religious groups, the laity participated much more in the regulation of religion than in traditional Brahmanism. . . .

The number of similar cases could be multiplied: the rise of the business class in Japan in the nineteenth century was associated with a special form of Buddhism – Zen, which again is a form of positive mysticism which is definitely individualistic and against many ritual religious forms. It stresses individual enlightenment or *satori* which is to be attained not by ritual or by "verbal implantation from the outside" but by the growth of "one's inner life". "Zen discipline is simple, direct, self-reliant, self-denying."[3] Its similarity to Quakerism has been suggested by many, but oddly enough in Japan it was the religion predominantly of the military caste – the *samurai*. And it was precisely from the *samurai* class that the "new economic leaders" were drawn in the late nineteenth century in Japan. Hagen feels that it was the "psychological frustrations" of the *samurai* arising from their increasingly "subordinated status" that drove them into business. Our view does not so much contradict as supplement and extend this. Presumably the *samurai* class would not have felt "frustrated" and reacted by counterstriving *unless they had had high* n *Achievement*, as their association with the mystical Zen Buddhist movement suggests to us that they did have at the time. Other groups have certainly been subordinated from higher status (e.g. the Catholics in England in the eighteenth century) without reacting by counterstriving, presumably because they had low *n* Achievement at the time.

Or finally, to take just one more example, it is a curious fact that the distinct business success of Jews within the past few generations has been associated with a strong antirabbinical mystical movement within Judaism known as Hassidism. Hassidism, like all these other religions, was an attempt to escape from "formalism and ecclesiastical systems" and to encourage the individual believer to feel that he could directly and joyously feel the presence of God. But, as we have repeatedly argued, multiplication of instances is not proof. What is needed is a careful and systematic test of a hypothesis suggested by these cases.

If we assume that these business communities were successful because of a higher average level of *n* Achievement, then it follows that their religious ideas should in some way be connected with a higher level of *n* Achievement. A simple summary of the evidence just reviewed would then run something as follows: institutionalized individualistic approaches to God (represented usually by some strain of positive mysticism) should be associated with higher levels of *n* Achievement. The data already systematically collected on the *n* Achievement levels of preliterate tribes permitted a systematic test of such a hypothesis. Four codes were developed for describing the nature of the religious views of each of these cultures. Each is described fully in Appendix V, but a brief summary will suffice here. The first recorded the extent to which the religions stress *individual versus ritual contact with the Divine*. Individual contact includes private prayer, or group contact (as in Quaker silent meetings, group trances, or revival meetings, etc.), or individual interpretation of oral or written tradition (as in the traditional Protestant practice of encouraging individual members to read the Bible and figure out the meaning of particular verses for their own lives). Ritual contact with the Divine, on the other hand, stresses exact memorization of

TABLE 9.8 RELIGIOUS ORIENTATIONS OF 45 PRELITERATE CULTURES CLASSIFIED AS HIGH AND LOW IN n ACHIEVEMENT ON THE BASIS OF FOLK-TALE CONTENT

Orientations	High n Achievement cultures $N = 23$	Low n Achievement cultures $N = 22$	Chi-square	p
I Per cent above median in individual over ritual contact with the Divine	65	23	8·30	<0·01
II Per cent below median in dependence on religious experts	52	18	5·61	<0·05
III Per cent placing high emphasis on ethics as opposed to self-improvement or worship as goals of religion	57	45		NS
IV Per cent having high internalization as opposed to externalization of the Sacred	48	45		NS

ritual formulas which gain their religious potency, so to speak, from being repeated often exactly as prescribed, as in Navaho, Buddhist, or Roman Catholic chants. Many religions, and certainly complex ones like Roman Catholicism, stress both approaches to the Divine to a certain extent, so that it was necessary to weight the order of importance of each of the approaches in each of the religions, which was done, of course, without any knowledge of the n Achievement content of the folk-tales for the culture. The resulting distribution of scores was broken at the median, and as Table 9.8 shows, the cultures high in n Achievement folk-tale content were significantly more often above the median on individualism in their approach to God.

The second code dealt with the extent to which *religious experts are necessary* in religious activity. For example, Jewish rabbis are useful and very important in the religious life of the Jewish community, but they are strictly speaking not *necessary* in the individual's performance of his religious duties. On the other hand, Roman Catholic priests have special powers directly granted them through the "laying on of hands" from the first heads of the church down to the present. At the other extreme are the Quakers who had practically no ministry at all and refused to believe that any person could perform a religious function for somebody else in a way that would substitute or be better than the person's doing it for himself. Every Quaker is at least theoretically qualified to perform all religious duties. Again, on this dimension, Table 9.8 shows that the preliterate cultures characterized by higher *n* Achievement also less often stressed the importance of religious experts, as *necessary* adjuncts to performing religious duties.

Two other codes, perhaps less directly related to the key hypothesis, did not show differences. The primary goal of the religion was also determined so far as possible in terms of three general objectives – ethical conduct of one man toward another, self-improvement (peace of mind, personal salvation, etc.), and, more strictly speaking *worship*, in the sense of *do ut des* or *do ut abeas*. Since many of the mystical sects described above appear to be characterized by interest in "good works" and an interest in man's relationship to his fellow man, it had been predicted that high *n* Achievement cultures would more often stress ethics as a goal of religion, but the prediction was not confirmed. Finally, since these same sects also appeared to be generally opposed to "externalization of the sacred", to the use of idols, sacred images, fixed places of worship, etc., it was also predicted that the cultures with high *n* Achievement would more often stress "internalization" of the sacred, as in the purely mystical forms of religion. Again, the hypothesis was not confirmed among these preliterate religions.

On the whole, however, our research has refined much more closely the core religious values associated with high *n* Achievement than a general comparison of such large amorphous religious bodies as contemporary Protestantism and Catholicism permitted. The key religious attitude is not unlike the general one we found to be associated with *n* Achievement in Chapters 6 and 7; that is, the person with high *n* Achievement wants to be responsible for his own decisions and the very act of making a decision implies some uncertainty as to the outcome. He is therefore "on his toes" in the same sense as the believer is in individualistic religions. In formal ritualistic ecclesiastical systems, on the other hand, the individual is "safe" if he does exactly what he is supposed to do, performs correct rituals, says his prayers often enough, calls in the right priest at the right time, etc. But here we run into the old chicken-and-egg problem: which came first, individualistic religion or *n* Achievement? No clear answer to the question can be given that would cover all cases, although some evidence on the point will be presented in the next chapter. However, theoretically either factor could "come first" and influence the development of the other. That is, Quaker parents with the religious views just described would certainly tend to behave toward their sons in ways that would be conducive to the development of high *n* Achievement. In this case the religion clearly comes first, and in fact since religion is one of the more stable persistent elements in many societies, it may often have "come first".

NOTES

1. A. L. Kroeber, *Configurations of Cultural Growth* (Berkeley: University of California Press, 1944), pp. 148–149.

2. R. M. Jones, *Studies in Mystical Religion* (London: The Macmillan Co., 1919), p. xxx.

3. D. T. Suzuki, *Zen and Japanese Culture*, rev. and enlarged 2nd ed. (New York: Pantheon Books and London: Routledge & Kegan Paul, 1959), pp. 10, 62.

8

INDIVIDUAL AND SOCIAL NARCISSISM*

Erich Fromm

In many of his writings Erich Fromm has also expressed deep concern about personal motivation. He has explored powerful dynamic factors such as man's fear of being morally alone (Escape from Freedom [*New York: Holt, Rinehart and Winston, 1941*], *published in Britain with title:* The Fear of Freedom [*London: Kegan Paul & Co., 1942*]), *his desire to lead a productive life* (Man for Himself [*New York: Holt, Rinehart and Winston, 1947 and London: Routledge & Kegan Paul, 1948*]), *and his will to love* (The Art of Loving [*New York: Harper and Row, 1956 and London: Allen & Unwin, 1957*]). *He has also explored the relationship between religion and personality in some detail* (Psychoanalysis and Religion [*New Haven: Yale University Press, 1950 and London: Victor Gollancz, 1951*] *and* Ye Shall Be as Gods [*New York: Holt, Rinehart and Winston, 1966 and London: Jonathan Cape, 1967*]). *Similar to Weber he has often focused upon the relationship between moral standards and the development of motives; unlike McClelland's study which is rigorously empirical and neutral in attitude toward both religion and personality types, Fromm's writings are moralistic. Fromm has long expressed the conviction that ethics must have an integral part in the personality sciences; in his writings there is manifest a deep humanistic faith in man combined with an increasing sense of urgency for man to use insights and appropriate methods to meet the dangers threatening his world. In the following chapter Fromm*

* A slightly edited version used by permission from Erich Fromm, *The Heart of Man* (New York: Harper and Row, 1964 and London: Routledge & Kegan Paul, 1965), pp. 62–94.

examines narcissism which, like prejudice, is a motivating factor that can have dire social consequences. He also considers how religion has both fostered narcissism and opposed it.

Questions for discussion: What does Fromm mean by narcissism and how is it distinct from his concept of mature existence? What are the social repercussions of narcissism? How has religion fostered narcissism? What kind of religion might oppose it and serve man's highest interests? How does his differentiation between types of religion compare with Allport's? What does Fromm think is the correlation between psychological insights and existential goals expressed by some religious leaders?

ONE OF the most fruitful and far-reaching of Freud's discoveries is his concept of narcissism. Freud himself considered it to be one of his most important findings, and employed it for the understanding of such distinct phenomena as psychosis ("narcissistic neurosis"), love, castration fear, jealousy, sadism, and also for the understanding of mass phenomena, such as the readiness of the suppressed classes to be loyal to their rulers. In this chapter I want to continue along Freud's line of thought and examine the role of narcissism for the understanding of nationalism, national hatred, and the psychological motivations for destructiveness and war.

I want to mention in passing the fact that the concept of narcissism found hardly any attention in the writings of Jung and Adler, and also less than it deserves in those of Horney. Even in orthodox Freudian theory and therapy the use of the concept of narcissism has remained very much restricted to the narcissism of the infant and that of the psychotic patient. It is probably due to the fact that Freud forced his concept into the frame of his libido theory that the fruitfulness of the concept has not been sufficiently appreciated. . . .

Let us begin our description of narcissism with two extreme examples: the "primary narcissism" of the newborn infant, and the narcissism of the insane person. The infant is not yet related to the outside world (in Freudian terminology his libido has not yet cathexed outside objects). Another way of putting it is to say that the outside world does not exist for the infant, and this to such a degree that it is not able to distinguish between the "I" and the "not I". We might also say that the infant is not "interested" (interesse = "to be in") in the world outside. The only reality that exists for the infant is itself: its body, its physical sensations of cold and warmth, thirst, need for sleep, and bodily contact.

The insane person is in a situation not essentially different from that of the infant. But while for the infant the world outside has *not yet emerged* as real, for the insane person it *has ceased* to be real. In the case of hallucinations, for instance, the senses have lost their function of registering outside events – they register subjective experience in categories of sensory response to objects outside. In the paranoid delusion the same mechanism operates. Fear or suspicion, for instance, which are subjective emotions, become objectified in such a way that the paranoid person is convinced that others are conspiring against him; this is precisely the difference to the neurotic person: the latter may be constantly afraid of being hated, persecuted, etc., but he still knows that this is what he *fears*. For the paranoid person the fear has been transformed into a fact.

A particular instance of narcissism which lies on the borderline between sanity and insanity can be found in some men who have reached an extraordinary degree of power. The Egyptian pharaohs, the Roman Caesars, the Borgias, Hitler, Stalin, Trujillo – they all show certain similar features. They have attained absolute power; their word is the ultimate judgment of everything, including life and death; there seems to be no limit to their capacity to do what they want. They are gods, limited only by illness, age, and death. They try to find a solution to the problem of human existence by the desperate attempt to transcend the limitation of human existence. They try to pretend that there is no limit to their lust and to their power, so they sleep with countless women, they kill numberless men, they build castles everywhere, they "want the moon", they "want the impossible".[1] This is madness, even though it is an attempt to solve the problem of existence by pretending that one is not human. It is a madness which tends to grow in the lifetime of the afflicted person. The more he tries to be god, the more he isolates himself from the human race; this isolation makes him more frightened, everybody becomes his enemy, and in order to stand the resulting fright he has to increase his power, his ruthlessness, and his narcissism. This Caesarian madness would be nothing but plain insanity were it not for one factor: by his power Caesar has bent reality to his narcissistic fantasies. He has forced everybody to agree that he is god, the most powerful and the wisest of men – hence his own megalomania seems to be a reasonable feeling. On the other hand, many will hate him, try to overthrow and kill him – hence his pathological suspicions are also backed by a nucleus of reality. As a result he does not feel disconnected from reality – hence he can keep a modicum of sanity, even though in a precarious state. . . .

Narcissism is a passion the intensity of which in many individuals can only be compared with sexual desire and the desire to stay alive. In fact, many times it proves to be stronger than either. Even in the average individual in whom it does not reach such intensity, there remains a narcissistic core which appears to be almost indestructible. This being so we might suspect that like sex and survival, the narcissistic passion also has an important *biological function*. Once we raise this question the answer comes readily. How could the individual survive unless his bodily needs, his interests, his desires, were charged with much energy? Biologically, from the standpoint of survival, man must attribute to himself an importance far above what he gives to anybody else. If he did not do so, from where would he take the energy and interest to defend himself against others, to work for his subsistence, to fight for his survival, to press his claims against those of others? Without narcissism he might be a saint – but do saints have a high survival rate? What from a spiritual standpoint would be most desirable – absence of narcissism – would be most dangerous from the mundane standpoint of survival. Speaking teleologically, we can say that nature had to endow man with a great amount of narcissism to enable him to do what is necessary for survival. This is true especially because nature has not endowed man with well-developed instincts such as the animal has. The animal has no "problems" of survival in the sense that its built-in instinctive nature takes care of survival in such a way that the animal does not have to consider or decide whether or not it wants to make an effort. In man the instinctive apparatus has lost most of its efficacy – hence narcissism assumes a very necessary biological function.

However, once we recognize that narcissism fulfills an important biological function, we are confronted with another question. Does not extreme narcissism have the function of making man indifferent to others, incapable of giving second place to his own needs when this is necessary for cooperation with others? Does not narcissism make man asocial and, in fact, when it reaches an extreme degree, insane? There can be no doubt that extreme individual narcissism would be a severe obstacle to all social life. But if this is so, narcissism must be said to be in *conflict* with the principle of survival, for the individual can survive only if he organizes himself in groups; hardly anyone would be able to protect himself all alone against the dangers of nature, nor would he be able to do many kinds of work which can only be done in groups.

We arrive then at the paradoxical result that narcissism is necessary for survival, and at the same time that it is a threat to survival. The solution of this paradox lies in two directions. One is that *optimal* rather than *maximal* narcissism serves survival; that is to say, the biologically necessary degree of narcissism is reduced to the degree of narcissism that is compatible with social cooperation. The other lies in the fact that individual narcissism is transformed into group narcissism, that the clan, nation, religion, race, etc., become the objects of narcissistic passion instead of the individual. Thus, narcissistic energy is maintained but used in the interests of the survival of the group rather than for the survival of the individual. Before I deal with this problem of group narcissism and its sociological function, I want to discuss the *pathology of narcissism.*

The most dangerous result of narcissistic attachment is the distortion of rational judgment. The object of narcissistic attachment is thought to be valuable (good, beautiful, wise, etc.) not on the basis of an objective value-judgment, but because it is me or mine. Narcissistic value-judgment is prejudiced and biased. Usually this prejudice is rationalized in one form or another, and this rationalization may be more or less deceptive according to the intelligence and sophistication of the person involved. In the drunkard's narcissism the distortion is usually obvious. What we see is a man who talks in a superficial and banal way, yet with the air and intonation of one voicing the most wonderful and interesting words. Subjectively he has a euphoric "on-top-of-the-world" feeling, while in reality he is in a state of self-inflation. All this does not mean to say that the highly narcissistic person's utterances are necessarily boring. If he is gifted or intelligent he will produce interesting ideas, and if he evaluates them highly, his judgment will not be entirely wrong. But the narcissistic person tends to evaluate his own productions highly anyway, and their real quality is not decisive in reaching this evaluation. (In the case of "negative narcissism" the opposite is true. Such a person tends to underevaluate everything that is his own, and his judgment is equally biased.) If he were aware of the distorted nature of his narcissistic judgments, the results would not be so bad. He would – and could – take a humorous attitude toward his narcissistic bias. But this is rare. Usually the person is convinced that there is no bias, and that his judgment is objective and realistic. This leads to a severe distortion of his capacity to think and to judge, since this capacity is blunted again and again when he deals with himself and what is his. Correspondingly, the narcissistic person's judgment is also biased against that which is not "he" or not his. The extraneous ("not me") world is inferior, dangerous, immoral. The narcissistic person, then, ends up with an enormous distortion. He and his are overevaluated.

Everything outside is underevaluated. The damage to reason and objectivity is obvious.

An ever more dangerous pathological element in narcissism is the emotional reaction to criticism of any narcissistically cathexed position. Normally a person does not become angry when something he has done or said is criticized, provided the criticism is fair and not made with hostile intent. The narcissistic person, on the other hand, reacts with intense anger when he is criticized. He tends to feel that the criticism is a hostile attack, since by the very nature of his narcissism he can not imagine that it is justified. The intensity of his anger can be fully understood only if one considers that the narcissistic person is unrelated to the world, and as a consequence is alone, and hence frightened. It is this sense of aloneness and fright which is compensated for by his narcissistic self-inflation. If he *is* the world, there is no world outside which can frighten him; if he is everything, he is not alone; consequently, when his narcissism is wounded he feels threatened in his whole existence. When the one protection against his fright, his self-inflation, is threatened, the fright emerges and results in intense fury. This fury is all the more intense because nothing can be done to diminish the threat by appropriate action; only the destruction of the critic – or oneself – can save one from the threat to one's narcissistic security.

There is an alternative to explosive rage as a result of wounded narcissism, and that is *depression*. The narcissistic person gains his sense of identity by inflation. The world outside is not a problem for him, it does not overwhelm him with its power, because he has succeeded in being the world, in feeling omniscient and omnipotent. If his narcissism is wounded, and if for a number of reasons, such as, for instance, the subjective or objective weakness of his position *vis-à-vis* his critic, he cannot afford to become furious, he becomes depressed. He is unrelated to and uninterested in the world; he is nothing and nobody, since he has not developed his self as the center of his relatedness to the world. If his narcissism is so severely wounded that he can no longer maintain it, his ego collapses and the subjective reflex of this collapse is the feeling of depression. The element of mourning in melancholia refers, in my opinion, to the narcissistic image of the wonderful "I" which has died, and for which the depressed person is mourning.

It is precisely because this narcissistic person dreads the depression which results from a wounding of his narcissism that he desperately tries to avoid such wounds. There are several ways of accomplishing this. One is to increase the narcissism in order that no outside criticism or failure can really touch the narcissistic position. In other words, the intensity of narcissism increases in order to ward off the threat. This means, of course, that the person tries to cure himself of the threatening depression by becoming more severely sick mentally, up to the point of psychosis.

There is, however, still another solution to the threat to narcissism which is more satisfactory to the individual, although more dangerous to others. This solution consists in the attempt to transform reality in such a way as to make it conform, to some extent, with his narcissistic self-image. An example of this is the narcissistic inventor who believes he has invented a *perpetuum mobile*, and who in the process has made a minor discovery of some significance. A more important solution consists in getting the consensus of one other person, and, if possible, in obtaining the consensus of millions. The former case is that of a *folie à deux* (some marriages and friendships rest on this basis), while the latter is that of public figures who prevent the open outbreak of their potential psychosis by gaining the acclaim and consensus of millions of people. The best-known example for this latter case is Hitler. Here was an extremely narcissistic person who probably could have suffered a manifest psychosis had he not succeeded in making millions believe in his own self-image, take his grandiose fantasies regarding the millennium of the "Third Reich" seriously, and even transforming reality in such a way that it seemed proved to his followers that he was right. (After he had failed he had to kill himself, since otherwise the collapse of his narcissistic image would have been truly unbearable.)

There are other examples in history of megalomaniac leaders who "cured" their narcissism by transforming the world to fit it; such people must also try to destroy all critics, since they cannot tolerate the threat which the voice of sanity constitutes for them. From Caligula and Nero to Stalin and Hitler we see that their need to find believers, to transform reality so that it fits their narcissism, and to destroy all critics, is so intense and so desperate precisely because it is an attempt to prevent the outbreak of insanity. Paradoxically, the element of insanity in such leaders makes them also successful. It gives them that certainty and freedom from doubt which is so impressive to the average person. Needless to say, this need to change the world and to win others to share in one's ideas and delusions requires also talents and gifts which the average person, psychotic or nonpsychotic, lacks.

In discussing the pathology of narcissism it is important to distinguish between two forms of narcissism – one *benign*, the other *malignant*. In the benign form, the object of narcissism is the result of a person's effort. Thus, for instance, a person may have a narcissistic pride in his work as a carpenter, as a scientist, or as a farmer. Inasmuch as the object of his narcissism is something he has to work for, his exclusive interest in what is *his* work and *his* achievement is constantly balanced by his interest in the process of work itself, and the material he is working with. The dynamics of this benign narcissism thus are self-checking. The energy which propels the work is, to a large extent, of a narcissistic nature, but the very fact that the work itself makes it necessary to be related to reality, constantly curbs the narcissism and keeps it within bounds. This mechanism may explain why we find so many narcissistic people who are at the same time highly creative.

In the case of malignant narcissism, the object of narcissism is not anything the person does or produces, but something he *has*; for instance, his body, his looks, his health, his wealth, etc. The malignant nature of this type of narcissism lies in the fact that it lacks the corrective element which we find in the benign form. If I am "great" because of some quality I *have*, and not because of something I *achieve*, I do not need to be related to anybody or anything; I need not make any effort. In maintaining the picture of my greatness I remove myself more and more from reality and I have to increase the narcissistic charge in order to be better protected from the danger that my narcissistically inflated ego might be revealed as the product of my empty imagination. Malignant narcissism, thus, is not self-limiting, and in consequence it is crudely solipsistic as well as xenophobic. One who has learned to achieve cannot help acknowledging that others have achieved similar things in similar ways – even if his narcissism may persuade him that his own achievement is greater than that of others. One who has achieved nothing will find it difficult to appreciate the achievements of others, and thus he will be forced to isolate himself increasingly in narcissistic splendor.

We have so far described the dynamics of individual narcissism: the phenomenon, its biological function, and its pathology. This description ought to enable us now to understand the phenomenon of *social narcissism* and the role it plays as a source of violence and war.

The central point of the following discussion is the phenomenon of the transformation of personal into group narcissism. We can start with an observation about the sociological function of group narcissism which parallels the biological function of individual narcissism. From the standpoint of any organized group which wants to survive, it is important that the group be invested by its members with narcissistic energy. The survival of a group depends to some extent on the fact that its members consider its importance as great as or greater than that of their own lives, and furthermore that they believe in the righteousness, or even superiority, of their group as compared with others. Without such narcissistic cathexis of the group, the energy necessary for serving the group, or even making severe sacrifices for it, would be greatly diminished.

In the dynamics of group narcissism we find phenomena similar to those we discussed already in connection with individual narcissism. Here, too, we can distinguish between benign and malignant forms of narcissism. If the object of group narcissism is an achievement, the same dialectical process takes place which we discussed above. The very need to achieve something creative makes it necessary to leave the closed circle of group solipsism and to be interested in the object it wants to achieve. (If the achievement which a group seeks is conquest, the beneficial effect of truly productive effort will of course be largely absent.) If, on the other hand, group narcissism has as its object the group as it is, its splendor, its past achievements, the physique of its members, then the countertendencies mentioned above will not develop, and the narcissistic orientation and subsequent dangers will steadily increase. In reality, of course, both elements are often blended.

There is another sociological function of group narcissism which has not been discussed so far. A society which lacks the means to provide adequately for the majority of its members, or a large proportion of them, must provide these members with a narcissistic satisfaction of the malignant type if it wants to prevent dissatisfaction among them. For those who are economically and culturally poor, narcissistic pride in belonging to the group is the only – and often a very effective – source of satisfaction. Precisely because life is not "interesting" to them, and does not offer them possibilities for developing interests, they may develop an extreme form of narcissism. Good examples of this phenomenon in recent years are the racial narcissism which existed in Hitler's Germany, and which is found in the American South today. In both instances the core of the racial superiority feeling was, and still is, the lower middle class; this backward class, which in Germany as well as in the American South has been economically and culturally deprived, without any realistic hope of changing its situation (because they are the remnants of an older and dying form of society), has only one satisfaction: the inflated image of itself as the most admirable group in the world, and of being superior to another racial group that is singled out as inferior. The member of such a backward group feels: "Even though I am poor and uncultured I am somebody important because I belong to the most admirable group in the world – I am white"; or, "I am an Aryan."

Group narcissism is less easy to recognize than individual narcissism. Assuming a person tells others, "I (and my family) are the most admirable people in the world; we alone are clean, intelligent, good, decent; all others are dirty, stupid, dishonest, and irresponsible," most people would think him crude, unbalanced, or even insane. If, however, a fanatical speaker addresses a mass audience, substituting the nation (or race, religion, political party, etc.) for the "I" and "my family", he will be praised and admired by many for his love of country, love of God, etc. Other nations and religions, however, will resent such a speech for the obvious reason that they are held in contempt. *Within* the favored group, however, everybody's personal narcissism is flattered and the fact that millions of people agree with the statements makes them appear as reasonable. (What the majority of people consider to be "reasonable" is that about which there is agreement, if not among all, at least among a substantial number of people; "reasonable", for most people, has nothing to do with reason, but with consensus.) Inasmuch as the group as a whole requires group narcissism for its survival, it will further narcissistic attitudes and confer upon them the qualification of being particularly virtuous.

The group to which the narcissistic attitude is extended has varied in structure and size throughout history. In the primitive tribe or clan it may comprise only a few hundred members; here the individual is not yet an "individual" but is still united to the blood-group by "primary bonds"[2] which have not yet been broken. The narcissistic involvement with the clan is thus strengthened by the fact that its members emotionally have still no existence of their own outside of the clan.

In the development of the human race we find an ever increasing range of socialization; the original small group based on blood affinity gives way to ever larger groups based on a common language, a common social order, a common faith. The larger size of the group does not necessarily mean that the pathological qualities of narcissism are reduced. As was remarked earlier, the group narcissism of the "whites" or the "Aryans" is as malignant as the extreme narcissism of a single person can be. Yet in general we find that in the process of socialization which leads to the formation of larger groups, the need for cooperation with many other and different people not connected among themselves by ties of blood, tends to counteract the narcissistic charge within the group. The same holds true in another respect, which we have discussed in connection with benign individual narcissism: inasmuch as the large group (nation, state, or religion) makes it an object of its narcissistic pride to achieve something valuable in the fields of material, intellectual, or artistic production, the very process of work in such fields tends to lessen the narcissistic charge. The history of the Roman Catholic Church is one of many examples of the peculiar mixture of narcissism and the counteracting forces within a large group. The elements counteracting narcissism within the Catholic Church are, first of all, the concept of the universality of man and of a "catholic" religion which is no longer the religion of one particular tribe or nation. Second, the idea of personal humility which follows from the idea of God and the denial of idols. The existence of God implies that no man can be God, that no individual can be omniscient or omnipotent. It thus sets a definite limit to man's narcissistic self-idolatry. But at the same time the Church has nourished an intense narcissism; believing that the Church is the only chance of salvation and that the pope is the Vicar of Christ, its members were able to develop an intense narcissism inasmuch as they were members of such an extraordinary institution. The same occurred in relation to God; while the omniscience and omnipotence of God should have led to man's humility, often the individual identified himself with God and thus developed an extraordinary degree of narcissism in this process of identification.

This same ambiguity between a narcissistic or an antinarcissistic function has occurred in all the other great religions, for example, in Buddhism, Judaism, Islam, and Protestantism. I have mentioned the Catholic religion not only because it is a well-known example, but mainly because the Roman Catholic religion was the basis both for humanism and for violent and fanatical religious narcissism at one and the same historical period: the fifteenth and sixteenth centuries. The humanists within the church and those outside spoke in the name of a humanism which was the fountainhead of Christianity. . . .

Group narcissism needs satisfaction just as individual narcissism does. On one level this satisfaction is provided by the common ideology of the superiority of one's group, and the inferiority of all others. In religious groups this satisfaction is easily provided by the assumption that *my* group is the only one which believes in the true God, and hence since *my* God is the only true one, all other groups are made up of misguided unbelievers. But even without reference to God as a witness for one's superiority, group narcissism can arrive at similar conclusions on a secular level. The narcissistic conviction of the superiority of whites over Negroes in parts of the United States and in South Africa demonstrates that there is no restraint to the sense of self-superiority or of the inferiority of another group. However, the satisfaction of these narcissistic self-images of a group requires also a certain degree of confirmation in reality. As long as the whites in Alabama or in South Africa have the power to demonstrate their superiority over the Negroes through social, economic, and political acts of discrimination, their narcissistic beliefs have some element of reality, and thus bolster up the entire narcissistic thought-system. The same held true for the Nazis; there the physical destruction of all Jews had to serve as proof of the superiority of the Aryans (for a sadist the fact that he can kill a man proves that the killer is superior). If, however, the narcissistically inflated group does not have available a minority which is sufficiently helpless to lend itself as an object for narcissistic satisfaction, the group's narcissism will easily lead to the wish for military conquests; this was the path of pan-Germanism and pan-Slavism before 1914. In both cases the respective nations were endowed with the role of being the "chosen nation", superior to all others, and hence justified in attacking those who did not accept their superiority. I do not mean to imply that "the" cause of the First World War was the narcissism of the pan-German and pan-Slavic movements, but their fanaticism was certainly one factor which contributed to the outbreak of the war. Beyond this, however, one must not forget that once a war has started, the various governments try to arouse national narcissism as a necessary psychological condition for the successful waging of the war.

If the narcissism of a group is wounded, then we find the same reaction of rage which we have discussed in connection with individual narcissism. There are many historical examples for the fact that disparagement of the symbols of group narcissism has often produced rage verging on insanity. Violation of the flag; insults against one's own God, emperor, leader; the loss of a war and of territory – these have often led to violent mass feelings of vengeance which in turn led to new wars. The wounded narcissism can be healed only if the offender is crushed and thus the insult to one's narcissism is undone. Revenge, individual and national, is often based on wounded narcissism and on the need to "cure" the wound by the annihilation of the offender.

One last element of narcissistic pathology must be added. The highly narcissistic group is eager to have a leader with whom it can identify itself. The leader is then admired by the group which projects its narcissism onto him. In the very act of submission to the powerful leader, which is in depth an act of symbiosis and identification, the narcissism of the individual is transferred onto the leader. The greater the leader, the greater the follower. Personalities who as individuals are particularly narcissistic are the most qualified to fulfill this function. The narcissism of the leader who is convinced of his greatness, and who has no doubts, is precisely what attracts the narcissism of those who submit to him. The half-insane leader is often the most successful one until his lack of objective judgment, his rage reactions in consequence of any setback, his need to keep up the image of omnipotence may provoke him to make mistakes which lead to his destruction. But there are always gifted half-psychotics at hand to satisfy the demands of a narcissistic mass.

We have so far discussed the phenomenon of narcissism, its pathology, and its biological and sociological function. As a result we might come to the conclusion that narcissism is a necessary and valuable orientation, provided it is benign and does not transcend a certain threshold. However, our picture is incomplete. Man is not only concerned with biological and social survival, he is also concerned with *values*, with the development of that by virtue of which he is human.

Looking at it from the standpoint of values it becomes evident that narcissism conflicts with reason and with love. This statement hardly needs further elaboration. By the very nature of the narcissistic orientation, it prevents one – to the extent to which it exists – from seeing reality as it is, that is, objectively; in other words, it restricts reason. It may not be equally clear that it restricts love – especially when we recall that Freud said that in all love there is a strong narcissistic component; that a man in love with a woman makes her the object of his own narcissism, and that therefore she becomes wonderful and desirable because she is part of him. She may do the same with him, and thus we have the case of the "great love", which often is only a *folie à deux* rather than love. Both people retain their narcissism, they have no real, deep interest in each other (not to speak of anyone else), they remain touchy and suspicious, and most likely each of them will be in need of a new person who can give them fresh narcissistic satisfaction. For the narcissistic person, the partner is never a person in his own right or in his full reality; he exists only as a shadow of the partner's narcissistically inflated ego. Nonpathological love, on the other hand, is not based on mutual narcissism. It is a relationship between two people who experience themselves as separate entities, yet who can open themselves to and become one with each other. In order to experience love one must experience separateness.

The significance of the phenomenon of narcissism from the ethical-spiritual viewpoint becomes very clear if we consider that the essential teachings of all the great humanist religions can be summarized in one sentence: *It is the goal of man to overcome one's narcissism.* Perhaps this principle is nowhere expressed more radically than in Buddhism. The teaching of the Buddha amounts to saying that man can save himself from suffering only if he awakens from his illusions and becomes aware of his reality; the reality of sickness, old age, and death, and of the impossibility of ever attaining the aims of his greed. The "awakened" person of whom Buddhist teaching speaks is the person who has overcome his narcissism, and who is therefore capable of being fully awake. We might put the same thought still differently: Only if man can do away with the illusion of his indestructible ego, only if he can drop it together with all other other objects of his greed, only then can he be open to the world and fully related to it. Psychologically this process of becoming fully awake is identical with the replacement of narcissism by relatedness to the world.

In the Hebrew and Christian traditions the same goal is expressed in various terms which also mean the overcoming of narcissism. The Old Testament says: "Love thy neighbor as thyself." Here the demand is to overcome one's narcissism at least to the point where one's neighbor becomes as important as oneself. But the Old Testament goes much further than this in demanding love for the "stranger". (You know the soul of the stranger, for strangers have you been in the land of Egypt.) The stranger is precisely the person who is not part of my clan, my family, my nation; he is not part of the group to which I am narcissistically attached. He is nothing other than human. One discovers the human being in the stranger, as Hermann Cohen has pointed out.[3] In the love for the stranger narcissistic love has vanished. For it means loving another human being in his suchness and his difference from me, and not because he is like me. When the New Testament says "love thine enemy" it expresses the same idea in a more pointed form. If the stranger has become fully human to you, there is no longer an enemy, because *you* have become truly human. To love the stranger and the enemy is possible only if narcissism has been overcome, if "I am thou".

The fight against idolatry, which is the central issue of prophetic teaching, is at the same time a fight against narcissism. In idolatry one partial faculty of man is absolutized and made into an idol. Man then worships himself in an alienated form. The idol in which he submerges becomes the object of his narcissistic passion. The idea of God, on the contrary, is the negation of narcissism because only

God – not man – is omniscient and omnipotent. But while the concept of an indefinable and indescribable God was the negation of idolatry and narcissism, God soon became again an idol; man identified himself with God in a narcissistic manner, and thus in full contradiction to the original function of the concept of God, religion became a manifestation of group narcissism.

The full maturity of man is achieved by his complete emergence from narcissism, both individual and group narcissism. This goal of mental development which is thus expressed in psychological terms is essentially the same as that which the great spiritual leaders of the human race have expressed in religious–spiritual terms. While the concepts differ, the substance and the experience referred to in the various concepts are the same.

We live in a historical period characterized by a sharp discrepancy between the intellectual development of man, which has led to the development of the most destructive armaments, and his mental–emotional development, which has left him still in a state of marked narcissism with all its pathological symptoms. What can be done in order to avoid the catastrophe which can easily result from this contradiction? Is it at all possible for man to take a step in the foreseeable future which, in spite of all religious teachings, he has never been able to take before? Is narcissism so deeply ingrained in man that he will never overcome his "narcissistic core", as Freud thought? Is there then any hope that narcissistic madness will not lead to the destruction of man before he has had a chance to become fully human? No one can give an answer to these questions. One can only examine what the optimal possibilities are which may help man to avoid the catastrophe.

One might begin with what would seem to be the easiest way. Even without reducing narcissistic energy in each person, the *object* could be changed. If *mankind*, the entire human family, could become the object of group narcissism instead of one nation, one race, or one political system being this object, much might be gained. If the individual could experience himself primarily as a citizen of the world and if he could feel pride in mankind and in its achievements, his narcissism would turn toward the human race as an object, rather than to its conflicting components. If the educational systems of all countries stressed the achievements of the human race instead of the achievements of an individual nation, a more convincing and moving case could be made for the pride in being man. If the feeling which the Greek poet expressed in Antigone's words, "There is nothing more wonderful than man", could become an experience shared by

all, certainly a great step forward would have been taken. Furthermore, another element would have to be added: the feature of all
benign narcissism, namely, that it refers to an achievement. Not one
group, class, religion, but all of mankind must undertake to accomplish tasks which allow everybody to be proud of belonging to
this race. Common tasks for all mankind are at hand: the joint fight
against disease, against hunger, for the dissemination of knowledge
and art through our means of communication among all the peoples
of the world. The fact is that in spite of all differences in political and
religious ideology, there is no sector of mankind which can afford to
exclude itself from these common tasks; for the great achievement of
this century is that the belief in the natural or divine causes of
human inequality, of the necessity or legitimacy of the exploitation
of one man by another, has been defeated to the point of no return.
Renaissance humanism, the bourgeois revolutions, the Russian,
Chinese, and colonial revolutions – all are based on one common
thought: the equality of man. Even if some of these revolutions have
led to the violation of human equality within the systems concerned,
the historical fact is that the idea of the equality of all men, hence of
their freedom and dignity, has conquered the world, and it is un-
thinkable that mankind could ever return to the concepts which
dominated civilized history until only a short time ago.

The image of the human race and of its achievements as the object
of benign narcissism could be represented by supranational organizations such as the United Nations; it could even begin to create its
own symbols, holidays, and festivals. Not the national holiday, but
the "day of man" would become the highest holiday of the year. But
it is clear that such a development can occur only inasmuch as many
and eventually all nations concur and are willing to reduce their
national sovereignty in favor of the sovereignty of mankind; not only
in terms of political, but also in terms of emotional, realities. A
strengthened United Nations and the reasonable and peaceful
solution of group conflicts are the obvious conditions for the possibility that humanity and its common achievements shall become the
object of group narcissism.[4]

Such a change in the object of narcissism from single groups to all
mankind and its achievements would indeed tend, as pointed out
before, to counteract the dangers of national and ideological narcissism. But this is not enough. If we are true to our political and
religious ideals, the Christian as well as the socialist ideal of unselfish-
ness and brotherhood, the task is to reduce the degree of narcissism
in each individual. Although this will take generations, it is now more

possible than ever before because man has the possibility to create the material conditions for a dignified human life for everybody. The development of technique will do away with the need for one group to enslave and to exploit another; it has already made war obsolete as an economically rational action; man will for the first time emerge from his half-animal state to a fully human one, and hence will not need narcissistic satisfaction to compensate for his material and cultural poverty.

On the basis of these new conditions man's attempt to overcome narcissism can be greatly helped by the scientific and the humanist orientations. As I have already indicated, we must shift our educational effort from teaching primarily a technical orientation to one that is scientific; that is, toward furthering critical thought, objectivity, acceptance of reality, and a concept of truth which is subject to no fiat and is valid for every conceivable group. If the civilized nations can create a scientific orientation as one fundamental attitude in their young, much will have been gained in the struggle against narcissism. The second factor which leads in the same direction is the teaching of humanist philosophy and anthropology. We cannot expect that all philosophical and religious differences would disappear. We could not even want this, since the establishment of one system claiming to be the "orthodox" one might lead to another source of narcissistic regression. But even allowing for all existing differences, there is a common humanist creed and experience. The creed is that each individual carries all of humanity within himself, that the "human condition" is one and the same for all men, in spite of unavoidable differences in intelligence, talents, height, and color. This humanist experience consists in feeling that nothing human is alien to one, that "I am you", that one can understand another human being because both share the same elements of human existence. This humanist experience is fully possible only if we enlarge our sphere of awareness. Our own awareness is usually confined to what the society of which we are members permits us to be aware. Those human experiences which do not fit into this picture are repressed. Hence our consciousness represents mainly our own society and culture, while our unconscious represents the universal man in each of us.[5] The broadening of self-awareness, transcending consciousness and illuminating the sphere of the social unconscious, will enable man to experience in himself all of humanity; he will experience the fact that he is a sinner and a saint, a child and an adult, a sane and an insane person, a man of the past and one of the future – that he carries within himself that which mankind has been and that which it will be.

A true renaissance of our humanist tradition undertaken by all religions, political, and philosophical systems claiming to represent humanism would, I believe, result in considerable progress toward the most important "new frontier" that exists today – man's development into a completely human being.

By presenting all these thoughts I do not mean to imply that teaching *alone* can be the decisive step for the realization of humanism, as the Renaissance humanists believed. All these teachings will have an impact only if essential social, economic, and political conditions change; a change from bureaucratic industrialism to humanist-socialist industrialism; from centralization to decentralization; from the organization man to a responsible and participating citizen; subordination of national sovereignties to the sovereignty of the human race and its chosen organs; common efforts of the "have" nations in cooperation with the "have-not" nations to build up the economic systems of the latter; universal disarmament and availability of the existing material resources for constructive tasks. Universal disarmament is also necessary for another reason: if one sector of mankind lives in fear of total destruction by another bloc, and the rest live in fear of destruction by both blocs, then, indeed, group narcissism cannot be diminished. Man can be human only in a climate in which he can expect that he and his children will live to see the next year, and many more years to come.

NOTES

1. Albert Camus, in his drama *Caligula* (London: Hamish Hamilton, 1948), has portrayed this madness of power most accurately.

2. Cf. the discussion of primary bonds in E. Fromm, *Escape From Freedom* (New York: Holt, Rinehart & Winston, 1941).

3. H. Cohen, *Die Religion der Vernunft aus den Quellen des Judentums* (Frankfurt-am-Main: F. Kaufman, 1929).

4. As an example of more specific measures for such an attempt, I want to mention only a few suggestions. History textbooks should be rewritten as textbooks of *world history*, in which the proportions of each nation's life remain true to reality and are not distorted, just as world maps are the same in all countries and do not inflate the size of each respective country. Furthermore, movies could be made which foster pride in the development of the human race, showing how humanity and its achievements are the final integration of many single steps undertaken by various groups.

5. Cf. E. Fromm, *Zen Buddhism and Psychoanalysis* (New York: Harper & Row and London: G. Allen & Unwin, 1960); and *Beyond the Chains of Illusion*, "Credo Perspectives", planned and edited by Ruth Nanda Anshen (New York: Simon and Schuster, 1962 and Pocket Books, 1963).

9

CHRIST, A SYMBOL OF
THE SELF*

Carl G. Jung

*In Fromm's view the personal world evolves through a conflict of
dynamic tendencies that pull man in opposite directions: toward self-
centeredness, destructiveness, and infantile dependence or toward love,
productiveness, and mature independence. Religion can function to
support either set of directions. The psychologist Carl Gustav Jung
shared many of the views and concerns of Fromm. Relevant to our
study, both formulated conceptions of positive personality development
in terms of dynamic self-realization and both examined the roles of
religion within this process. While Fromm has emphasized reason's role
in directing tendencies toward fulfillment, Jung, on the other hand,
called special attention to dynamics of the Unconscious which he
believed to be important. Particularly significant, he claimed, are
unconscious symbols, such as mandalas, which motivate psychic energy
in the process of individuation. Mandalas are ancient religious symbols
which, according to Jung, are also psychological archetypes representing psychic wholeness; in the West the Christ symbol, often associated
with mandalas, has played a significant role in self-realization. In the
following chapter Jung analyzed the Christ symbol, not in terms of
stories about a historical Jesus but in view of a theological tradition
that has emphasized the divine purity of Christ's being. It is not easy*

* This is an abridged version of a chapter entitled "Christ, A Symbol of the
Self", from *The Collected Works of C. G. Jung*, Bollingen Series XX, ed. by
G. Adler, Michael Fordham, and H. Read, trans. by R. F. C. Hull, Vol. 9, 2; *Aion:
Researches into the Phenomenology of the Self*, rev. edition, © 1968. Published by
Princeton University Press and Routledge & Kegan Paul, Ltd., London; used
by permission of both publishers and the Bollingen Foundation.

reading, in part because Jung was addressing difficult and sometimes obscure texts, though much of the intricate textual analysis has been deleted here. Using his psychological insights he criticized this religious symbol where he felt it was deficient and had harmful effects on individuals and society.

Some questions for discussion: To what extent does Jung believe the Christ symbol is an inadequate self-symbol? What are the repercussions of its inadequacies in personality formation and in society? How do Jung's views of psychic mechanisms of such phenomena relate to insights into projection and prejudice? What are Jung's reasons for believing that some early Christian theology reflected a healthier self-symbol? What features should be included in an adequate, mature self-symbol? What features, if any, do you feel that Jung has omitted in consideration of an adequate self-symbol?

For further reading see also C. G. Jung, Psychology and Religion: West and East *(Bollingen Series XX; Princeton: Princeton University Press, 1958). For an investigation into the religious symbol of Satan from a psychological viewpoint see the article by Henry A. Murray, "The Personality and Career of Satan",* The Journal of Social Issues, XVIII *(October, 1962),* 36–54.

WHY – my reader will ask – do I discourse here upon Christ and his adversary, the Antichrist? Our discourse necessarily brings us to Christ, because he is the still living myth of our culture. He is our culture hero, who, regardless of his historical existence, embodies the myth of the divine Primordial Man, the mystic Adam. It is he who occupies the center of the Christian *mandala*, who is the Lord of the Tetramorph, i.e. the four symbols of the evangelists, which are like the four columns of his throne. He is in us and we in him. His kingdom is the pearl of great price, the treasure buried in the field, the grain of mustard seed which will become a great tree, and the heavenly city.[1] As Christ is in us, so also is his heavenly kingdom.

These few familiar references should be sufficient to make the psychological position of the Christ symbol quite clear. *Christ exemplifies the archetype of the self.*[2] He represents a totality of a divine or heavenly kind, a glorified man, a son of God *sine macula peccati*, unspotted by sin. As Adam *secundus* he corresponds to the first Adam before the Fall, when the latter was still a pure image of God, of which Tertullian says: "And this therefore is to be considered as the image of God in man, that the human spirit has the same motions and sense as God has, though not in the same way as God has them." . . .

There can be no doubt that the original Christian conception of the *imago Dei* embodied in Christ meant an all-embracing totality that even includes the animal side of man. Nevertheless, the Christ symbol lacks wholeness in the modern psychological sense, since it does not include the dark side of things but specifically excludes it in the form of a Luciferian opponent. Although the exclusion of the power of evil was something the Christian consciousness was well aware of, all it lost in effect was an insubstantial shadow, for, through the doctrine of the *privatio boni* first propounded by Origen, evil was characterized as a mere diminution of good and thus deprived of substance. According to the teachings of the church, evil is simply "the accidental lack of perfection". . . .

If we see the traditional figure of Christ as a parallel to the psychic manifestation of the self, then the Antichrist would correspond to the shadow of the self, namely, the dark half of the human totality, which ought not to be judged too optimistically. So far as we can judge from experience, light and shadow are so evenly distributed in man's nature that his psychic totality appears, to say the least of it, in a somewhat murky light. The psychological concept of the self, in part derived from our knowledge of the whole man, but for the rest depicting itself spontaneously in the products of the unconscious as an archetypal quaternity bound together by inner antinomies, cannot omit the shadow that belongs to the light figure, for without it this figure lacks body and humanity. In the empirical self, light and shadow form a paradoxical unity. In the Christian concept, on the other hand, the archetype is hopelessly split into two irreconcilable halves, leading ultimately to a metaphysical dualism – the final separation of the kingdom of heaven from the fiery world of the damned. . . .

Just as we have to remember the gods of antiquity in order to appreciate the psychological value of the anima/animus archetype, so Christ is our nearest analogy of the self and its meaning. It is naturally not a question of a collective value artificially manufactured or arbitrarily awarded, but of one that is effective and present *per se*, and that makes its effectiveness felt whether the subject is conscious of it or not. Yet, although the attributes of Christ (consubstantiality with the Father, coeternity, filiation, parthenogenesis, crucifixion, Lamb sacrificed between opposites, One divided into Many, etc.) undoubtedly mark him out as an embodiment of the self, looked at from the psychological angle he corresponds to only one half of the archetype. The other half appears in the Antichrist. The latter is just as much a manifestation of the self, except that he consists of its dark aspect. Both are Christian symbols, and they have the same meaning as the image of the Savior crucified between two thieves. This great symbol tells us that the progressive development and differentiation of consciousness leads to an ever more menacing awareness of the conflict and involves nothing less than a crucifixion of the ego, its agonizing suspension between irreconcilable opposites. Naturally there can be no question of a total extinction of the ego, for then the focus of consciousness would be destroyed, and the result would be complete unconsciousness. The relative abolition of the ego affects only those supreme and ultimate decisions which confront us in situations where there are insoluble conflicts of duty. This means, in other words, that in such cases the ego is a suffering bystander who decides nothing but must submit to a decision and surrender unconditionally. The "genius" of man, the higher and more spacious part of him whose extent no one knows, has the final word. It is therefore well to examine carefully the psychological aspects of the individuation process in the light of Christian tradition, which can describe it for us with an exactness and impressiveness far surpassing our feeble attempts, even though the Christian image of the self – Christ – lacks the shadow that properly belongs to it. . . .

In the world of Christian ideas Christ undoubtedly represents the self.[3] As the apotheosis of individuality, the self has the attributes of uniqueness and of occurring once only in time. But since the psychological self is a transcendent concept, expressing the totality of conscious and unconscious contents, it can only be described in antinomial terms;[4] that is, the above attributes must be supplemented by their opposites if the transcendental situation is to be characterized correctly. We can do this most simply in the form of a quaternion of opposites:

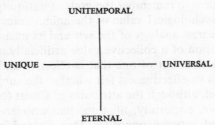

This formula expresses not only the psychological self but also the dogmatic figure of Christ. As an historical personage Christ is unitemporal and unique; as God, universal and eternal. Likewise the self: as an individual thing it is unitemporal and unique; as an archetypal symbol it is a God-image and therefore universal and eternal.[5] Now if theology describes Christ as simply "good" and "spiritual", something "evil" and "material" – or "chthonic" – is bound to arise on the other side, to represent the Antichrist. The resultant quaternion of opposites is united on the psychological plane by the fact that the self is not deemed exclusively "good" and "spiritual"; consequently its shadow turns out to be much less black. A further result is that the opposites of "good" and "spiritual" need no longer be separated from the whole:

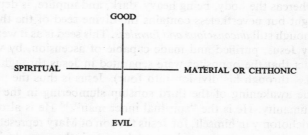

This *quaternio* characterizes the psychological self. Being a totality, it must by definition include the light and dark aspects, in the same way that the self embraces both masculine and feminine and is therefore symbolized by the marriage *quaternio*.[6] This last is by no means a new discovery, since according to Hippolytus it was known to the Naassenes.[7] Hence individuation is a *"mysterium coniunctionis"*, the self being experienced as a nuptial union of opposite halves[8] and depicted as a composite whole in mandalas that are drawn spontaneously by patients.

It was known, and stated, very early that the man Jesus, the son of Mary, was the *principium individuationis*. Thus Basilides[9] is reported by Hippolytus as saying: "Now Jesus became the first sacrifice in the separation of categories [φυλοκρίνησις], and the Passion came to pass for no other reason than the separation of composite things. For in this manner, he says, the sonship that had been left behind in a formless state [ἀμορφία] . . . needed separating into its components [φυλοκρινηθῆναι], in the same way that Jesus was separated."[10] According to the rather complicated teachings of Basilides, the "non-existent" God begot a threefold sonship (υἱοτῆς). The first "son", whose nature was the finest and most subtle, remained up above with the Father. The second son, having a grosser (παχυμερέστερα) nature, descended a bit lower, but received "some such wing as that with which Plato . . . equips the soul in his *Phaedrus*".[11] The third son, as his nature needed purifying (ἀποκαθάρσις), fell deepest into "formlessness". This third "sonship" is obviously the grossest and heaviest because of its impurity. In these three emanations or manifestations of the nonexistent God it is not hard to see the trichotomy of spirit, soul, and body (πνευματικόν, ψυχικόν, σαρκικόν). Spirit is the finest and highest; soul, as the *ligamentum spiritus et corporis*, is grosser than spirit, but has "the wings of an eagle",[12] so that it may lift its heaviness up to the higher regions. Both are of a "subtle" nature and dwell, like the ether and the eagle, in or near the region of light, whereas the body, being heavy, dark, and impure, is deprived of the light but nevertheless contains the divine seed of the third sonship, though still *unconscious and formless*. This seed is as it were awakened by Jesus, purified and made capable of ascension, by virtue of the fact that the opposites were separated in Jesus through the Passion (i.e. through his division into four). Jesus is thus the prototype for the awakening of the third sonship slumbering in the darkness of humanity. He is the "spiritual inner man".[13] He is also a complete trichotomy in himself, for Jesus the son of Mary represents the incarnate man, but his immediate predecessor is the second Christ, the son of the highest archon of the hebdomad, and his first prefiguration is Christ the son of the highest archon of the ogdoad, the demiurge Yahweh.[14] This trichotomy of Anthropos figures corresponds exactly to the three sonships of the nonexisting God and to the division of human nature into three parts. We have therefore three trichotomies:

I	II	III
First sonship	*Christ of the Ogdoad*	*Spirit*
Second sonship	*Christ of the Hebdomad*	*Soul*
Third sonship	*Jesus the Son of Mary*	*Body*

It is in the sphere of the dark, heavy body that we must look for the ἀμορφία, the "formlessness" wherein the third sonship lies hidden. As suggested above, this formlessness seems to be practically the equivalent of "unconsciousness". Attention has been drawn to the concepts of ἀγνωσία in Epiphanius[15] and ἀνόητον in Hippolytus,[16] which are best translated by "unconscious". Ἀμορφία, ἀγνωσία, and ἀνόητον all refer to the initial state of things, to the potentiality of unconscious contents, aptly formulated by Basilides as οὐκ ὄν σπέρμα τοῦ κόσμου πολύμορφον ὁμοῦ καί πολυούσιον (the nonexistent, many-formed, and all-empowering seed of the world).[17]

This picture of the third sonship has certain analogies with the medieval *filius philosophorum* and the *filius macrocosmi*, who also

symbolize the world-soul slumbering in matter.[18] Even with Basilides
the body acquires a special and unexpected significance, since in it
and its materiality is lodged a third of the revealed Godhead. This
means nothing less than that matter is predicted as having considerable numinosity in itself, and I see this as an anticipation of the
"mystic" significance which matter subsequently assumed in alchemy
and – later on – in natural science. From a psychological point of
view it is particularly important that Jesus corresponds to the third
sonship and is the prototype of the "awakener" because the opposites were separated in him through the Passion and so became conscious, whereas in the third sonship itself they remain unconscious
so long as the latter is formless and undifferentiated. This amounts to
saying that in unconscious humanity there is a latent seed that corresponds to the prototype Jesus. Just as the man Jesus became conscious only through the light that emanated from the higher Christ
and separated the natures in him, so the seed in unconscious humanity is awakened by the light emanating from Jesus, and is thereby
impelled to a similar discrimination of opposites. This view is entirely
in accord with the psychological fact that the archetypal image of the
self has been shown to occur in dreams even when no such conceptions exist in the conscious mind of the dreamer.[19]

I would not like to end this chapter without a few final remarks that
are forced on me by the importance of the material we have been
discussing. The standpoint of a psychology whose subject is the
phenomenology of the psyche is evidently something that is not easy·
to grasp and is very often misunderstood. If, therefore, at the risk of
repeating myself, I come back to fundamentals, I do so only in order
to forestall certain wrong impressions which might be occasioned by
what I have said, and to spare my reader unnecessary difficulties.

The parallel I have drawn here between Christ and the self is not
to be taken as anything more than a psychological one, just as the
parallel with the fish is mythological. There is no question of any
intrusion into the sphere of metaphysics, i.e. of faith. The images of
God and Christ which man's religious fantasy projects cannot avoid
being anthropomorphic and are admitted to be so; hence they are
capable of psychological elucidation like any other symbols. Just as
the ancients believed that they had said something important about
Christ with their fish symbol, so it seemed to the alchemists that their
parallel with the stone served to illuminate and deepen the meaning
of the Christ-image. In the course of time, the fish symbolism disappeared completely, and so likewise did the *lapis philosophorum*.

Concerning this latter symbol, however, there are plenty of statements to be found which show it in a special light – views and ideas which attach such importance to the stone that one begins to wonder whether, in the end, it was Christ who was taken as a symbol of the stone, rather than the other way round. This marks a development which – with the help of certain ideas in the epistles of John and Paul – includes Christ in the realm of immediate inner experience and makes him appear as the figure of the total man. It also links up directly with the psychological evidence for the existence of an archetypal content possessing all those qualities which are characteristic of the Christ-image in its archaic and medieval forms. Modern psychology is therefore confronted with a question very like the one that faced the alchemists: Is the self a symbol of Christ, or is Christ a symbol of the self?

In the present study I have affirmed the latter alternative. I have tried to show how the traditional Christ-image concentrates upon itself the characteristics of an archetype – the archetype of the self. My aim and method do not purport to be anything more in principle than, shall we say, the efforts of an art historian to trace the various influences which have contributed toward the formation of a particular Christ-image. Thus we find the concept of the archetype in the history of art as well as in philology and textual criticism. The psychological archetype differs from its parallels in other fields only in one respect: it refers to a living and ubiquitous psychic fact, and this naturally shows the whole situation in a rather different light. One is then tempted to attach greater importance to the immediate and living presence of the archetype than to the idea of the historical Christ. As I have said, there is among certain of the alchemists, too, a tendency to give the *lapis* priority over Christ. Since I am far from cherishing any missionary intentions, I must expressly emphasize that I am not concerned here with confessions of faith but with proven scientific facts. If one inclines to regard the archetype of the self as the real agent and hence takes Christ as a symbol of the self, one must bear in mind that there is a considerable difference between *perfection* and *completeness*. The Christ-image is as good as perfect (at least it is meant to be so), while the archetype (so far as known) denotes completeness but is far from being perfect. It is a paradox, a statement about something indescribable and transcendental. Accordingly the realization of the self, which would logically follow from a recognition of its supremacy, leads to a fundamental conflict, to a real suspension between opposites (reminiscent of the crucified Christ hanging between two thieves), and to an approximate state of wholeness that lacks perfection. To strive after τελείωσις – completion – in this sense is not only legitimate but is inborn in man as a peculiarity which provides civilization with one of its strongest roots. This striving is so powerful, even, that it can turn into a passion that draws everything into its service. Natural as it is to seek perfection in one way of another, the archetype fulfills itself in completeness, and this is a τελείωσις of quite another kind. Where the archetype predominates, completeness is *forced* upon us against all our conscious strivings, in accordance with the archaic nature of the archetype. The individual may strive after perfection ("Be you therefore perfect – τέλειοι – as also your heavenly Father is perfect."[20]) but must suffer from the opposite of his intentions for the sake of his completeness. "I find then a law, that, when I would do good, evil is present with me."[21]

The Christ-image fully corresponds to this situation: Christ is the perfect man who is crucified. One could hardly think of a truer picture of the goal of ethical endeavor. At any rate the transcendental idea of the self that serves psychology as a working hypothesis can never match that image because, although it is a symbol, it lacks the character of a revelatory historical event. Like the related ideas of *atman* and *tao* in the East, the idea of the self is at least in part a product of cognition, grounded neither on faith nor on metaphysical speculation but on the experience that under certain conditions the unconscious spontaneously brings forth an archetypal symbol of wholeness. From this we must conclude that some such archetype occurs universally and is endowed with a certain numinosity. And there is in fact any amount of historical evidence as well as modern case material to prove this.[22] These naïve and completely uninfluenced pictorial representations of the symbol show that it is given central and supreme importance precisely because it stands for the conjunction of opposites. Naturally the conjunction can only be understood as a paradox, since a union of opposites can be thought of only as their annihilation. Paradox is a characteristic of all transcendental situations because it alone gives adequate expression to their indescribable nature.

Whenever the archetype of the self predominates, the inevitable psychological consequence is a state of conflict vividly exemplified by the Christian symbol of crucifixion – that acute state of unredeemedness which comes to an end only with the words "*consummatum est*". Recognition of the archetype, therefore, does not in any way circumvent the Christian mystery; rather, it forcibly creates the psychological preconditions without which "redemption" would appear meaningless. "Redemption" does not mean that a burden is taken from one's shoulders which one was never meant to bear. Only the "complete" person knows how unbearable man is to himself. So far as I can see, no relevant objection could be raised from the Christian point of view against anyone accepting the task of individuation imposed on us by nature, and the recognition of our wholeness or completeness, as a binding personal commitment. If he does this consciously and intentionally, he avoids all the unhappy consequences of repressed individuation. In other words, if he voluntarily takes the burden of completeness on himself, he need not find it "happening" to him against his will in a negative form. This is as much to say that anyone who is destined to descend into a deep pit had better set about it with all the necessary precautions rather than risk falling into the hole backwards.

The irreconcilable nature of the opposites in Christian psychology is due to their moral accentuation. This accentuation seems natural to us, although, looked at historically, it is a legacy from the Old Testament with its emphasis on righteousness in the eyes of the law. Such an influence is notably lacking in the East, in the philosophical religions of India and China. Without stopping to discuss the question of whether this exacerbation of the opposites, much as it increases suffering, may not after all correspond to a higher degree of truth, I should like merely to express the hope that the present world situation may be looked upon in the light of the psychological rule alluded to above. Today humanity, as never before, is split into two apparently irreconcilable halves. The psychological rule says that when an inner situation is not made conscious, it happens outside, as fate. That is to say, when the individual remains undivided and does not become conscious of his inner contradictions, the world must perforce act out the conflict and be torn into opposite halves.

NOTES

1. For "city", cf. *Collected Works of C. G. Jung*, Vol. 12: *Psychology and Alchemy*, pp. 104 ff.

2. Cf. my observations on Christ as archetype in "A Psychological Approach to the Dogma of the Trinity", *Collected Works of C. G. Jung*, Vol. 11: *Psychology and Religion*.

3. It has been objected that Christ cannot have been a valid symbol of the self, or was only an illusory substitute for it. I can agree with this view only if it refers strictly to the present time, when psychological criticism has become possible, but not if it pretends to judge the pre-psychological age. Christ did not merely *symbolize* wholeness, but, as a psychic phenomenon, he *was* wholeness. This is

proved by the symbolism as well as by the phenomenology of the past, for which – be it noted – evil was a *privatio boni*. The idea of totality is, at any given time, as total as one is oneself. Who can guarantee that our conception of totality is not equally in need of completion? The mere concept of totality does not by any means posit it.

4. Just as the transcendent nature of light can only be expressed through the image of waves *and* particles.

5. Cf. *Psychology and Alchemy*, pp. 99 ff., and "The Relations between the Ego and the Unconscious", *Collected Works of C. G. Jung*, Vol. 7: *Two Essays on Analytical Psychology*.

6. Cf. "Psychology of the Transference", *Collected Works of C. G. Jung*, Vol. 16: *The Practice of Psychotherapy*, pp. 222 ff.

7. *Elenchos*, V, 8, 2 (trans. by F. Legge, I, p. 131).

8. *Psychology and Alchemy*, p. 219, and "Psychology of the Transference", pp. 246 ff.

9. Basilides lived in the second century.

10. *Elenchos*, VII, 27, 12 (cf. Legge trans., II, p. 79).

11. *Ibid.*, VII, 22, 10 (cf. II, pp. 69–70).

12. *Ibid.*, VII, 22, 15 (II, p. 70). The eagle has the same significance in alchemy.

13. *Ibid.*, VII, 27, 5 (II, p. 78).

14. *Ibid.*, VII, 26, 5 (II, p. 75).

15. *Panarium*, XXXI, 5 (Oehler ed., I, p. 314).

16. *Elenchos*, VII, 22, 16 (Legge trans., II, p. 71).

17. *Ibid.*, 20, 5 (cf. II, p. 66). Quispel, "Note sur 'Basilide'".

18. With reference to the psychological nature of Gnostic sayings, see Quispel's "Philo und die altchristliche Häresie", p. 432, where he quotes Irenaeus (*Adv. haer.*, II, 4, 2): "*Id quod extra et quod intus dicere eos secundum agnitionem et ignorantiam, sed non secundum localem sententiam*" (In speaking of what is outward and what is inward, they refer, not to place, but to what is known and what is not known). (Cf. Legge, I, p. 127.) The sentence that follows immediately after this – "But in the Pleroma, or in that which is contained by the Father, everything that the demiurge or the angels have created is contained by the unspeakable greatness, as the centre in a circle" – is therefore to be taken as a description of unconscious contents. Quispel's view of projection calls for the critical remark that projection does not do away with the *reality* of a psychic content. Nor can a fact be called "unreal" merely because it cannot be described as other than "psychic". Psyche is reality *par excellence*.

19. Cf. *Psychology and Alchemy*, pp. 47 ff. and 91 ff., and "A Study in the Process of Individuation", *Collected Works of C. G. Jung*, Vol. 9, 1: *The Archetypes and the Collective Unconscious*.

20. Matthew 5 : 48 (DV).

21. Romans 7 : 21 (AV).

22. Cf. the last two papers in *The Archetypes and the Collective Unconscious*.

IO

FATHER AND SON IN CHRISTIANITY AND CONFUCIANISM*

Robert N. Bellah

The focus thus far has largely been upon the meaning of religion in terms of the emergence of certain patterns of perception, thinking, feeling, and significant factors in motivation within the development of a personal world. All these are important to the development of a personal self; but equally important are relations to other people, particularly intimate relationships with significant other persons. One of the most serious tasks and problems facing social scientists today is the analysis and understanding of interpersonal relationships. It is especially important in the study of religion; in many types of religion some of the most significant rites and beliefs apply to interpersonal relationships. Unfortunately too little attention has been given to this area. In the following chapter the sociologist Robert Bellah makes a very significant contribution to the particular study represented by this volume; his focus is upon certain religious symbols and their impact upon intimate relationships as these exist in families. By correlating dominant religious symbols which were incorporated into practices important in the Christian tradition with an emergent pattern of father and son relationships and then comparing this constellation to a similar correlation in Confucianism, he indicates the marked effect different types of religious symbols may have upon relationships, family structure, indi-

* Reprinted with permission of both the *Review* and the author from Robert N. Bellah, "Father and Son in Christianity and Confucianism", *The Psychoanalytic Review*, (Summer, 1965), 92–114.

vidual development, and society. Elsewhere Bellah has focused upon the interrelationship between religion and cultural factors in: Tokugawa Religion: The Values of Pre-Industrial Japan *(New York: The Free Press, 1957); Religion and Progress in Modern Asia, ed. (New York: The Free Press, 1965); and "Civil Religion in America", Daedalus (Winter, 1967).*

Some questions for discussion: To what extent does Bellah think Freud's theory of Oedipal complex is inadequate to account for religious symbolism and family relationships? What similarities exist between the constellation of religious symbols and family structure in Judaism and that found in Confucianism? What are the most significant differences between them? How does the constellation of these factors in Christianity differ from the previous two traditions? How does Bellah's concept of Christ as a symbol differ from that suggested by Jung? What specifically did the distinctive Christian religious symbols do to father–son relationships and family structure? What is the relationship between this symbolism and emergent attitudes toward authority, freedom, and responsibility?

I

ARISTOTLE, in the first book of the *Politics*, briefly discusses the relation between the family and religious symbolism. He says that the earliest form of social organization is the family, that the earliest form of political organization is simply an extension of the family in which the patriarch of an extended family is king, and finally that men speak of Zeus being the father of gods and men or of the gods having a king on the analogy of their own way of life.[1] Though noting that, "He who thus considers things in their first growth and origin, whether a state or anything else, will obtain the clearest view of them",[2] Aristotle apparently considers this peculiar relation between the family and the early modes of organization of gods and men as sufficiently obvious to warrant no great amount of time being spent on its explanation. It must be admitted that Aristotle's insight provides a fundamental reference point for us even today and that in fact the analysis of the problem has not gone as much beyond Aristotle as might be imagined. However, our evident advantage over Aristotle in the systematic understanding of human behavior and in the amount of comparative data available to us should allow us to push the analysis considerably farther. This essay is intended as a brief reconnaissance in that direction.

Aristotle's notion that men think of the gods on the analogy of their own way of life is perhaps close to what some modern psychiatrists mean when they speak of religion as a projection. Freud very significantly contributed to our understanding of the relation between the family and religious symbolism when he traced the structure of conflicts within the family which might give rise to such projection. In the Oedipus complex Freud had found the nucleus of all neurosis. In *Totem and Taboo* he asserted that the major aspects of human society and culture found their origin in the same place. Religion, morals, and society, he said, arise out of and are means of dealing with problems and conflicts within the family, especially "one single concrete point – man's relation to his father". In particular he held that the function of religious symbolism and religious ritual is to give expression to the love and fear, respect and guilt, obedience and rebellion generated in man's relation to his father in a way which will not be socially disruptive. For example, he analyzed the totemic sacrifice as a symbolic substitute for the actual murder of the father. In the ritual the hostile impulses together with the guilt feelings could both be appeased in such a way that cultural values and social norms would be reinforced rather than destroyed. In *The Future of an Illusion* Freud stated even more clearly the projective function of religion and dealt with it mainly as a defense against anxiety generated in the process of growing up in a family. On the basis of Freud's general view a number of psychologists and anthropologists have dealt with religion as a fairly direct projective mechanism which can be explained almost entirely in terms of the typical family structure in a given society and the way in which it channels the anxieties of growing children. The work of Abram Kardiner is perhaps the best known example of such an approach and a number of interesting studies of religion in various primitive societies have been made from this point of view.

While accepting the Freudian analysis in general terms and adopting Freud's insistence on the importance of the father–son relationship as at least a convenient focus for investigation, I will argue that the relation between the family and religious symbolism is not quite so simple as the projective hypothesis might lead us to assume. In particular I will argue that religious symbolism cannot be treated as merely a dependent variable of family structure. Elements of motivation derived from family experiences are very profoundly involved in religion but it is my thesis that in the religious sphere these motivational elements may be reformulated in such a way as to affect dramatically the structure of the family itself and the motivation of people in family and society generally. Interestingly enough, Freud, who earlier seems to have been supporting a rather straightforward projective interpretation, in *Moses and Monotheism* is clearly cognizant of the creative historical role of religion and of the consequences for personality and society which changes in religious symbolism might have.

As a stimulus for the tentative explorations which will be presented here it has seemed useful to compare two diverse examples of religions in which the family or family symbolism are evidently central, though in contrasting ways: Christianity and Confucianism. It seems obvious that no great religion has concentrated more on familial symbolism than has Christianity. Above all, the father–son relation is symbolically absolutely central. And yet Christian civilization relative to the other great civilizations has not placed an especial stress on the family and one could argue that the father–son tie, though certainly important, was less so than in Islamic, Indian, or East Asian society. And it is clear that modern Western society which has grown out of traditional Christian civilization is based less exclusively on the family than any other known society.

In contrast, China, of all the great civilizations, made the family most central. The family has been the core of Chinese society for millennia and the breakup of the traditional family system in this century has been accompanied by the drastic disruption and perhaps end of classical Chinese civilization. And yet in Chinese religious symbolism familial figures are far from central. Though there is no civilization which has placed greater emphasis on the father–son tie, this is not reflected in the ultimate religious symbolism. For example, the *Tao* was never even anthropomorphic, much less a father, and *T'ien* was only vestigially and non-essentially paternal, at least from mid-Chou times. It would seem that an investigation of these two cases, in which the relation between the actual position of the family and the place of familial symbolism in religion is not exactly what one would have expected on the basis of the projective hypothesis, may be useful in elucidating the problem in hand.

Let us begin by analyzing the place of familial symbolism in Christianity and some of its motivational implications. Freud (in *Totem and Taboo* but especially in *Moses and Monotheism*) gives a useful starting-point for analysis.

The story of Adam's fall states narratively what the doctrine of original sin states essentially about the sinful nature of man. In *Totem and Taboo* Freud chose characteristically to state narratively in terms of the archetypal father-murder in the primal horde his own theory as to the essential disturbance in human nature, which he elsewhere put more analytically in terms of the Oedipal conflicts inevitable in the process of growing up in a family. In analyzing Christianity he identified original sin with the archetypal father-murder and interpreted Christ as bringing redemption from original sin by sacrificing his own life and thus allaying the guilt of the company of brothers responsible (hereditarily) for committing the original crime. It is a case of a life for a life. Christ's death obtains satisfaction through the law of talion for the murder of the father. But in accordance with the law of ambivalence which always displays itself in Oedipal situations, the very act which atones most completely for the original crime is in a way the complete fulfillment of the wishes which motivated that crime. For through the atonement the son becomes united with the father in such a way that he effectively replaces the father not only as redeemer but as creator. But a further consequence of this development which displays again the characteristic ambivalence is that the atoning death is also a father-murder, for if Christ is God then it is God who has been murdered. The Christian eucharist gathers up all these motives and repeats them in a continual symbolic re-enactment of the original deed. Freud attributes the effectiveness of Christianity to the relatively undisguised manner in which this complex of motives was acknowledged.

Before dealing with the limitations in Freud's analysis, let us consider whether it sheds light on the meaning of Christ for Christians in New Testament and later times. It is in Paul perhaps that we can find the most explicit confirmation of Freud's interpretation. Paul says, "For as by one man's disobedience many were made sinners, so by one man's obedience many will be made righteous" (Romans 5:19). Through Adam sin and death came into the world just as through Christ have come acquittal and life. The pattern of implications which Paul sets up in his parallelisms between Adam and Christ can leave but one conclusion: Christ was obedient to his father unto death; Adam was disobedient to his father unto murder. Or at any rate, Adam's disobedience, his denial of God's authority, opened the door to a sinfulness in man which could and eventually did reach the extreme of the murder of God.

The same motivational components are clearly revealed in an important counterplot in the Gospels in which Judas portrays a parody of Christ. Judas was certainly a father-murderer, for in accordance with Jewish ideas of the time a man's spiritual master was to be treated as a father to whom, if anything, more honor and reverence was due than to the literal father.[4] Furthermore, at least by implication Judas was not the only one of the company of brothers to harbor murderous impulses. Peter was dismayed to discover in himself a degree of betrayal which he had not thought possible. In order to expiate his crime Judas goes willingly to his death – that is, he commits suicide. Through the starkest contrast he illustrates the motivational components which are involved in the crucifixion of the innocent Christ.

Christ is not just victim; he is also hero. He accepts the father's command to do what is required even though he must suffer. He willingly gives his life for the sake of others: "Greater love has no man than this, that a man lay down his life for his friends" (John 15:13). He struggles with death and overcomes it. Many writers through the centuries have emphasized this heroic aspect of Christ. Aquinas, for example, wrote that Christ gave us an example "by overcoming bravely the sufferings of the flesh" and in love exposing himself to the dangers of death.[5] None goes further than Calvin in stressing the heroic accomplishments of Christ undertaken in spite of the dread arising from his sensitive nature. Calvin says:

> Nothing had been done if Christ had only endured corporeal death. In order to interpose between us and God's anger, and satisfy his righteous judgment, it was necessary that he should feel the weight of divine vengeance. Whence also it was necessary that he should engage, as it were, at close quarters with the powers of hell and the horrors of eternal death.[6]

Calvin expressly rejects a passive interpretation of Christ's sacrifice:

> . . . Nor are we to understand that by the curse which he endured he was himself overwhelmed, but rather that by enduring it he repressed, broke, annihilated all its force.[7]

Through withstanding the worst, Christ won the right to sit at the right hand of the Father. He who emptied himself and took the form of a servant became the one to whom every knee shall bow. Thus Christ does not merely expiate the original crime. As Freud said, he also fulfills, though of course innocently in Christian terms, part of the motivation behind the original crime, namely the desire to replace the father, to participate in his power rather than be simply subjected to it.

Freud posited the effectiveness of Christianity in the fact that Christians identify with Christ and participate in the working through of the motives involved in his life and sacrificial death. Of course this is merely his way of putting what is thoroughly evident in the New Testament and later Christian thought. The gospel is indeed the message that Christ's victory over death is mankind's victory, that all men can and indeed actually do participate in it. Christ is the only begotten son of God. But through Christ all men can become sons of God. Augustine says:

> For God doth this thing, out of sons of men He maketh sons of God; because out of the Son of God He hath made the Son of Man. Mark what this participation is. There hath been promised to us a participation of Divinity.[8]

Paul speaks of the church as the body of Christ, thus emphasizing the participation of the believers in the divine life. The identification with Christ, however, to be real must be total. As Augustine says:

> ... Whatever He hath suffered, therein we also have suffered; and that which we suffer, He also suffers in us ... In Him we are dead, and in Him we are risen again; and He dieth in us and in us riseth again; for He is the unity of the Head and the Body.[9]

Paul asks the brethren "to present your bodies as a living sacrifice, holy and acceptable to God" (Romans 12:1) and Augustine says that the cross is for the whole of life.[10]

It is precisely in the eucharist, the center of the Christian liturgy from the earliest times, that the sacrificial identification of the church with the body of Christ was made most plainly manifest. Again it is Augustine who says:

> This is the sacrifice of Christians: we, being many, are one body in Christ. And this also is the sacrifice which the Church continually celebrates in the sacrament of the altar, known to the faithful, in which she teaches that she herself is offered in the offering she makes to God.[11]

In fact, without the eucharist it is hardly possible to speak of a church at all, and yet there could be no eucharist until Christ had sacrificed himself. The church had to lose Christ in order to become Christ, a point recognized in the Fourth Gospel where Jesus says in his farewell speech:

> Nevertheless I tell you the truth: it is to your advantage that I go away, for if I do not go away, the Counselor will not come to you; but if I go, I will send him to you. (John 16:7)

The descent of the Counselor or Holy Spirit into the assembled believers on the day of Pentecost marks the foundation of the church. Through the recurrent eucharist the church celebrates both the loss of the beloved object and its own identification with that object. The psychological mechanisms involved in the process of identification with the lost object were first pointed out by Freud in his brilliant paper "Mourning and Melancholia", and later even more explicitly in *The Ego and the Id*,[12] though he did not have the eucharist in mind.

Having sampled briefly some of the implications of the father–son symbolism in Christian belief and ritual, what are we to make of it? It would seem that Freud's analysis in terms of Oedipal themes has much to recommend it. Nevertheless it becomes obvious upon reflection that the Christian symbolism is not *explained* by the Oedipus complex. If it were simply a direct projection of the Oedipus complex, then since the Oedipus complex is universal so would Christian symbolism be. But this is clearly far from the case. Christian symbolism is in fact highly unique, emerging from a particular historical context and bearing a particular historical role, a fact which Freud seems to have recognized. The particular qualities of the Christian symbolism emerge in the first instance from the Christian notion of God, around which the whole symbolic structure hangs. This notion is neither general nor obvious and has, in fact, emerged only once in history and that once historically traceable to Israel at the moment of the Mosaic revelation.[13] There the notion of one God, rejecting all magic and known through his ethical demands rather than any philosophical speculation, was first clearly discerned. As the recent work of George Mendenhall[14] and others has pointed out, the social analogies on which the Mosaic covenant was based were political and not familial. God was conceived in terms of the Near Eastern great king, not a father. Though memories of the Abrahamic covenant with its more patriarchal conception of Jahwe remained, the use of the term "father" with respect to him was eschewed and any suggestions of the more naturalistic relations with divinity found in the widespread Near Eastern fertility cults was violently rejected. God was to be known through his will, which gradually became codified as his law. In the face of such an overwhelming and demanding God the temptation to respond with an obsessive compulsive legalism was strong. Nevertheless the sense of God's love and faithfulness was not lost and, by the time of Jesus, references to God as Father or Father in Heaven were not infrequent.

Whatever may have been Jesus' own understanding of his role and mission, and this is in dispute among New Testament scholars, the early church soon proclaimed his divine sonship. In this way for the first time in the history of Israel the family symbolism was taken up explicitly into the religious sphere and worked out there. The life and death of Jesus then provided a pattern or model for the working through of the father–son relationship with such a father as the God of Israel. The church emerged as the body of those who identified with Jesus and participated in his action. As such it was a collectivity of a different kind from that of the Jewish community bound together by its hereditary connection with the patriarchs and its adherence to the law. This new religious collectivity which was the Christian church had enormous sociological consequences which we will return to briefly later. Here we can only state that the radical extent to which this new collectivity involved elements of familial motivation transformed on the religious plane has something to do with its dynamism. It must of course be noticed that this familial motivation is not just projection, for the religious symbolism differs drastically from the fundamental family pattern. There is no mother, for the One God is a Father.[15] Any other solution would have involved a violation of Israel's idea of God and so have been no solution at all.

If we are right that the Oedipus complex itself cannot explain the difference between Christian symbolism and that of other religions, including, as we shall see, Confucianism, perhaps marked differences in family structure, of the sort which anthropologists have studied in primitive societies, can explain the difference. Let us compare briefly the Jewish family at the time of Christ with the Chinese family and then consider whether Confucian religious symbolism is illuminated by such a contrast.

Filial piety, according to George Foot Moore, was considered by the Jews at the time of Christ as "among all the commandments the 'weightiest of the weighty'".[16] The fifth of the ten commandments was of course, "Honor thy father and thy mother, that thy days may be long upon the land which the Lord thy God giveth thee" (Exodus 20 : 12). Custom provided detailed forms of reverence in word and act which a son owed his parents. A son who strikes a parent or who is stubborn and rebellious may be put to death, according to the Mosaic law.[17] Only in one instance was disobedience countenanced: a son should not transgress one of the commandments of the law even if bidden to do so by a parent.

With the exception of the last point the teaching of Confucianism was in agreement with that of Judaism. This is not surprising as the family systems in China and Palestine were in broad outline not markedly dissimilar. Both Confucian and Jewish families were patrilineal and patrilocal with a strong emphasis on the authority of the father and a relatively subordinate position for women. Again, if we were to follow the hypothesis that religious symbolism is essentially projected from the family situation then we should expect to find in Confucianism a set of religious symbols broadly similar to that found in Judaism or early Christianity.[18] Unfortunately, this is not the case.

We have already noted that the main characteristics of Jahwe in the Old Testament were formed on a political analogy rather than a familial one. While the political analogy is also of great importance in Chinese religious thought there was no Chinese equivalent to Jahwe. There were a number of highest terms only partially integrated with each other. Some like *T'ien* and *Shang Ti* have a clearly anthropomorphic background and may have originally meant the ancestor or ancestors of the tribe (who dwell in heaven, *T'ien*).[19] But by late Chou times these terms were largely depersonalized. *T'ien*, which remains an important conception up to modern times, is frequently joined with *Ti*, earth, and joined or not, tends to mean the order of nature. Therefore, even when *T'ien* is said to have a *ming*, decree, what is implied is an impersonal normative pattern, not a personal ethical command. There is no conception of a creator deity. In addition to these terms of anthropomorphic origin there were several terms with a quality of ultimacy which never had any personal referent, such as *Tao* and later *T'ai Ch'i* (Supreme Ultimate). If Granet's admittedly speculative analysis is correct, *Tao*, literally "the way", may originally have been derived from *Wang Tao*, the magico-political action or "way" of the king whereby he orders the social and cosmic universe.[20] At any rate in the *Analects*, *Tao* clearly means the way of the former kings or the way of the ancestors and only later does it take on its more philosophical significance.

In short, the Chinese conception differs radically from that of Judaism or Christianity. Confucianism tends to view the universe as a single social cosmic totality in which the *Tao* of heaven, earth, and man are the same. For example, the twenty-second chapter of the *Chung Yung* tells us that a man of utmost sincerity "may form a trinity with heaven and earth". Legge translates "he may with heaven and earth form a ternion", and says in a note, "*ts'an* is a 'file of three', and I employ 'ternion' to express the idea, just as we use 'quaternion' for a file of four. What is it but extravagance thus to file man with the Supreme Power?"[21] And so in the instinctive reaction of the Reverend James Legge, we see the difference between the Jewish and Christian view of the divine human relation and that of the Chinese.

The *Lü-shih Ch'un Ch'iu* says, "Heaven, Earth, and all things are like the body of one man, and this is what is called the Great Unity."[22] In early texts such as the *Shih Ching* and the *Shu Ching* the king is not infrequently referred to as the "One man". It is in this context that we can understand how the ruler came to be called the "son of Heaven". An early etymology for the character for *wang* or king (which happens to be false etymologically but valuable symbolically) interprets the three horizontal lines of which it is composed as Heaven, Man, and Earth and the vertical line which unites them as the king.[23] The ruler is to maintain order in society by taking as his model the orderly pattern of the heavens. Because the conception of heaven was so impersonal the conception of a son of heaven did not indicate much in the way of a personal relationship. Nor did it when Chuang Tzu appropriated the term for the Taoist adept.[24]

What I am trying to indicate is that though familial symbolism does appear in a religious context, it was not basic. It was not meant to indicate a pattern of relationships which was *essentially* personal and familial but rather to enrich with familial symbolism a pattern which had other bases. Thus when we come to Tung Chung-shu in the Han period and find him saying, "What produces (man) cannot (itself) be man, for the creator of man is Heaven. The fact that men are men derives from Heaven", and even, "Man's vigor is directed to love (*jen*) through the transforming influence of Heaven's will (*chih*)", we assume a pattern of relationship between Heaven and man not dissimilar to that with which we are familiar. But on closer inspection we find this to be not quite the case. For example, we are told that "Heaven has Five Elements . . . Wood produces fire, fire earth, earth metal, metal water, and water wood. Such is their father and son (relationship)." And again, "Man's likes and dislikes are influenced by Heaven's warmth and purity. Man's joy and anger are influenced by Heaven's cold and heat . . . The duplicate of Heaven lies in man, and man's feelings and nature derive from Heaven."[25] Here we see that the relationship of Heaven and man is one of organic correspondences, hardly the Jewish or Christian conception. Perhaps it is wrong to call the Chinese notion impersonal. In the Chinese view the whole cosmos is a closely interrelated community or organism with a continuous flow of sympathy between its parts. But the analogy of biological organism is far closer to the essence of the position than is familial relationship.

I do not, however, want to overstate my case. Familial symbolism, though not particularly central, is fairly constant in the East Asian religious tradition and occasionally attains an unmistakable seriousness, as for example in the following passage from the seventeenth-century Japanese Confucian Kaibara Ekken:

All men may be said to owe their birth to their parents, but a further inquiry into their origins reveals that men come into being receiving their principle of life from heaven and earth. Thus all men in the world are children born of heaven and earth, and heaven and earth are the great parents of us all. The Book of History says, "Heaven and earth are the father and mother of all things" (T'ai-shih 1). Our own parents are truly our parents; but heaven and earth are the parents of everyone in the world. Moreover, though we are brought up after birth through the care of our own parents and are sustained on the graciousness of the ruler, still if we go to the root of the matter, we find that we sustain ourselves using the things produced by heaven and earth for food, dress, housing, and implements. Thus, not only do all men at the outset come into being receiving their principles of life from heaven and earth, but from birth till the end of life they are kept in existence by the support of heaven and earth. Man surpasses all other created things in his indebtedness to the limitless bounty of heaven and earth. It will be seen therefore that man's duty is not only to do his best to serve his parents, which is a matter of course, but also to serve heaven and earth throughout his life in order to repay his immense debt. That is one thing all men should keep in mind constantly.[26]

Nevertheless I doubt if any Confucian would have felt comfortable with the following statement of Karl Barth:

It is therefore not as if the Father–Son relationship were itself a reality originally and properly creaturely, as if God in some hidden source of His essence were nevertheless something other than Father and Son, and as if therefore these names were optional and ultimately meaningless symbols, symbols the original and proper, non-symbolic content of which consisted in the said creaturely reality. On the contrary, it is precisely in God that the Father–Son relationship, like all creaturely relationships, has its original and proper reality. The mystery of the generation is originally and properly not a creaturely but a divine mystery, perhaps we ought to say outright, *the* divine mystery.[27]

The Confucian would simply not see the necessity for drawing the line between creaturely and divine in that way. This consideration leads us to the core of familial symbolism in Confucianism.

We have seen that heaven and earth may be considered the parents of men and that the ruler is called the son of Heaven. The ruler may also be called the parent of the people.[28] But all of these usages are rather peripheral. The core of familial involvement in Confucianism is not really in one sense symbolic at all, for it is the family itself. The subject of the present paper is the family in a religious context, but for Confucianism the family in many respects *is* the religious context. Honor thy father and thy mother is very nearly the whole of it. At least there is the fairly clear assumption that if that is achieved everything else will follow naturally. For example, the *Hsiao Ching* (*Classic of Filial Piety*) says:

Serving parents when alive with love and affection and when dead with grief and sorrow – this completely exhausts the basic duties of living men. (ch. 18.)

Filial piety is the root of virtue and that from which teaching comes. (ch. 1.)

Filial piety is heaven's pervading principle, earth's fundamental meaning, and the people's duty. (ch. 7.)

The relative vagueness and impersonality of religious concepts such as *T'ien* and *Tao* is certainly not unrelated to the fact that the religious sphere *par excellence* is the highly personal domestic scene itself. It is father and mother who have the first claim on reverence and it is father and mother who, after their death, will form the center of the family cultus. It is the family cult which is in the foreground. It is the family cult which monopolizes the drama and the intense personal feelings of the religious life. Other objects of religious reverence are mediated to the individual only through the family and so to speak have but a reflected light. A passage from Nakae Toju, a seventeenth-century Japanese Confucianist who made filial piety almost into a cosmic principle, illustrates the point:

> When we seek to investigate origins [we find that] our body is received from our parents, our parents' bodies are received from heaven and earth, heaven and earth are received from the universe (*taikyo*), and therefore since basically our body is a branch and transformation of the universe and the gods (*shimmei*), we are clearly one with the universe and the gods.[29]

Since one's relation to the universe is mediated through the parents, one's primary religious obligation is filial piety. It is thus that one expresses one's unity with the universe.

A consideration of the family cultus itself is extremely revealing for our purposes. It is interesting that nearly one-fourth of the *Li Chi*, by far the most important early source on ritual practice, is devoted to mourning rites. In order to give an indication of what these involved I would like to quote a rather extended passage from the *Li Chi*:

> Immediately after his father's death, (the son put off his cap, and) kept his hair, with the pin in it, in the bag (of silk); went barefoot, with the skirt of his dress tucked up under his girdle; and wailed with his hands across his breast. In the bitterness of his grief, and the distress and pain of his thoughts, his kidneys were injured, his liver dried up, and his lungs scorched, while water or other liquid did not enter his mouth, and for three days fire was not kindled (to cook anything for him). On this account the neighbors prepared for him gruel and rice-water, which were his (only) meat and drink. The internal grief and sorrow produced a change in his outward appearance; and with the severe pain in his heart, his mouth could not relish any savoury food, nor his body find ease in anything pleasant.
>
> Someone may ask, "Why does the dressing not commence till three days after death?" and the answer is: – When his parent is dead, the filial son is sad and sorrowful, and his mind is full of trouble. He crawls about and bewails his loss; – how can he hurriedly take (the corpse) and proceed to dress it? Therefore, when it is said that the dressing does not begin till after three days, the meaning is, that (the son) is waiting that time to see if (his father) will come to life. When after three days there is no such return, the father is not alive, and the heart of the filial son is still more downcast . . .
>
> On the third day there was the (slighter) dressing (of the corpse) . . . At the moving of the corpse, and lifting up of the coffin, (the son) wailed and leaped, times without number. Such was the bitterness of his heart, and the pain of his thoughts, so did his grief and sorrow fill his mind and agitate his spirit, that he

bared his arms and leaped, seeking by the movement of his limbs to obtain some comfort to his heart and relief to his spirit.

In presenting the sacrifice (of repose) in the ancestral temple, (the son) offered it (to his parent) in his disembodied state, hoping that his shade would per- adventure return (and enjoy it). When he came back to the house from com- pleting the grave, he did not venture to occupy his chamber, but dwelt in the mourning shed, lamenting that his parent was now outside. He slept on the rushes, with a clod for his pillow, lamenting that his parent was in the ground. Therefore he wailed and wept, without regard to time; he endured the toil and grief for three years. His heart of loving thoughts showed the mind of the filial son, and was the real expression of his human feelings.[30]

Though the more extreme aspects of the procedure were greatly modified in later times the mourning observances remained extremely important. The three-year (actually twenty-seven months) period was strictly observed by the literati, and government officials left office temporarily to do so.

Before making some interpretative remarks let us consider a few examples of what the *Li Chi* has to say about sacrifices to the ances- tral tablets, the so-called ancestor worship, which is both an attenu- ated form of the mourning ritual and the basic periodic ritual of the family cult:

King Wan, in sacrificing, served the dead as if he were serving the living. He thought of them dead as if he did not wish to live (any longer himself). On the recurrence of their death-day, he was sad; in calling his father by the name else- where forbidden, he looked as if he saw him. So sincere was he in sacrificing that he looked as if he saw the things which his father loved, and the pleased expression of his face: such was King Wan! The lines of the ode (II, v, ode 2),

> *When early dawn unseals my eyes,*
> *Before my mind my parents rise,*

might be applied to King Wan. On the day after the sacrifice, when the day broke, he did not sleep, but hastened to repeat it; and after it was finished, he still thought of his parents. On the day of sacrifice his joy and sorrow were blended together. He could not but rejoice in the opportunity of offering the sacrifice; and when it was over, he could not but be sad.

When a filial son is about to sacrifice, he is anxious that all preparations should be made beforehand; and when the time arrives, that everything necessary should be found complete; and then, with a mind free from all preoccupation, he should address himself to the performance of his sacrifice.

. . . He sets forth the stands with the victims on them; arranges all the cere- monies and music; provides the officers for the various ministries. These aid in sustaining and bringing in the things, and thus he declares his mind and wish, and in his lost abstraction of mind seeks to have communion with the dead in their spiritual state, if peradventure they will enjoy his offerings, if peradventure they will do so. Such is the aim of the filial son (in his sacrifices)![31]

This do in remembrance of me. If the ancestral sacrifices be com- pared to the eucharist then the mourning rites are concerned with

Calvary itself. For the death of the father is the death of the son's most religiously significant object. Freud said that the death of a man's father is the most poignant moment in his life. The Confucians made it the most religiously significant as well. All the ambivalence that is normally found in Oedipal situations is revealed in the mourning rites: Love and hostility, respect and fear. The aggression against the self and the guilt this indicates are of course normal in the grief work, but the intensity of the reaction probably displays the extent of the unconscious aggression against the father, unconscious because so profoundly disapproved in this society. The three-year mourning period gives a socially approved opportunity to accomplish the grief work and internalize the lost object. This transition is crucial socially as well as psychologically since upon the death of one's father one becomes in a new sense the head of a family and the family cult. Only then, in a sense, has one really become a father, even though one may have married and had children long before.

The Chinese, of course, have no monopoly on filial piety. Legge, for all his misgivings, could still write, "We are justified in looking on the long-continued existence and growth of the [Chinese] nation as a verification of the promise attached to our fifth commandment, 'Honour thy father and mother, that thy days may be long in the land which Jehovah thy God giveth thee.'"[32] But as we will have occasion to see in a moment, the place of filial piety in Christianity had quite different consequences than in Confucianism.

II

We have now completed a cursory glance at father–son symbolism in the context of Christianity and Confucianism. While there are common elements the configurations in the two instances are quite different. Let us briefly consider some of the spheres in which these differences expressed themselves.

In the sphere of religious organization the early church saw a rich development of familial symbolism. Abbot, the word for the head of a monastic community, is from the Aramaic for father. Pope, which in the early church was synonymous with bishop, is from the Greek for father. These terms, together with the common term "father" for priest, were used to indicate the appropriately familial relationships which should obtain within the Christian community. The power which made the priests "fathers", however, was not derived from the natural family as such but delegated from God through Christ. Even when the demands of the church contravened those of the natural family the church could claim a higher right to be a true family than could the natural family, in terms of Christian assumptions. This is one of the practical implications of Karl Barth's point mentioned above – that creaturely paternity derives from divine.

No such conception is possible on Confucian assumptions and there is no basis for a structurally independent religious community. For the Confucian any religious community which caused disturbance to actual family relations could only be a perversion. Chu Hsi points this out as follows:

> Beneath Heaven, it is only this normative Principle that unto the end we cannot but follow. The Buddhists and Taoists, for example, even though they would destroy the social relationships [by becoming monks], are nevertheless quite unable to escape them. Thus, lacking (the relationship of) father and son, they nevertheless on the one hand pay respect to their own preceptors (as if they were fathers), and on the other treat their acolytes as sons. The elder among them become elder brother preceptors, while the younger become younger brother preceptors. They are thereby clinging to something false, whereas it is the (Confucian) sages and worthies who have preserved the reality.[33]

For Chu Hsi it is not conceivable that these religious communities could have a higher basis of legitimation than the family. Rather he perceives them as subject to the pervasive family principle itself, but in a perverted and destructive way.

Christianity, again, while it can in accordance with its basic assumptions validly use familial terms for religious offices, can equally well reject such terms. The Reformers rejected the mediatorial function of the clergy and held that Christians are directly related to the triune God without intermediaries.[34] The Reformed churches consequently dropped the use of paternal terminology for their clergy lest any suggestion of spiritual hierarchy remain. Whether the familial terminology is used or dropped the legitimation on Christian assumptions must be divine authority.

The Christian attitude toward political and familial authority is again based on the premise of the derivative nature of such authority, as is well brought out in the following passage from Calvin:

> The end of this precept [the fifth commandment] is, that since the Lord God desires the preservation of the order he has appointed, the degrees of preeminence fixed by him ought to be inviolably preserved. The sum of it, therefore, will be that we should reverence them whom God has exalted to any authority over us, and should render them honour, obedience, and gratitude.[35]

It is on the basis of authority derived from God that parents and rulers should be reverenced. Calvin goes on to develop his point with considerable warmth.

For to those, to whom he gives any pre-eminence, he communicates his own authority, as far as is necessary for the preservation of that pre-eminence. The titles of Father, God, and Lord, are so eminently applicable to him, that, whenever we hear either of them mentioned, our minds cannot but be strongly affected with a sense of majesty. Those, therefore, on whom he bestows these titles, he illuminates with a ray of his splendour, to render them all honourable in their respective stations. Thus in a father we ought to recognize something Divine; for it is not without reason that he bears one of the titles of the Deity. Our prince, or our Lord, enjoys an honour somewhat similar to that which is given to God.[36]

Wherefore it ought not to be doubted that God here lays down a universal rule for our conduct; namely, that to everyone, whom we know to be placed in authority over us by his appointment, we should render reverence, obedience, gratitude, and all the other services of our power. Nor does it make any difference, whether they are worthy of his honour, or not. For whatever is their character, yet it is not without the appointment of the Divine providence, that they have attained that station, on account of which the supreme Legislator has commanded them to be honoured. He has particularly enjoined reverence to our parents, who have brought us into this life, which nature itself ought to teach us. For those who violate the parental authority are monsters. Therefore the Lord commands all those, who are disobedient to their parents, to be put to death, as having rendered themselves unworthy to enjoy the light, by their disregarding those by whose means they were introduced to it.[37]

Calvin seems to be determined to use every argument in support of absolute authority. The penalty of disobedience to one illumined by a ray of his splendor is death. He goes on to an involved discussion of the promise of long life attached to the fifth commandment and then near the end of his discussion adds as a sort of after-thought what is, in fact, a delayed action bomb which places what went before in a new light:

But it must be remembered by the way, that we are commanded to obey them "in the Lord"; and this is evident from the foundation before laid; for they preside in that station to which the Lord has exalted them by communicating to them a portion of his honour. Wherefore the submission exercised towards them ought to be a step towards honouring the Supreme Father. Therefore, if they instigate us to any transgression of the law, we may justly consider them not as parents, but as strangers, who attempt to seduce us from obedience to our real Father. The same observation is applicable to princes, lords and superiors of every description. For it is infamous and absurd, that their eminence should avail to depreciate the pre-eminence of God, upon whom it depends, and to which it ought to conduct us.

Unillumined by a ray of his splendor our fathers and princes are strangers.

Of course that "We must obey God rather than men" (Acts 5 : 29) is good New Testament doctrine, but the Reformation pushed it relentlessly through in every sphere of life. Luther, Calvin, Beza, and others of the Reformers disobeyed their fathers at critical junctures of their lives when they felt a divine calling to do so. They were able not only to disobey the pope but abandon the monarchical principle in the church, when they felt it did not accord with divine intent. And it was not long before English Calvinists would behead an English king, and put a permanent crimp in the monarchical principle in the state as well. No wonder Calvin protested his devotion to authority in such extreme language. He was unable to admit to himself how revolutionary the implications of his own position were, nor could the aging Luther. The especial violence with which both execrated the Anabaptists reveals that they had to deny in the world what they could not face in themselves. In the case of Luther, Erikson has helped us to understand the special guilt which attaches to a man who has made a great step toward freedom. Calvin, I think, had the same guilt. They had, in a sense, dared too much and they tried to repair the damage in their later years. It is clear that it was only their reliance on an absolute God which made it psychologically possible for them to question every accepted authority in their world without being completely overwhelmed in the process. They bore the guilt for their followers who could proceed to carry through the implications of their teaching with much less inner conflict.

Let us turn to the Confucian attitude toward political and familial authority. There does not seem to be any point of leverage in the Confucian symbol system from which disobedience to parents could be justified. This does not mean parents could not be criticized. When they did not live up to the pattern of the ancestors there was indeed a positive duty to remonstrate, but they could not be disobeyed. Thus the *Li Chi* says:

> If a parent have a fault, (the son) should with bated breath, and bland aspect, and gentle voice, admonish him. If the admonition do not take effect he will be the more reverential and the more filial; and when the father seems pleased, he will repeat the admonition. If he should be displeased with this, rather than allow him to commit an offense against any one in the neighborhood or countryside, (the son) should strongly remonstrate. If the parent be angry and (more) displeased, and beat him till the blood flows, he should not presume to be angry and resentful, but be (still) more reverential and more filial.[38]

By suffering patiently and by being even more reverential and filial the son can silently reproach his father. But that is all, at least all that is legitimate within the framework of the Confucian system.

It is true that rebellion against tyrannical rulers has a classical justification in Confucianism, notably in the famous passages in Mencius. Nevertheless there was a strong tendency in Confucianism, especially in neo-Confucianism, to regard political rebellion as virtually in the category of disobedience to parents. It is notable that major rebellions were initially usually justified in terms of some Taoist or Buddhist ideology and only when successful was the Confucian stamp of approval received. Of course there was the obligation, as in the case of the family, to remonstrate with an erring superior. But there was little in the Confucian position to justify going beyond that. In this connection the notes of the censor Tso Kuang-tou written to his sons just before he was tortured to death by the emperor on a trumped-up charge in 1625 are psychologically very revealing:

At this moment my pain and distress are extreme; I can no longer even walk a step. In the middle of the night the pain gets still worse. If I want water to drink, none is at hand. Death! Death! Only thus can I make recompense to the Emperor and to the two imperial ancestors . . . The bones of my whole body are broken, and my flesh is bloodlogged . . . This loyal heart came to be at odds with powerful villains and brought about this sore calamity. All sorts of punishments I have willingly endured. Since I have already argued at the risk of my life, why need I shrink from running against the spear and dying? My body belongs to my ruler-father. I am lucky I shall not die in the arms of my wife and children; for I have found the proper place to die! I only regret that this blood-filled heart has not been able to make recompense to my ruler, and that my aged parents cannot once again see my face. This will be my remorse in Hades! . . . My misery is extreme; my pain is extreme. Why do I live on? Why do I cling to life? Death! Only thus can I make recompense to the Emperor and to the two imperial ancestors in Heaven.[39]

There is in such an attitude a truly heroic loyalty which refuses to waver even at such a moment. The roots of the strength and endurance of a great civilization are displayed in these words. But at the same time we see how the Confucian phrasing of the father–son relationship blocks any outcome of Oedipal ambivalence except submission – submission not in the last analysis to a person but to a pattern of personal relationships which is held to have ultimate validity. An outcome which could lead to creative social innovation as in the Protestant case was precluded by the absence of a point of transcendent loyalty which could provide legitimation for it. In the West from the time of the Mosaic revelation every particular pattern of social relations was in principle deprived of ultimacy. In China filial piety and loyalty became absolutes. In the West it was God alone who in the last analysis exercised power. In China the father continued to dominate.

Before concluding I would like to suggest two other lines of inquiry which we might pursue if there were time. It is a generally admitted fact that in East Asia there is no literary genre which we might call tragic. There are conquering heroes and there are suffering heroes but there are not tragic heroes in the Western sense, men whose agony calls into question the justice of the cosmos itself; in other words, there is no Chinese Job. This is not unrelated, it seems to me, to the patterns of father–son symbolism we have been suggesting. The particularly tragic note in the West seems to require a double motion which never quite gets started in China. In the first motion the world is criticized from the point of view of God, but then by a subtle reversal it is God himself who is questioned. Christianity, it is claimed, overcomes the tragic. Perhaps so, but as long as it carries near the heart of its critical narrative the words "My God, My God, Why hast thou forsaken me?" it does not destroy the tragic. However much exegetical effort one makes to explain this away, the fact remains that it is a question. Even when the question is in a sense answered it is not blotted out. The capacity to ask questions of the ultimate is perhaps a consequence of shifting the locus of ultimacy from the natural social order to a transcendent reference point. From the point of view of the transcendent everything natural has only relative value and can be questioned. But the questioning leads to the question of the ultimate itself.[40]

One last point. Both Christianity and Confucianism repress rather drastically certain forms of aggression. Communism is to be explained in part as an aggressive parody of the religion of divine love. In the Orozco mural at Dartmouth this is stunningly illustrated in the giant figure of Christ who stands, legs apart, his left hand raised in a clenched fist salute, his right hand holding the axe with which he has just cut down the cross and behind him an immense pile of broken idols and symbols of the religions of the world. In its origin Communism can be understood only in relation to the Christian symbolizations which preceded it, and its appeal in various Western countries has been partly conditioned by the variety of Christianity prevailing in them. I would suggest that Chinese Communism must be understood in terms of the particular background of Confucian symbolization. It has apparently succeeded in tapping at last the age-long repressed aggression of sons against fathers as is indicated by the symbolic denunciation of the father which forms the high point of Chinese Communist "re-education". But it could do so only by bringing in a basic reference point which transcends the given social and familial order. The capacity of Communism to do this derives in part from its own Christian lineage. And so Christianity, in parody form at least, has come closer in the last fifteen years to the missionaries' dream of "total evangelization" than in the whole preceding century of effort. The subtle dialectic between surviving elements of the Confucian tradition and crypto-Christian Communism helps to explain the dynamism of current Chinese society.

The burden of this brief comparison is that we must take seriously the content and structure of historical religious symbols. The Oedipus complex and the patriarchal family help us to understand much in the Christian and Confucian cases, but they do not explain the differences between them. In fact, we have seen on closer inspection that the phrasing and outcome of the Oedipus complex and the structure of the family may themselves be profoundly affected by particular modes of religious symbolization.

NOTES

1. *Politics*, 1252b, 1259b.
2. *Ibid.*, 1252a.
3. James Strachey's translation, *Collected Works*, Vol. 13 (New York: W. W. Norton, 1952 and London: Hogarth Press, 1955), p. 157.
4. G. F. Moore, *Judaism*, Vol. II (Boston: Harvard University Press, 1927), p. 134.
5. *Summa Contra Gentiles*, book iv, ch. 55, par. 14, 18.
6. *Institutes*, book ii, ch. xvi, par. 10.
7. *Ibid.*, par. 6.
8. E. Przywara, *An Augustine Synthesis* (New York: Harper Torchbooks, 1958), p. 305.
9. *Ibid.*, p. 287.
10. *Ibid.*, p. 290.
11. *City of God*, x, 6.
12. London: Hogarth Press, 1947.
13. On this point see E. Voegelin, *Order and History*, Vol. I: *Israel and Revelation* (Baton Rouge, Louisiana: Louisiana State University Press, 1956 and Oxford: Oxford University Press, 1957), ch. 12.
14. G. Mendenhall, "Law and Covenant in Israel and the Ancient Near East", *The Biblical Archaeologist*, XVII (1954).
15. The problem of female symbolism in Christianity is a complicated one and lies beyond the scope of this paper. The central point for present purposes is that none of the members of the Godhead is explicitly female. We cannot here pursue the problems which arise in connection with the Virgin Mary, the feminization of Jesus, or the church itself as a feminine symbol. On the last point Kenneth Burke's essay on Augustine in *The Rhetoric of Religion* (New York: Beacon Press, 1961), pp. 43–171, is especially illuminating.
16. *Op. cit.*, Vol. II, p. 131.
17. *Ibid.*, p. 134.
18. The historical transformation of religious symbolism within and between Judaism and Christianity is a problem of great importance but a systematic treatment of it is beyond the scope of this paper. Here we can only stress the main

differences between Judaism and Christianity on the one hand and Confucianism on the other.

19. A. Waley, *The Analects of Confucius* (London: Allen & Unwin, 1938), pp. 40–43; see also H. G. Creel, *et al.*, *Literary Chinese*, Vol. I (Chicago, 1948), p. 66.

20. *La Pensée Chinoise* (Paris: Albin Michel, 1934), pp. 300–339.

21. *The Chinese Classics*, Vol. I (Oxford: Clarendon Press, 1893), p. 416.

22. Fung Yu-lan, *A History of Chinese Philosophy*, Vol. I (Princeton, New Jersey: Princeton University Press, 1953), p. 168.

23. Granet, *op. cit.*, p. 319.

24. *Chuang Tzu*, x.

25. Fung, *op. cit.*, Vol. II, pp. 20–21, 32.

26. Ryusaku Tsunoda and others, *Sources of the Japanese Tradition* (New York: Columbia University Press, 1958), p. 376. Translation slightly revised after consultation with *Ekken Zenshu*, Vol. 3, p. 2.

27. *Church Dogmatics*, Vol. I.1: *Doctrine of the Word of God* (New York: Charles Scribner's Sons and Edinburgh: T. & T. Clark, 1936), p. 495.

28. Legge, *The Chinese Classics*, Vol. III, p. 125.

29. *Okina Mondo*, Iwanami ed., pp. 54–55.

30. Legge's translation, *Sacred Books of the East*, Vol. XXVIII (Oxford: The Clarendon Press, 1885), pp. 375–377. The paragraphs have been somewhat rearranged for greater clarity of exposition.

31. *Ibid.*, pp. 210–214 (with omissions).

32. *The Religions of China* (London: Hodder & Stoughton, 1880), p. 88.

33. Fung, *op. cit.*, Vol. II, p. 569.

34. E.g. Calvin, *Institutes*, book iii, ch. 20, par. 37.

35. *Ibid.*, book ii, ch. 8, par. 35.

36. *Ibid.*

37. *Ibid.*, par. 36.

38. *Sacred Books of the East*, Vol. XXVII, pp. 456–457.

39. Translated in C. O. Hucker, "Confucianism and the Chinese Censorial System", *Confucianism in Action*, eds. David S. Nivison and Arthur F. Wright (Stanford, California: Stanford University Press, 1959), p. 208.

40. The emergence of tragedy in Greece is closely related to the philosophical questioning of the inherited myth and ritual pattern from the point of view of a more transcendental conception of reality. On this point see E. Voegelin, *Order and History*, Vol. II: *The World of the Polis* (Baton Rouge, Louisiana: Louisiana State University Press, 1957), ch. 10.

II

RELIGIOUS ASPECTS OF
PEAK-EXPERIENCES*

Abraham H. Maslow

As witnessed by the studies in this section there can be little question that religion can have dramatic effects upon the formation of a personal world; however, it is sometimes dubious if the effects are beneficial to either individuals or groups. Some studies have indicated the positive contribution religion can make to personality development, while pointing out that certain types of religion can be harmful. What begins to emerge as a tentative conclusion is that from the viewpoint of the personality sciences there are at least two basic forms of religion. Allport applied the labels intrinsic and extrinsic; independent of his analysis, other social scientists have reached a similar conclusion. In the following chapter the psychologist Abraham Maslow has also examined two types of religion in terms of their respective impact upon personality. Like many of the contributors he has concentrated upon motivation (Motivation and Personality [*New York: Harper and Row, 1954*]), *and he has emphasized the dynamic power of values in the process of self-realization* (New Knowledge and Human Values, ed. [*Harper and Row, 1959*] and Toward a Psychology of Being, *2nd ed.* [*New York: Van Nostrand, 1968*]). *While other personality scientists have often concentrated upon everyday aspects of the personal world, Maslow has followed up one suggestion made earlier by James and has investigated the high points of human existence. In the following chapter he*

* A compilation of several portions, used with permission of the author and of Kappa Delta Pi, an Honor Society in Education, owner of the copyright, from Abraham H. Maslow, *Religions, Values and Peak-experiences* (Columbus: Ohio State University Press, 1964).

studies these high points, what he refers to as peak-experiences, in relationship to religion. He claims that a peak-experience is the core of religion, or at least some forms of it.

Like many of these studies, Maslow's chapter is provocative, raising numerous questions. What are the characteristic features of a peak-experience and how do they compare with James's description of the effects of authentic religious experience? What is the relationship between peak-experiences, values, and religion? Considering peak-experiences as influencing a distinctive life style, what is characteristic of a life style in which peak-experiences are absent? What does Maslow believe should be the proper attitude of organized religion toward peak-experiences? What insight does an analysis of peak-experiences provide to our understanding of human potentialities? What aspects of religion do you feel are important which Maslow omits in his view of an ideal religion? Is a peak-experience as he defines it a sufficient criterion to evaluate mature personality and mature religion?

For further reading, in addition to the above-mentioned books by Maslow, one might consult Laski's study cited in this text by Maslow and an article by Carl R. Rogers, "Toward a Modern Approach to Values: The Valuing Process in the Mature Person", The Journal of Abnormal and Social Psychology, 68 (1964), 160–167.

I

THIS LECTURE is in a direct line with James's *Varieties of Religious Experience*, Dewey's *A Common Faith*, and Fromm's *Psychoanalysis and Religion*. They examined religious experiences as psychologists examine any experience, descriptively, empirically, objectively, humanistically, in the effort to be as truthful as possible. This is what I have also tried to do in this lecture.

In 1963, it is possible to be more precise about these matters than it was in 1902 and in 1934. I have based my discussion mostly on the investigations of what I prefer to call "peak-experiences", rather than upon narrowly religious experiences or mystical experiences. This is because it has been discovered that this same kind of subjective experimental response (which has been thought to be triggered only in religious or mystical contexts, and which has, therefore, been considered to be only religious or mystical) is also triggered by many other stimuli or situations, e.g. experiences of the aesthetic, of the creative, of love, of sex, of insight, etc. If we insist on calling the peak-experience a religious experience, then we must say that religious experiences can be produced by sexual love, or by philosophical insight, or by athletic success, or by watching a dance performance, or by bearing a child. This inevitably means, as James and Dewey both saw, that we must take the word "religious" out of its narrow context of the supernatural, churches, rituals, dogmas, professional clergymen, etc., and distribute it in principle throughout the whole of life. Religion becomes then not one social institution among others, but rather a state of mind achievable in almost any activity of life, if this activity is raised to a suitable level of perfection.

Peak-experiences, as I have defined them for this analysis, are secularized religious or mystical or transcendent experiences; or, more precisely, peak-experiences are the raw materials out of which not only religions can be built but also philosophies of any kind: educational, political, aesthetic, etc. Not only are these experiences not dependent on churches or specific religions, as James and Dewey saw, they do not necessarily imply any supernatural concepts. They are well within the realm of nature, and can be investigated and discussed in an entirely naturalistic way. . . .

This thesis that religious experiences are natural experiences could be seen by churchmen with dismay, as simply and only a further instance of science carving another chunk out of the side of organized religion – which, of course, it is. But it is also possible for a more perceptively religious man to greet this development with enthusiasm, when he realizes that what the mystics have said to be essential to the *individual's* religion is now receiving empirical support and no longer needs rest only on tradition, blind faith, temporal power, exhortation, etc. If this development is a secularizing of all religion, it is also a religionizing of all that is secular. This lecture is a critique, not only of traditional, conventional religion, but also of traditional and conventional atheism. As a matter of fact, I am addressing myself much more to the latter than to the former. Religion is easy to criticize but difficult to explain. It begins to be clear to me that in throwing out *all* of religion and everything to do with it, the atheists have thrown out too much. Also, religion has been "reduced" too much, e.g. by Freud, by Feuerbach, etc. Undoubtedly correct to a large extent, yet they went too far in their generalizations and, in any case, were, I think, attacking organized religions more than private, transcendent experiences. Also, it is clear that they didn't realize, as we do today, how deep and possibly even "instinctoid" is the need for a framework of values (Fromm), for meaning (Frankl), for understanding (Maslow). Nor did they anticipate that a psychology of ends (an ontopsychology, a psychology of Being) could become possible, offering us in the distance not too far ahead the possibility of a "scientific" or objective value system. (In a fuller treatment I would also bring up the possibility of a "need for transcendence" beyond the need for understanding, as Fromm has.)

One more lesson that we have learned from the peak-experiences makes a difference between the psychologist of 1902 and the psychologist of today. William James assumed, with his time, that many of the religious experiences he discussed were abnormal and pathological. We know now this is true far less often than James thought. If anything, peak-experiences are more characteristic of health than of neurosis or psychosis. They *may* be pathological, but more often they are not. They are more often to be valued than to be feared.

The dichotomy between "higher" and "lower" is also being transcended here. It is equally possible to call a peak-experience or any other "serious" experience *either* a reaching up to the heights *or* a probing to the depths of experience. This is true in the sense also that "mind" or "spirit" or "spiritual values" do not soar someplace "higher" in space or "above" the body, the animal, the instincts. A whole school of psychologists now believe that "spiritual values" are *in* the organism, so much a part of a well-functioning organism as to be *sine qua non* "defining-characteristics" of it.

I do not wish to be understood as reducing religion – either theistic or non-theistic – to a code of ethics only. Peak-experiences are also epistemological and ontopsychological. They have to do with the nature of reality, of man's relation to it, of knowledge of it, and of the values inherent in it. They can be trans-moral, transcending distinctions between good and evil.

This lecture is more a set of notes than a finished product. But, this air of a progress report, of a struggle still going on, this incompleteness, is actually more true and authentic than a polished and final product would have been. I plan to keep on trying to draw the consequences of my investigations of psychological health for the theory of values, of ethics, of education, of psychotherapy, or "religion", of work, etc.

II

Practically everything that happens in the peak-experiences, naturalistic though they are, could be listed under the headings of religious happenings, or indeed have been in the past considered to be only religious experiences.

1. For instance, it is quite characteristic in peak-experiences that the whole universe is perceived as an integrated and unified whole.

This is not as simple a happening as one might imagine from the bare words themselves. To have a clear perception (rather than a purely abstract and verbal philosophical acceptance) that the universe is all of a piece and that one has his place in it – one is a part of it, one belongs in it – can be so profound and shaking an experience that it can change the person's character and his Weltanschauung forever after. In my own experience I have two subjects who, because of such an experience, were totally, immediately, and permanently cured of (in one case) chronic anxiety neurosis and, in the other case, of strong obsessional thoughts of suicide.

This, of course, is a basic meaning of religious faith for many people. People who might otherwise lose their "faith" will hang onto it because it gives a meaningfulness to the universe, a unity, a single philosophical explanation which makes it all hang together. Many orthodoxly religious people would be so frightened by giving up the notion that the universe has integration, unity, and, therefore, meaningfulness (which is given to it by the fact that it was all created by God or ruled by God or *is* God) that the only alternative for them would be to see the universe as a totally unintegrated chaos.

2. In the cognition that comes in peak-experiences, characteristically the percept is exclusively and fully attended to. That is, there is tremendous concentration of a kind which does not normally occur. There is the truest and most total kind of visual perceiving or listening or feeling. Part of what this involves is a peculiar change which can best be described as non-evaluating, non-comparing, or non-judging cognition. That is to say, figure and ground are less sharply differentiated. Important and unimportant are also less sharply differentiated, i.e. there is a tendency for things to become equally important rather than to be ranged in a hierarchy from very important to quite unimportant. For instance, the mother examining in loving ecstasy her new-born infant may be enthralled by every single part of him, one part as much as another one, one little toenail as much as another little toenail, and be struck into a kind of religious awe in this way. This same kind of total, non-comparing acceptance of everything, as if everything were equally important, holds also for the perception of people. Thus it comes about that in peak-experience cognition a person is most easily seen *per se*, in himself, by himself, uniquely and idiosyncratically as if he were the sole member of his class. Of course, this is a very common aspect not only of religious experience but of most theologies as well, i.e. the person is unique, the person is sacred, one person in principle is worth as much as any other person, everyone is a child of God, etc.

3. The cognition of being (B-cognition) that occurs in peak-experiences tends to perceive external objects, the world, and individual people as more detached from human concerns. Normally we perceive everything as relevant to human concerns and more particularly to our own private selfish concerns. In the peak-experiences, we become more detached, more objective, and are more able to perceive the world as if it were independent not only of the perceiver but even of human beings in general. The perceiver can more readily look upon nature as if it were there in itself and for itself, not simply as if it were a human playground put there for human purposes. He can more easily refrain from projecting human purposes upon it. In a word, he can see it in its own Being (as an end in itself) rather than as something to be used or something to be afraid of or something to wish for or to be reacted to in some other personal, human, self-centered way. That is to say, B-cognition, because it makes human irrelevance more possible, enables us thereby to see more truly the nature of the object in itself. This is a little like talking about god-like perception, superhuman perception. The peak-experience seems to lift us to greater than normal heights so that we can see and perceive in a higher than usual way. We become larger, greater, stronger, bigger, taller people and tend to perceive accordingly.

4. To say this in a different way, perception in the peak-experiences can be relatively ego-transcending, self-forgetful, egoless, unselfish. It can come closer to being unmotivated, impersonal, desireless, detached, not needing or wishing. Which is to say, that it becomes more object-centered than ego-centered. The perceptual experience can be more organized around the object itself as a centering point rather than being based upon the selfish ego. This means in turn that objects and people are more readily perceived as having independent reality of their own.

5. The peak-experience is felt as a self-validating, self-justifying moment which carries its own intrinsic value with it. It is felt to be a highly valuable – even uniquely valuable – experience, so great an experience sometimes that even to attempt to justify it takes away from its dignity and worth. As a matter of fact, so many people find this so great and high an experience that it justifies not only itself but even living itself. Peak-experiences can make life worthwhile by their occasional occurrence. They give meaning to life itself. They prove it to be worthwhile. To say this in a negative way, I would guess that peak-experiences help to prevent suicide.

6. Recognizing these experiences as end-experiences rather than

as means-experiences makes another point. For one thing, it proves to the experiencer that there are ends in the world, that there are things or objects or experiences to yearn for which are worthwhile in themselves. This in itself is a refutation of the proposition that life and living is meaningless. In other words, peak-experiences are one part of the operational definition of the statement that "life is worthwhile" or "life is meaningful".

7. In the peak-experience there is a very characteristic disorientation in time and space, or even the lack of consciousness of time and space. Phrased positively, this is like experiencing universality and eternity. Certainly we have here, in a very operational sense, a real and scientific meaning of "under the aspect of eternity". This kind of timelessness and spacelessness contrasts very sharply with normal experience. The person in the peak-experiences may feel a day passing as if it were minutes or also a minute so intensely lived that it might feel like a day or a year or an eternity even. He may also lose his consciousness of being located in a particular place.

8. The world seen in the peak-experiences is seen only as beautiful, good, desirable, worthwhile, etc., and is never experienced as evil or undesirable. The world is accepted. People will say that then they understand it. Most important of all for comparison with religious thinking is that somehow they become reconciled to evil. Evil itself is accepted and understood and seen in its proper place in the whole, as belonging there, as unavoidable, as necessary, and, therefore, as proper. Of course, the way in which I (and Laski also) gathered peak-experiences was by asking for reports of ecstasies and raptures, of the most blissful and perfect moments of life. Then, of course, life *would* look beautiful. And then all the foregoing might seem like discovering something that had been put in *a priori*. But observe that what I am talking about is the perception of evil, of pain, of disease, of death. In the peak-experiences, not only is the world seen as acceptable and beautiful, but, and this is what I am stressing, the bad things about life are accepted more totally than they are at other times. It is as if the peak-experience reconciled people to the presence of evil in the world.

9. Of course, this is another way of becoming "god-like". The gods who can contemplate and encompass the whole of being and who, therefore, understand it must see it as good, just, inevitable, and must see "evil" as a product of limited or selfish vision and understanding. If we could be god-like in this sense, then we, too, out of universal understanding would never blame or condemn or be disappointed or shocked. Our only possible emotions would be pity,

charity, kindliness, perhaps sadness or amusement. But this is precisely the way in which self-actualizing people do at times react to the world, and in which all of us react in our peak-experiences.

10. Perhaps my most important finding was the discovery of what I am calling B-values or the intrinsic values of Being. When I asked the question, "How does the world look different in peak-experiences?", the hundreds of answers that I got could be boiled down to a quintessential list of characteristics which, though they overlap very much with one another, can still be considered as separate for the sake of research. What is important for us in this context is that this list of the described characteristics of the world as it is perceived in our most perspicuous moments is about the same as what people through the ages have called eternal verities, or the spiritual values, or the highest values, or the religious values. What this says is that facts and values are not totally different from each other; under certain circumstances, they fuse. Most religions have either explicitly or by implication affirmed some relationship or even an overlapping or fusion between facts and values. For instance, people not only existed but they were also sacred. The world was not only merely existent but it was also sacred.

11. B-cognition in the peak-experience is much more passive and receptive, much more humble, than normal perception is. It is much more ready to listen and much more able to hear.

12. In the peak-experience, such emotions as wonder, awe, reverence, humility, surrender, and even worship before the greatness of the experience are often reported. This may go so far as to involve thoughts of death in a peculiar way. Peak-experiences can be so wonderful that they can parallel the experience of dying, that is of an eager and happy dying. It is a kind of reconciliation and acceptance of death. Scientists have never considered as a scientific problem the question of the "good death"; but here in these experiences, we discover a parallel to what has been considered to be the religious attitude toward death, i.e. humility or dignity before it, willingness to accept it, possibly even a happiness with it.

13. In peak-experiences, the dichotomies, polarities, and conflicts of life tend to be transcended or resolved. That is to say, there tends to be a moving toward the perception of unity and integration in the world. The person himself tends to move toward fusion, integration, and unity and away from splitting, conflicts, and oppositions.

14. In the peak-experiences, there tends to be a loss, even though transient, of fear, anxiety, inhibition, of defense and control, of perplexity, confusion, conflict, of delay and restraint. The profound

fear of disintegration, of insanity, of death, all tend to disappear for the moment. Perhaps this amounts to saying that fear disappears.

15. Peak-experiences sometimes have immediate effects or after-effects upon the person. Sometimes their aftereffects are so profound and so great as to remind us of the profound religious conversions which forever after changed the person. Lesser effects could be called therapeutic. These can range from very great to minimal or even to no effects at all. This is an easy concept for religious people to accept, accustomed as they are to thinking in terms of conversions, of great illuminations, of great moments of insight, etc.

16. I have likened the peak-experience in a metaphor to a visit to a personally defined heaven from which the person then returns to earth. This is like giving a naturalistic meaning to the concept of heaven. Of course, it is quite different from the conception of heaven as a place somewhere into which one physically steps after life on this earth is over. The conception of heaven that emerges from the peak-experiences is one which exists all the time all around us, always available to step into for a little while at least.

17. In peak-experiences, there is a tendency to move more closely to a perfect identity, or uniqueness, or to the idiosyncracy of the person or to his real self, to have become more a real person.

18. The person feels himself more than at other times to be responsible, active, the creative center of his own activities and of his own perceptions, more self-determined, more a free agent, with more "free will" than at other times.

19. But it has also been discovered that precisely those persons who have the clearest and strongest identity are exactly the ones who are most able to transcend the ego or the self and to become selfless, who are at least relatively selfless and relatively egoless.

20. The peak-experiencer becomes more loving and more accepting, and so he becomes more spontaneous and honest and innocent.

21. He becomes less an object, less a thing, less a thing of the world living under the laws of the physical world, and he becomes more a psyche, more a person, more subject to the psychological laws, especially the laws of what people have called the "higher life".

22. Because he becomes more unmotivated, that is to say, closer to non-striving, non-ending, non-wishing, he asks less for himself in such moments. He is less selfish. (We must remember that the gods have been considered generally to have no needs or wants, no deficiencies, no lacks, and to be gratified in all things. In this sense, the unmotivated human being becomes more god-like.)

23. People during and after peak-experiences characteristically feel lucky, fortunate, graced. A common reaction is "I don't deserve this". A common consequence is a feeling of gratitude, in religious persons, to their God, in others, to fate or to nature or to just good fortune. It is interesting in the present context that this can go over into worship, giving thanks, adoring, giving praise, oblation, and other reactions which fit very easily into orthodox religious frameworks. In that context we are accustomed to this sort of thing – that is, to the feeling of gratitude or all-embracing love for everybody and for everything, leading to an impulse to do something good for the world, an eagerness to repay, even a sense of obligation and dedication.

24. The dichotomy or polarity between humility and pride tends to be resolved in the peak-experiences and also in self-actualizing persons. Such people resolve the dichotomy between pride and humility by fusing them into a single complex superordinate unity, that is by being proud (in a certain sense) and also humble (in a certain sense). Pride (fused with humility) is not hubris nor is it paranoia; humility (fused with pride) is not masochism.

25. What has been called the "unitive consciousness" is often given in peak-experiences, i.e. a sense of the sacred glimpsed *in* and *through* the particular instance of the momentary, the secular, the worldly.

It has been demonstrated again and again that the transcendent experiences have occurred to some people in any culture and at any time and of any religion and in any caste or class. All these experiences are described in about the same general way; the language and the concrete contents may be different, indeed must be different. These experiences are essentially ineffable (in the sense that even the best verbal phrasings are not quite good enough), which is also to say that they are unstructured (like Rorschach ink-blots). Also throughout history, they have never been understood in a naturalistic way. Small wonder it is then that the mystic, trying to describe his experience, can do it only in a local, culture-bound, ignorance-bound, language-bound way, confusing his description of the experience with whatever explanation of it and phrasing of it is most readily available to him in his time and in his place.

Laski discusses the problem in detail in her chapters on "Overbeliefs" and in other places and agrees with James in disregarding them.[1] For instance, she points out, "To a substantial extent the people in the religious group knew the vocabulary for such experiences before they knew the experience; inevitably when the experiences are known, they tend to be recounted in the vocabulary already accepted as appropriate."

To summarize, it looks quite probable that the peak-experience may be the model of the religious revelation or the religious illumination or conversion which has played so great a role in the history of religions. But, because peak-experiences are in the natural world and because we can research with them and investigate them, and because our knowledge of such experiences is growing and may be confidently expected to grow in the future, we may now fairly hope to understand more about the big revelations, conversions, and illuminations upon which the high religions were founded.

(Not only this, but I may add a new possibility for scientific investigation of transcendence. In the last few years it has become quite clear that certain drugs called "psychedelic", especially LSD and psilocybin, give us some possibility of control in this realm of peak-experiences. It looks as if these drugs often produce peak-experiences in the right people under the right circumstances, so that perhaps we need not wait for them to occur by good fortune. Perhaps we can actually produce a private personal peak-experience under observation and whenever we wish under religious or non-religious circumstances. We may then be able to study in its moment of birth the experience of illumination or revelation. Even more important, it may be that these drugs, and perhaps also hypnosis, could be used to produce a peak-experience, with core-religious revelation, in non-peakers, thus bridging the chasm between these two separated halves of mankind.)

To approach this whole discussion from another angle, in effect what I have been saying is that the evidence from the peak-experiences permits us to talk about the essential, the intrinsic, the basic, the most fundamental religious or transcendent experience as a totally private and personal one which can hardly be shared (except with other "peakers"). As a consequence, all the paraphernalia of organized religion – buildings and specialized personnel, rituals, dogmas, ceremonials, and the like – are to the "peaker" secondary, peripheral, and of doubtful value in relation to the intrinsic and essential religious or transcendent experience. Perhaps they may even be harmful in various ways. From the point of view of the peak-experiencer, each person has his own private religion, which he develops out of his own private revelations in which are revealed to him his own private myths and symbols, rituals and ceremonials, which may be of the profoundest meaning to him personally and yet completely idiosyncratic, i.e. of no meaning to anyone else. But to say it even more simply, each "peaker" discovers, develops, and retains his own religion.

In addition, what seems to be emerging from this new source of data is that this essential core-religious experience may be embedded either in a theistic, supernatural context or in a non-theistic context. This private religious experience is shared by all the great world religions including the atheistic ones like Buddhism, Taoism, Humanism, or Confucianism. As a matter of fact, I can go so far as to say that this intrinsic core-experience is a meeting ground not only, let us say, for Christians and Jews and Moslems but also for priests and atheists, for communists and anti-communists, for conservatives and liberals, for artists and scientists, for men and for women, and for different constitutional types, that is to say, for athletes and for poets, for thinkers and for doers. I say this because our findings indicate that all or almost all people have or can have peak-experiences, and all kinds of constitutional types have peak-experiences, but, although the content of the peak-experiences is approximately as I have described for all human beings, the situation or the trigger which sets off peak-experiences, for instance in males and females, can be quite different. These experiences can come from different sources, but their content may be considered to be very similar. To sum it up, from this point of view, the two religions of mankind tend to be the peakers and the non-peakers, that is to say, those who have private, personal, transcendent, core-religious experiences easily and often and who accept them and make use of them, and, on the other hand, those who have never had them or who repress or suppress them and who, therefore, cannot make use of them for their personal therapy, personal growth, or personal fulfillment.

NOTE

1. Margharita Laski, *Ecstasy: A Study of Some Secular and Religious Experiences* (Bloomington: Indiana University Press, 1961).

PART THREE: THE ROLE OF RELIGION IN EXISTENTIAL CRISES

12

RELIGION IN TIMES OF SOCIAL DISTRESS*

Thomas F. O'Dea

For many people religion has not been associated with moments of ecstasy and creative innovation but with times of distress and unhappiness. David Hume observed:

> When a man is in a cheerful disposition, he is fit for business, or company, or entertainment of any kind; and he naturally applies himself to these and thinks not of religion. When melancholy and dejected, he has nothing to do but brood upon the errors of the invisible world, and plunge himself still deeper in affliction.

Some more recent interpretations of religion have shared Hume's view. Freud saw religion as arising out of man's sense of helplessness and fear; and even James suggested authentic religion emerges essentially as a cry for "help". In the preceding section, the scientific study of religion and personality has enlarged the above perspective and has indicated a complex relationship between the two. Though religion has been observed to have damaging effects upon the formation of a personal world, it has also been found to provide a positive influence in developing patterns of perception, motivation toward achievement, self-realization, creativity, and new forms of interpersonal relationships and social institutions. Maslow has even suggested that positive forms

* Used by permission from Thomas F. O'Dea, *The Sociology of Religion* (Englewood Cliffs, New Jersey: Prentice-Hall, Inc., 1966), pp. 59–65.

of religion arise from peak-experiences of ecstatic transcendence. Yet there is some truth in Hume's remark. At least some people do find that religion attains its greatest meaning in times of strain, frustration, and even disintegration. In this section three chapters examine the important meaning religion can have for individuals in their attempts to cope with major existential crises.

In a time of radical social change a man's whole way of life can be altered, including some of his most firmly held convictions. In the following chapter the sociologist Thomas O'Dea gives special attention to the function of religion in times of social distress. In periods of stability religion may function to assure individuals of the rightness of the status quo; yet when a man is uprooted from his familiar world and his old norms and values become irrelevant and untrustworthy, then new and urgent needs arise which may lead him to search for a different kind of religion that will somehow satisfy them. Thus, in periods of social distress new religious movements emerge to meet these needs; in such situations we also frequently find the significant phenomenon of conversion. O'Dea here examines various ways religion serves individuals in such periods; in particular he concentrates upon the Pentecostal churches in New York City which draw heavily upon Puerto Ricans. In addition to the role of religion in the lives of individual members of minority groups he also considers how religion functions in times of radical social change and transition.

Some questions for consideration: What are the most significant factors pertinent to conversion? How does the meaning of the religion described by O'Dea compare with that described by Lee? What are the significant differences? In what sense does religion function as an ideology for individuals as well as for groups in periods of crisis and transition?

For further reading the well-known work by Erik Erikson, Young Man Luther, *published by W. W. Norton & Co. (New York, 1958) and Faber & Faber (London, 1959), is particularly worthwhile and relevant, especially chapter VI: "The Meaning of 'Meaning it'". Erikson also examined the possible role religion may play in personality formation in terms of ideology. His focus, however, is upon a transitional period in an individual's life history in which a person experiences a profound identity crisis that propels him to discover or invent a new ideology. According to Erikson, man is motivated not merely by drive fragments but also by a need to find appropriate life meanings and values; at certain stages of development man needs a new ideological orientation which will provide him with a sense of individual identity. In this particular study Erikson investigated the personal development of the young Martin Luther, using psychoanalysis as a historical tool to understand the identity crisis Luther went through. Similar to many authors represented in this volume Erikson also interpreted an individual's religious writings in terms of their psychological significance so as to understand more clearly the meaning profound religious experiences had upon that individual's personality development. Though Erikson's study concentrates upon one famous personality, it provides far reaching insight into forces at work in many crises of identity, including both forces which tend to aggravate crises and those which help resolve them; and it richly complements O'Dea's investigation. Other studies also helpful to the issue raised here include:* Ideology and Utopia *by Karl Mannheim, available in a paperback edition by Harcourt, Brace, and World (New York) and by Routledge & Kegan Paul (London);* The Religions of the Oppressed *by Vittorio Lanternari published by Alfred A. Knopf (New York, 1963); and the previously cited works by Durkheim, Nock, and Weber.*

SITUATIONS OF social distress have often given rise to messianic movements led by charismatic leaders promising this-worldly or otherworldly salvation to the oppressed.[1] Such movements have been found throughout the world. While in our day such movements tend to be politically oriented and only quasi-religious, most of them in the past have had a definite religious character. Oppressed social strata experiencing the need to be saved from their unhappy situations have evolved utopian ideas concerning divine intervention and the establishment of a kingdom of God on earth. In Judaism such ideas were linked up with the expected coming of the Messiah and the beginning of a messianic age. In Christianity, such ideas have been connected with the second coming of Christ and his reign for a thousand years upon a renewed earth. In other religions, they have taken other forms from sophisticated theological messianism to cargo cults among primitive peoples.[2] Mannheim, the great pioneer in the study of the sociology of knowledge, has shown how out of the perspective of oppressed strata and their longings for deliverance, utopias are born in the minds of men.[3] We saw in the last chapter that the development of specifically religious organizations gave rise to protest movements within such groups. Such manifestations of protest are frequently the result of a combination of both religious and social opposition to developments in both society and religion.

Weber also pays attention to different religious propensities of women. He found that women display a "great receptivity" to "all religious prophecy except that which is exclusively military in orientation". He also stated that women tended to participate in religious activity with greatly intensified emotional involvement even to the point of what he called hysterical.[4]

What Weber offers the reader are profound insights into tendencies with respect to the relation between social stratification and affinity for religious doctrines. These are not sociological "laws"; they do not claim to state simple and sovereign factors shaping the religious sensitivities of men. Life conditions affect men's religious propensities, and life conditions are significantly correlated with the facts of stratification in all societies. Yet the institutionalization of certain ideas, values, and practices in a society can affect all classes, strata, and groups in that society. When men are socialized in a society and culture, they learn to accept its dominant ideas and values, and this learning is supported by the general opinion of their fellows – by consensual validation. Weber has shown that classes which might never have originated a type of religion can in this way become affected by it. Moreover, certain religious ideas tend to have a universal appeal. Once they are established, for example, salvation-religions have a very wide appeal. In the Middle Ages the warrior aristocracy put Christianity and a fighting man's ethic together in the code of chivalry. Weber has said: "Periods of strong prophetic or reformist religious agitation have frequently pulled the nobility in particular into the path of prophetic ethical religion, because this type of religion breaks through all classes and estates, and because the nobility has generally been the first carrier of lay education."[5]

CONVERSION

In our consideration above of Weber and Durkheim, three things become quite clear. First, inclination toward certain kinds of religious doctrines on the part of people is highly influenced by their social position in society. Secondly, some religious ideas reflect more universal characteristics of the human condition and therefore have a wide appeal which transcends the divisions of social stratification. Thirdly, social change, and especially social disorganization, result in a loss of cultural consensus and group solidarity, and set men upon a "quest for community" – that is, looking for new values to which they might adhere and new groups to which they might belong. This implies that conversion – the acceptance of new religions – is itself closely related to needs and aspirations which are highly affected by the social circumstances of the people involved, although social conditions are not a simple and unique causal element in such cases.

The new doctrines proclaimed by a charismatic leader or by his missionizing followers are in fact a complex mixture of the new and old. Unless they found people's minds in some measure prepared, they would not gather converts. But at the same time they proclaim something new, or something old in a new way. In this way they are able to appeal to those who are seeking for new values. A. D. Nock, in his classic study of conversion, states: "The originality of a prophet lies commonly in his ability to fuse into a white heat combustible material which is there, to express and to appear to meet the half-formed prayers of some at least of his contemporaries."[6]

The kind of situation in which conversion takes place may be seen in the early history of the Christian church. Christianity entered the world outside Palestine at a time when the Roman Empire had united a vast area into one political unit and had gone far in breaking down local cultural and ethnic barriers. Urbanization had progressed far – as far, perhaps, as such a development could go before modern industrialism. The breakdown of traditional groups and traditional values was creating a need for a larger world view and a new kind of community in the face of urbanization and its accompanying anomie. Moreover, Christianity came to Europe only after the Roman Empire had established a measure of social and economic stability. The ancient world had gone through several centuries, from the Peloponnesian War to the time of the Gracchi, in which bitter and shattering class struggles were common. Moreover, during this period political ideas of various kinds were widely diffused. But with the rise of the Hellenistic empires in the East and then of Rome, social and economic conditions for large numbers improved. Exploitation and misery for the poor lessened and there was a reduction of the slave markets as a consequence of the *pax Romana*. As a result a middle class rose again. Moreover, there was a decline of this-worldly political ideals, and a marked turn to other-worldly religious and philosophical interests. Troeltsch says: "From the second century, to a great extent, the transcendental interest was paramount, and the desire to improve social conditions in any practical way had died down. . . . The iron stability of the Monarchy influenced the whole spirit of social and political order, and all free movement retired into the sphere of personal, interior life, into the domain of ethical and religious reflection."[7]

Most of the early converts to Christianity came from the lower middle classes of the large cities, who shared in the gradual economic improvement that took place at the time. Yet converts were also made among the very poor, and, as time went on, increasingly among the upper classes as well. Moreover, the largest early conversions were made in the East, where social cleavages were fewer than in the West. Troeltsch states that in general outlook these new communities of Christians were middle class.[8]

CONTEMPORARY CONVERSION

A study of store-front Pentecostal churches among the Puerto Ricans in New York illustrates both the affinity of certain strata for certain religious messages and how membership in a religious organization offers a way out of anomie. Many migrants found themselves uprooted from old groups, alone, and often mistreated in the new metropolis. The rise of the Pentecostal movement among these immigrants is a typical example of the formation of new religious groups. The study suggests that the formation of these groups represents "a reaction to the anomie involved in migration".[9] It is an example of both the re-formation of solidarity and the development of new values and attitudes. The study details the close and warm solidarity characteristic of the new community of the store-front church and the enthusiasm for the new values espoused by its members. The acceptance of these is experienced by the converts as "regeneration" – a radical break with the past and immersion in a new life. The authors conclude that the formation of these groups is the response to the need for solidarity and the search for new values. It is the "attempt to redevelop the community in the new urban situation".[10] In this conversion too we find that the new ideas and values are not altogether new. Most of the converts were brought up at least nominally as Catholics. Despite the remoteness of institutionalized Catholicism from many of their needs, their background was such as to prepare them to be receptive to the evangelical message of the Pentecostals.[11]

The congruence of the religious message of the Pentecostal movement with the life experience of migrants suffering isolation and disorientation in the metropolis is also evident. The study reports that those interviewed spoke frankly about their conversion. They considered such frank description as a "testimony", a bearing of witness to the work of the Holy Spirit. But the study points out that despite the spontaneity of this witness, there is a degree of stereotyping in the way the conversion is related.

It would appear that each convert has heard many testimonies and makes the attempt to interpret and fit his own experience into a normatively desired pattern. They usually go this way: "I used to drink . . . I was a drug addict . . . I used to run around with women . . . I was on the wrong path . . . but one day I received the Spirit, I got to know the 'Word'." They always attribute a great sinfulness to their previous life. The form of the testimony emphasizes a great experience of sinfulness and the religious experience of being possessed by the Spirit. And the latter appears to give them a certitude of regeneration.[12]

The study points out that conceptualization in terms of *sinfulness–conversion–regeneration* bears a striking congruity with the actual experience of the converts. The period they see as sinful is that of personal and social disorganization at the time when they were alone and in a genuine sense "lost" in the large city. Conversion means a personal reorganization brought about by identification with the new group and its values. Regeneration describes the state in which as regular members of the new highly solidary and supportive religious group they are sustained in the new values which they now share with their fellow converts.

A. D. Nock, in his study of conversion in the ancient world, has pointed out that Christianity made a much more profound and radical conversion demand than did the other competing religions of the time. One could adhere to the various other groups, but none of them demanded or made possible the full conversion in the Christian and Judaic sense. These religions required a complete turning away from the old and a complete immersion in the new.[13] Only in Greek philosophy, with its idea of a higher life to which it bade men turn, did one find anything really like conversion in the Jewish and Christian sense.[14] Today in New York (and in fact in large cities in Europe and Latin America) such enthusiastic sects bring this message of conversion to men suffering the anxieties and disorientation of anomie. Because their fundamental message, constructed upon the model of *sinfulness–conversion–regeneration*, possesses a strong resonance with the experience of those suffering from anomie and its disorganizing consequences for their lives, these groups are able to convert people and in fact lead them to a new kind of life – to give them the subjective experience of *being saved*.

But we have also seen that in our times religion surrogates perform many of the functions traditionally fulfilled by religion itself. Disprivileged strata under modern circumstances often exhibit a need for salvation and a propensity to accept salvation doctrines, but their specific affinity is for salvation doctrines in non-religious rather than religious form. The socialist movement in the nineteenth and first part of the twentieth century offered to members of the working class who had little or no stake in a developing capitalist society such a salvation doctrine. The socialist movement not only offered new ideas and values but also satisfied a quest for community with its trade union and party organizations. In the present century the growth of communism and nationalism offer a similar spectacle. Such secularized quasi-religious movements offer a kind of belongingness – they satisfy to some degree the quest for community. They also offer an ideological answer to the problem of meaning. Thus to those uprooted and experiencing the anomie and deprivation involved in that condition, secular movements – communism, nationalism, national socialism, etc. – bring the community and sense of worth and meaning formerly associated with religious movements.

Hannah Arendt, in her brilliant work on the origins of totalitarianism, has shown the relation between the quest for community and the search for meaning, and the identification of people with such secular quasi-religious movements. At the core of such phenomena she points to a kind of pseudo-mystical identification with "the movement". The "forces of race" or of "history" become a kind of obscure ultimate that finds its embodiment – its incarnation, to use religious language – in the "party". Similarly, in the new nationalisms, the "nation" offers a similar phenomenon.[15]

RELIGION AS THE IDEOLOGY OF TRANSITION

In traditional societies, the goals of individuals and groups, and even of society itself, are established and recognized over long periods of time. When, because of contact with other cultures or developments internal to a society, new goals arise and new values come into existence, the leadership of society finds itself in need of an ideology to explain and rationalize the new goals and the values supporting them. "When elites come to power in periods of crisis, they do so in part by their ability to rally the community around a drive for new goals and by their skill in propounding a new value system acceptable usually to a majority of the community. This system of ideas and aims provides the framework within which the elite organizes a new structure of power and control."[16] In modern times, at least in Europe and America, such new value systems and the ideologies justifying them have been of a secular character.

The American elite ... were the direct heirs of the British Whig revolution and the exponents of the value system of Locke and his friends. They laid down in the Declaration of Independence, the Constitution, and the Bill of Rights the rules under which we still operate, rules for protecting "life, liberty and property", to use Locke's phrase, for which Jefferson substituted "life, liberty, and the pursuit of happiness". These are the rules whereby the elite of a national political economy can administer a private enterprise system and a market economy.[17]

Today in the developing nations, national leaders, in order to explain to themselves and to others and to justify the changes they introduce and propose to introduce in their countries, develop statements of interpretation of their histories which set forth goals and render them meaningful. These statements of beliefs and values are ideologies in that "they elicit an emotional commitment by the leadership and their followers and are directed toward action".[18] Thus the ideologies of nationalism and socialism explain and justify the course of transition and the goals involved in it.

In earlier periods of history, religions often fulfilled this function of serving as the *ideology of transition*. In the eighth century, Christianity provided the ideology for the re-establishment of empire for Charlemagne and those about him. Later, in the tenth century, with the establishment of the Holy Roman Empire, it provided the same thing. Perhaps this may be seen most strikingly in the example of the Norse. The conversion of the Nordic peoples to Christianity coincided with the attainment of national unity and a vast process of expansion. Christian kingship, consecrated by ecclesiastical rites and given the sacred charisma of church approval, was an element aiding the development of such unity. Christianity supported and in fact partially inspired these efforts of unification. This can be seen in the lives of men like King Canute in Denmark, and Olaf Trygvason and St. Olaf in Norway. One historian has written: "It was, in fact, only through the authority of a new universal religion that the national monarchy acquired the prestige necessary to overcome the conservativism of the old peasant culture and the independence of the old tribal kingdoms. . . ."[19]

This need of new elites and of peoples in transitions for an ideology is similar to the need of people suffering from anomie for a new value system and a new kind of community. In fact the two needs are often found together. While leaders emerge with a need to develop a definition of their mission in order to know how to act in the situation facing them and in order to legitimate themselves as leaders, followers suffering the anomie of social change search for new values to which they can adhere and new groups to which they can belong. Thus in movements built upon ideologies – whether religious or secular – the leaders find a needed *ideology of transition*, while the followers (and often the leaders too) find satisfaction in their *quest for community* and their *search for new values*.

NOTES

1. Bernard Barber, "Acculturation and Messianic Movement", *American Sociological Review*, 6 (October 1941), 663–669.

2. See Vittorio Lanternari, *The Religions of the Oppressed*, trans. by Lisa Sergio (New York: New American Library, 1965).

3. Karl Mannheim, *Ideology and Utopia* (New York: Harcourt, Brace & World, 1949), pp. 190–191.

4. Max Weber, *The Sociology of Religion* (Boston: Beacon Press, 1964 and London: Methuen & Co., 1965), p. 104.

5. *Ibid.*, p. 86.

6. A. D. Nock, *Conversion* (Oxford: Oxford University Press, 1961), pp. 9–10.

7. Ernst Troeltsch, *The Social Teaching of the Christian Churches*, Vol. I, trans. by Olive Wyon (New York: Macmillan and London: G. Allen & Unwin, 1931), pp. 40–42.

8. *Ibid.*

9. Renato Poblete, S.J., and Thomas F. O'Dea, "Anomie and the 'Quest for Community': The Formation of Sects among the Puerto Ricans of New York", *American Catholic Sociological Review*, 21 (Spring 1960), 25–26.

10. *Ibid.*, p. 29.

11. *Ibid.*, p. 35.

12. *Ibid.*, pp. 31–32.

13. Nock, *op. cit.*, p. 114.

14. *Ibid.*

15. Hannah Arendt, *The Origins of Totalitarianism* (New York: Meridian Books, The World Publishing Company, 1958).

16. Robert K. Lamb, "Political Elites and the Process of Economic Development", *The Progress of Underdeveloped Areas*, ed. Bert F. Hoselitz (Chicago: University of Chicago Press, 1952), p. 34.

17. *Ibid.*, p. 35.

18. Paul E. Sigmund, Jr., ed., *The Ideologies of the Developing Nations* (New York and London: Frederick A. Praeger, 1963), p. 4.

19. Christopher Dawson, *Religion and the Rise of Western Culture* (Garden City, New York: Doubleday Anchor Books, 1958), p. 95.

13

CRISES IN PERSONALITY DEVELOPMENT*

Anton Boisen

Personal crises are often turbulent; they do not, however, usually have the disintegrating effect upon one's personal world that one encounters in cases of severe mental illness. The following chapter was written by a hospital chaplain, Anton Boisen, who specialized in a ministry to the mentally ill. He himself was hospitalized several times because of psychotic attacks; yet he recovered from them to lead a highly productive life. He was instrumental in establishing a new form of ministry for clergymen that is specifically geared toward persons suffering mental illness; and in numerous publications he contributed toward the analysis and understanding of schizophrenia. Boisen was convinced that in a therapeutic encounter with severe crises which threaten mental health one may find a deeply religious struggle between healing and destroying forces. Sometimes the powerful emotions which erupt from such crises can have a shattering effect upon the personal world; yet sometimes, he pointed out, these experiences can signify psychological and religious awakening. When this happens, the person may find stability and new meaning with which to lead a more productive life than before the crisis. Thus he argued that intense personality crises can have a creative aspect, so that the individual can emerge from them a stronger, better person.

* A slightly edited version, used with permission, from Anton Boisen, *Religion in Crisis and Custom* (New York: Harper and Row, 1945, 1955), pp. 41–70. Portions of this chapter were originally published in the *Journal of Religion* and *Psychiatry*, 5 (1942), 209-218. Permission to reprint has been granted by both journals and The William Alanson White Psychiatric Foundation, Inc.

Questions for discussion: Apart from physiological factors, what did Boisen think contributes to disintegrating personal upheavals? What are the religious dimensions of such experiences? What are the most common ways of facing such crises? How can they become creative experiences? What role does religion play in helping the person resolve the crisis in the direction of maturity? In what sense might such a crisis be considered a peak-experience?

His earlier The Exploration of the Inner World *and his autobiography,* Out of the Depths, *are worth consulting; both were published by Harper and Row (New York), 1936 and 1960 respectively. An illuminating exploration of the creative possibilities encountered when facing severe illness is provided in* The Voice of Illness *by Aarne Siirala, published by The Fortress Press (Philadelphia), 1964. Samuel Klausner in* Psychiatry and Religion, *published by The Free Press (New York) and Collier-Macmillan (London), 1964, provides an informative description of the new role of the minister of religion in a religio-psychiatric clinic.*

THE ENORMOUS amount of mental illness which we found in the small village considered in the last chapter led to the suggestion that mental illness may be the price we have to pay for being human and having the power of choice and the capacity for growth. This chapter presents evidence in support of that suggestion. It attempts to show that certain forms of mental illness are themselves manifestations of healing power. These forms, to be sharply distinguished from those in which some adaptation to defeat and failure has been made and accepted, are associated with periods in the development of the personality in which fate hangs in the balance and destiny is in large measure determined.

In such periods of crisis religious concern is much in evidence and the creative forces are exceptionally active. So also are the forces of destruction. These are periods of seething emotion which tend either to make or to break. We therefore frankly acknowledge that religion is associated with mental illness. This follows from the fact that religion is concerned with that which is not yet but ought to be both in personal character and in social order, and that it is ever religion's task to disturb the consciences of men regarding the quality of the life they are living and the failure to achieve their true potentialities.

For light upon this problem we turn to the laboratory of life and examine the experiences of those who are breaking or who have broken under the strain of moral crisis. From them we may learn that crisis experiences are associated with religious quickening, and tend to set in motion forces which have the capacity to transform the personal and social life. We shall try to discover the conditions under which religious concern is likely to appear and the conditions under which defeat or victory is likely to result.

TYPES OF PERSONAL CRISIS

1. *Crises in Normal Development*

Crisis periods are characteristic of normal growth. Any individual in the course of development is sure to pass through some critical periods: coming of age, getting married, birth of children, advent of old age, bereavement, and death. In the development of the religious life such crisis periods are likely to be of decisive importance. The man who normally goes his way somewhat carelessly, occupied with his daily work, with the sports page, or with the movie offerings, doing little serious thinking, may at such times feel himself face to face with life's ultimate issues. His eyes may be opened to unsuspected possibilities and he may accept for himself a role which completely changes his course in life.

Evidence of the religious significance of these normal crises in personal development may be found in the extent to which they are associated with religious ceremonies. Civil marriages and mortuary chapels in America may be increasing in number, but funerals and weddings are still prevailingly functions of the church. And not only in America but also in non-Christian lands religious ceremonies are associated with marriage, with the birth of children, with the burial of the dead, and, especially among certain primitive peoples, with coming of age.

But religious quickening does not always occur at such times. There are many who, passing through what should be crisis periods, remain blind to the issues at stake. Some come to grief. One very large group, found in every mental hospital, has been given the label "dementia praecox" because the types of reaction which it represents seemed to be associated with adolescence. Serious disturbances are also associated with the birth of children; and they are not limited to mothers; they befall fathers also. The onset of old age is another critical period in which a new level of development must be achieved. It also is associated with liability to disturbance.

2. *Situational Frustration*

Frustration may be a condition of growth. It is generally recognized that, if we got everything we wanted when we wanted it, we would not become men. There would be no thinking and no feeling. Character and personality develop through the overcoming of difficulties. So also do cultures.[1]

Even serious frustrations may bring blessing with them. But they also bring danger. Such experiences as disappointment in love, domestic tragedy, vocational failure, business reverses, and chronic illness or disability may result in religious quickening. There are those who come through with flying colors. There are also those who take to drink, those who accept the situation with listless resignation, those who go to pieces, and those who pass into a physical decline.

Here, for example, is a man who was faced with a serious domestic tragedy. He was a minister of religion, an Armenian who came of a long line of village priests. As a boy of twelve he had seen both his parents massacred. After completing college he took a church and married a beautiful but illiterate woman. He then came to America leaving his wife and children in the old country. Within three years he was able to send for them. When they arrived, in company with an uncle of his, it was at once apparent that something was wrong. Three months later the wife gave birth to a child by his uncle.

What is a man to do in such a situation? There have been those who, in the face of very similar tragedy, have emerged with blessing. It was thus that the prophet Hosea discovered God's love for his erring people. Not so this man. His reaction was outwardly proper. He made quiet arrangements for a divorce. He gave up his church and took a teaching position. But deep bitterness, rooted perhaps in his tragic childhood, took possession of him. Finally he attempted to shoot his eldest daughter.

In the hospital where he was sent he was neat, orderly, intelligent, and somberly prepossessing in appearance. But he was always bitter. The more one did for him, the more he demanded. It was clear that with his church he had also given up his religion. While he still loved to talk theology, that theology was of a peculiar sort. The golden rule, which he was always quoting, was invariably in reverse. It was what others ought to do for him, not what he should do for others.

One can sympathize with this man in the bitterly trying experiences through which he had passed. It was easy to understand his reaction, but that reaction was nonetheless malignant. He was regarded as one of the most dangerous men in the institution and because of his extreme bitterness no hope could be entertained for his recovery.

This case is of interest because we see many similarly embittered persons in this war-torn world. It also exemplifies a reaction pattern common not only in mental hospitals but in any normal community. There are many who in the face of life's frustrations develop malignant attitudes and become so set in their ways that little can be done to change them. In this case some measure of self-respect was maintained and the personality was thus preserved, but only at the cost of isolation from human fellowship.

In one respect this case is not typical of situational disturbances. The outlook is extremely gloomy. Among the cases which come to a mental hospital a classification of "situational psychosis" usually carries with it the hope of a favorable outcome. It is only when situational frustration is combined with deep-seated weakness of character that the outlook is hopeless.

3. *Intrapsychic Conflict*

Why did this minister adopt such an unfortunate way of dealing with his problem? Of one thing we may be sure: the more serious nonorganic disorders which come to a mental hospital are to be explained, as a rule, not in terms of the immediate situation but rather in terms of some defect in the structure of the personality. The experience of seeing his parents massacred must have been a factor in this man's bitterness. We may suspect that there were other factors. There may have been long-standing conflict between the loyalty which he professed and interests which should long since have been outgrown. His bitterness may then have served as a defense against some sense of personal failure and unworthiness. Crisis experiences reveal hidden elements of strength and of weakness. In bereavement, for example, exaggerated display of grief is often due to a lurking sense of guilt rather than to deep affection. In any case the symptoms of a neurosis may be best explained as reactions to an accumulation of unassimilated experience which, like ill-digested food, gives the sufferer no peace until in some way it is taken care of.

REACTION PATTERNS

Among the various ways of dealing with trial and frustration and the sense of personal failure we may recognize a number of common patterns.

First of all is that of throwing in the sponge. It is represented by those who in the face of growing uneasiness and difficulty merely shut their eyes and drift, getting perhaps easy satisfactions through drink or daydream. In such persons there is little religious concern. Their end is progressive disintegration.

Another pattern is that of "saving face" and keeping up appearances. It is represented by those who refuse to admit defeat or error and resort to various concealment devices. Like the Armenian minister they may dwell on their grievances and become suspicious and bitter. They may exaggerate their own importance and build their world on the basis of some grandiose idea of themselves. They may take refuge in physical incapacitation, securing for themselves sympathy and attention. Religious concern is little in evidence in this group, least of all in those who are embittered and who blame others for their difficulties. And few such persons recover. . . .

ACUTE SCHIZOPHRENIC REACTIONS

The following case of acute mental disturbance represents a crisis experience which is of peculiar interest from the standpoint of this study.

The patient in question was brought to the hospital because of an attempt at suicide. He had been found in his home with the gas turned on and both wrists cut. According to the commitment papers, the motive was self-sacrifice. He wanted to relieve the world of its sin. The onset of the illness, according to the patient, was "quite long – it was a whole week". The wife states that she had not noticed anything out of the way until two days before. There had been a previous commitment thirteen years before. Then also the onset had been sudden, the disturbance severe, and the duration brief.

In appearance Oscar, as we will call him, was a stocky man of fifty-three with barrel chest and heavy muscles. When he was first seen, the disturbed condition had already passed. For one who had emerged from so searching an ordeal he showed a surprising degree of quiet self-assurance. He talked frankly of his experience in a sensible and matter-of-fact manner.

The case history showed that he was of good, middle-class Swedish stock, second in a family of nine, of whom seven were boys. All of the children lived to maturity and have given a good account of themselves.

Oscar considered himself to have been a fairly normal boy. He went through seven grades of school without repeating any grades, but his scholastic standing was only fair and he hated school. In a fight, however, he was "not so dumb". He could lick any boy in his room. After leaving school he served an apprenticeship as a mechanic and worked for a time as a journeyman. Then at the age of twenty-one he went to sea. After seven years of roving he settled down in the United States and at the age of thirty-one he married. His vocational record was excellent. His trade, however, was a highly specialized one and the assignment of jobs was determined by the union. For this reason he was often idle.

Of his sex adjustments he talked frankly. There had been the usual difficulty with masturbation in the adolescent period, but he thought it had not been excessive. While at sea he sometimes went with his mates to houses of prostitution in some of the ports they visited, but he contracted no venereal disease and apparently he kept within the limits of respectability as judged by his particular group.

His wife at the time he met her was a working girl. He became interested in her and then discovered that she came from his native town in Sweden. According to him the marital adjustments had been happy on both sides. The wife also admitted no irregularities. One inferred, however, that the home was somewhat of a matriarchy. The wife was a quick, attractive, businesslike person, accustomed apparently to having her own way. She said of him, "He always says anything I say is all right." He said of himself that he had good willpower and that whenever he wanted anything he did not hesitate to assert himself. One got the impression that he did not choose to assert himself very often.

Oscar and his wife were both brought up in the Lutheran Church. Of his early training he said that he was dragged off to church and Sunday school and that he hated it. He "never did grab anything in religion". He claimed to be something of a free-thinker. In politics he inclined toward socialism. In religion he came from Missouri. He wanted proof before he was ready to believe. Neither he nor his wife was ever active in church.

According to the wife the first indication that anything was wrong was an increasing self-absorption and loss of sleep. She noticed this first on Friday. By Sunday he had become extremely agitated. He kept pacing the floor, moaning and lost in thought. When spoken to, he was irritable, especially toward her. He asked her to go away and leave him alone. This she finally did. The suicide attempt was made during her absence.

Oscar was quite ready to tell of his experience and allowed me to get it down pretty much word for word. Here is his report:

I must give it to you in order. You can't understand unless we go back to the beginning thirteen years ago. You must know how the whole thing started, how I made a sort of bet with God. I was at a socialist meeting one night. A man there spoke of Jesus and of his giving his life for others. He asked if there were not many other men who would be willing to do that.

That night I was thinking about what the socialist speaker said and that I would gladly give up my life for my family alone. In the night I was waked up and a voice said, "You must be put to the test to see if you will really give up your life." It seemed as though God were right in front of me, and the voice seemed to be God's voice, and words from the Bible came into my head. I began to feel very nervous. It seemed as though something were getting into me. I did not tell my wife. I felt she would not understand. I got up and ran out into the street in my underwear. Of course that was a very strange thing to do, but it was just like the old Greek who found out how to weigh a ship. He was in his bathtub at the time the idea came to him and he got so excited that he jumped up and ran out without anything on. You get an idea so big it just carries you away. But a policeman brought me back and I slept until eight or nine o'clock in the morning.

I think it was the same night that blood came into my mouth and something said it took almost two thousand years to produce a man like me. I had lived for two thousand years. It was just like I had gone through many generations. Sometimes I was born rich and sometimes I was born poor. . . .

About a week after that I was sent to the hospital. After that dream I was nervous. I had a feeling like when they bind up your arm and give you a blood test. I was sort of filled up. It was a queer feeling – something you don't understand what it is. I had the feeling that there were two sides and that I had to go to one side or the other in order to get salvation. . . .

In the hospital I was put in a strait-jacket. The first night I had a dream. I seemed to be crucified and the whole room was full of devils. They were trying to hurt me, but I was full of power. You see I was in a delirium. I dreamed I was dead. I dreamed I was lying in the grave just like Jesus did.

In about three days my mind came back and I was released at the end of three weeks. I got along very well after that. I had steady work and there was nothing to worry about. During the last three years work has been scarce and there has been plenty of time to think. No, I had not been thinking much about religion. My wife was told at the hospital that the trouble came from reading the Bible, so I put the Bible in the attic. I didn't want to make her nervous. And I didn't go to church.

The last attack came when something told me to go and get the Bible. I had started then to pray to God. I had been feeling lonesome and I had it in my mind that there is a God. Then it came to me that I had a second installment to pay. I had to finish paying my bet with God. I came then into a state of fear. Something said to me, "Are you willing to commit suicide?" And it was just like I had to do it. I turned on the gas. That was for my wife. Then I slashed my wrists, one for one daughter and the other for the other daughter. But everything I have done before came to a good end and I have the feeling that this will too. I just felt that I had to do it to keep my promise. I have the feeling now that I am a new man. All this is over. I have done my part.

No, I didn't hear anything. It's just like when you sit and think. Something comes to you. Sometimes it comes quick just like something talk to you. I suppose it comes from God. I can't see any other explanation. Yes, it came from the best part of myself.

Yes, I did say that when this came on it was just like I hypnotized myself. When I talk with a doctor I talk about self-hypnotizing. A doctor understand that. He don't understand about religion.

Did I think of myself as Christ? Yes, I guess I did. That was before I understand. You get happy and you wake up and think you are it. You get puzzled as to who you are.

My plans? I want to get to work as soon as possible and get along the same as before. I don't want to take any more of them fits. When this thing came on, I thought I was going to have to preach, but the voice said, "You was going right the way you was. I don't need you to preach. I have other men I can send to do that."

Oscar's case is typical of the acute phase of those profound disturbances of the personality which are known as schizophrenia, or dementia praecox. It is typical not in the sense that it is the usual picture, but rather in that it presents a constellation of phenomena which statistical studies have shown to be related and presents them freed to an unusual degree from complicating features.

Here is a desperate attempt at reorganization which was actually in some measure successful. It occurred in a man who had many assets and relatively few liabilities. He was well adjusted vocationally. He was happily married and had two attractive daughters to whom he was genuinely attached. And he was unusually free from the malignant attitudes of suspicion, hostility, and eroticism. More than that, the disturbance developed quite abruptly. As in the case of Rudolph, it followed a period of preoccupation and sleeplessness and it began with an "idea so big it just carries you away". He thought that God was talking to him. Then as he obeyed the prompting to sacrifice himself for the sake of his family, he found that he was a far more important person than he had ever dreamed. He had lived two thousand years. He was one with Christ. Sometimes he had been born rich and sometimes he had been poor. A great responsibility was resting upon him, that of relieving the world of its sins. He thought he was going to have to preach, but the voice said to him, "You was going right the way you was. I don't need you to preach. I have other men I can send."

Among our excited schizophrenics ideas of prophetic mission are characteristic, and not always does the voice give such sound advice. Characteristic also is the idea that God is talking to them or that the devil is on their trail. Usually the disturbed period begins with some supposed manifestation of the superhuman which shatters the basis of their accepted beliefs and judgments. Such a patient does not know what to believe. There is utter perplexity regarding the very foundations of his being. "Who am I?" "What is going to happen?" become for him questions of life and death to which he sees new answers.

In many cases his eyes are opened to the fact that he is more important than he had ever dreamed. "It comes to him", or "something tells him", or "the voice says" that a great responsibility has been resting upon him and that his failure has brought misery to those he loves. Perhaps the entire world has been hanging in the balance, its fate dependent upon him. He has been remiss and it is now about to be destroyed; but there is still a chance to save it. To accomplish this he must sacrifice his own life. His readiness to do this is commonly followed by the sense of being identified with God or with Christ. It may also come to him that he is about to be reborn or that he has lived before in previous incarnations.

We find such ideas in case after case in disturbances of this type. They crop out spontaneously regardless of previous indoctrination. Where we find one we are likely to find the others also. Such disturbances are to be regarded, according to my view, not as evils but as problem-solving experiences of a desperate and dramatic variety.[2]

What now was the particular problem with which Oscar was grappling? The key may be found in the beginning of the first disturbed period. He had gone to a socialist meeting and the speaker had asked if there were not other men besides Jesus who were willing to give their lives for others. That night, he tells us, he kept thinking about what the socialist speaker had said, and the question came to him, "Would you be willing to give your life for your wife and family?" It came to him that he must be put to the test.

We must, of course, be careful not to draw too many inferences from the immediate occasion of a disturbance. We know that we have to do with an accumulation of inner stresses, especially in the acute disorders, and that the upsetting factor may be the merest touch. But this factor must have some relationship to the central problem. We notice, then, that the question with which the disturbance began had to do with Oscar's relationship to his wife and family. Examining the story from this standpoint, what do we find?

The picture seems fairly clear. Here is a reasonably steady, self-reliant person who, after serving his apprenticeship as a mechanic, goes to sea. There are in this period some irregularities, but nothing which goes beyond the bounds of respectability as judged by his group. After several years of wandering he marries a young woman from his native town in Sweden whom he meets in America. She is an attractive person of considerable force of character.

With his marriage, his entire manner of life is changed. He becomes now a devoted husband and father. His evenings are spent at home or at least in the company of his wife and daughters. Aside from his labor union, he belongs to no organizations. It is therefore clear that his wife is now supreme in his system of loyalties. His entire life is built around her, and his love for her has for him been a substitute for a religion.

There is in this nothing unusual. Sex love, as Professor Hocking points out,[3] is closely associated with religion. It is not that religion can be explained in terms of sex, but that sex love at its best approaches religion. Both want somewhat the same things: union with the idealized Other-than-self. But it is also true that sex love seeks something beyond the finite object of affection and that it cannot be satisfied with the finite. This is the law which is exemplified in the old story of Dante and Beatrice. It seems fair to assume that it was operative also in the case of this simple mechanic.

It was not sufficient for him to have reorganized his life around his love for his wife. He had undoubtedly, after the manner of lovers, sworn his readiness to give up everything for her; and his picture of himself was that of a devoted husband and father. But the actualities would be sometimes a bit trying. As a rugged, self-reliant male he found it not always easy to submit to her domination. Probably he became uncomfortably aware of attitudes within himself which were at variance with the devotion he professed. The socialist speaker had asked a question which for him was a live one. We may hazard the guess that the source of strain in this case was not merely the sense of guilt due to the presence of repressed hostility so much at variance with his accepted role but also the need of achieving a higher level of adjustment. I refer to the level represented by the psychoanalytic doctrine of autonomy and the Christian doctrine of the sovereignty of God.

During the fourteen years which elapsed between this man's release from the hospital and his death from carcinoma, he passed through a period of stress when he returned voluntarily to the hospital. This occurred six years later in a period of enforced idleness. He was, however, adjudged "not insane" and remained only a week. Aside from this period he worked steadily and there is reason to believe that a higher level of adjustment was in some measure achieved. Cases of profound mental disorder with clearly constructive solutions are the exception rather than the rule, but they form a continuum with cases of dramatic religious experience. They have thus great significance.

In reactions of another type the patient sees no way out. The situation seems to him utterly hopeless. He himself must therefore die; or perhaps he is already dead with nothing to hope for but rebirth. The picture then is one of depression, or stupor.[4]

In still other cases ideas of mysterious hostile forces are dominant.

Ideas that evil forces are at work and that great danger is impending are common in acute disturbances, and when the prevailing attitude is one of bitterness, as in the case of our Armenian minister, when there is a marked tendency to transfer blame on to other persons and to nurse grievances and suspicions, the chances of recovery are anything but favorable.

During the stormy phases of schizophrenia there may be no serious disarrangement of the thinking processes. Seeming incoherence is often due to the very quickening of the mental life, to the tendency to accept as valid all the ideas that come surging in, and to the difficulty of keeping pace with the thoughts. In such states meaning far outstrips symbol. Not only does the excited schizophrenic have to find new words to express the strange ideas which come thronging in upon him, ideas for which the conventional language is inadequate, but he has no longer any language of which he is sure. Only one thing appears certain: things are not what they seem. In everything that happens he sees hidden meanings. . . .

It is important to recognize that the acute disturbances, though gravely serious, are transitional. Like the conversion experience, as exemplified in the case of Rudolph, they are manifestations of nature's power to heal. They tend either to make or to break. If the problem is more or less solved, the patient returns to his normal condition, sometimes changed for the better, usually somewhat damaged in his self-esteem. In many cases there is no reconstruction. Instead the patient loses faith in himself and gives up the fight. We have then a progressive fragmentation of the personality. In other cases the personality is rebuilt on the basis of beliefs regarding oneself implanted during the disturbed period which others do not accept.

An instructive case is that of a Polish longshoreman with a superb physique and an excellent industrial record who, after a period of anxiety regarding his sexual potency, went to a Pentecostal meeting and got the "baptism of the Spirit". Within a couple of days he passed into an acute schizophrenic condition in which it was told him that the end of the world was at hand and that he was the Christ of this present age. In the hospital where he was sent he prostrated himself upon the floor with his arms outstretched at right angles to represent a cross. He performed many other symbolic acts.

From this condition he emerged in about ten days, making a recovery apparently as satisfactory as that of Oscar. He talked rationally and was even ready to laugh regarding the queer ideas he had had. But in about three weeks there was another disturbance, then another recovery, then a third disturbance. From this he emerged with the unshakable conviction that he was indeed the Christ of this present age and that a new era was at hand. Upon this new role he rebuilt his life. The strong emotion passed and he became a remarkably well-unified person, free from all bitterness and from ideas of persecution. Very striking in him was a certain quiet reserve of strength which was felt even by his fellow patients on the disturbed ward, where he was kept because of his refusal to work. But his universe was little bigger than himself. To an unusual degree his system of delusions had succeeded in preserving the integrity of his personality, but only at the cost of a really satisfactory social adjustment.

The freedom from bitterness and from ideas of persecution is unusual in such delusional reconstructions, but common to them all is the reliance upon the reasoning processes for the maintenance of the integrity of the personality and for keeping the head above water. There is in such cases no breakdown of reason but rather its accentuation. This is reflected in the coherent thinking characteristic of this type as distinguished from those cases in which the personality has gone to pieces and in which we find the "word-salads", the disjointed sentences, and the disorderly thinking so often mistakenly regarded as characteristic of all schizophrenic patients.[5]

A somewhat extended consideration has been given to these less familiar, though common, types of experience because they represent personal crisis in its most easily accessible and striking forms. They also throw a flood of light upon the social basis of the personality, upon language as a factor in personality structure, and upon the social significance of the idea of God. They tell us what happens when an individual feels himself cut off from the inwardly conceived fellowship of the best. They tell us what happens when he feels himself face to face with a social order which he regards as superior and different and when his concept of himself is radically altered. They tell us of the imperative need of organization in the personality and of faith in oneself.

In the light of these experiences we see that the idea of God stands for something which is operative in the lives of all men, even though they may not call themselves religious. It is the symbol of that which is supreme in the interpersonal relationships and corresponds closely to what Mead has called the "generalized other". It stands also to the individual in the time of his extremity for that fellowship without which he cannot live and of which his system of values is merely a function. These considerations help us to understand the emotional impact of experiences which are interpreted as manifestations of the divine. The ancient Hebrew question, Can a man see God and live?

suggests that men have long recognized the destructive aspects of mystical experience as we see it in the acute disorders.[6] But they have also recognized it as constructive and have given credence to those who, like our Polish longshoreman, have emerged from such an experience with the deep conviction that they have found ultimate reality. . . .

RECONSIDERATION

This chapter has shown that crisis periods tend to be associated with religious quickening. Men are naturally lazy. They do no more hard thinking than they are forced to do. In periods of normality, therefore, they do their thinking in an accepted currency of ideas, and their attention is free to apply itself to the commonplace duties of life. In time of crisis, however, when their fate is hanging in the balance, they are likely to think and feel intensely. Under such conditions new ideas come flashing into the mind, often so vividly that they seem to come from an outside source. Crisis periods have therefore creative possibilities. They are also periods of danger. They may either make or break.

Crises are likely to arise in the normal course of development. Coming of age, getting married, birth of children, and bereavement are experiences which few persons escape. And few escape more or less serious situational frustration. The more serious crises are those resulting from inner stress and maladjustment in which the sense of estrangement from the inwardly conceived fellowship of the best is the primary factor.

The emotional disturbance which often characterizes such experiences is not to be regarded as an evil, even when it becomes definitely pathological. In the face of difficult life situations and serious personality maladjustments, the really malignant reactions are those of withdrawal and concealment in its various forms. Anxiety and self-blame, in so far as they represent the honest facing of the facts, are likely to result in constructive solutions, even though they may induce actual psychosis. Such disturbances may be regarded as manifestations of nature's power to heal. They are characterized by marked religious concern and, when severe, by a constellation of ideas which crop out spontaneously, apparently without regard to the individual's particular culture: ideas of death, of rebirth, of previous incarnation, of cosmic catastrophe, of cosmic identification, and of prophetic mission.

Pathological experiences are frequently attended by religious concern, and religious experience of the dramatic type by pathological features. This is explained by the fact that both may be attempts to solve some difficult and vital problem. When the outcome is constructive, we are likely to recognize it as religious experience. When it is destructive or inconclusive, we call it "mental disorder".

The outcome of an acute disturbance is dependent upon the assets and liabilities which the individual brings to the crisis experience. The nature and value of the insights which come to him will depend upon the problem with which he is grappling and upon his own previous preparation.

In these considerations we have the key with which to approach the problem of religion in its relation to personal and social organization.

NOTES

1. See Arnold J. Toynbee, *The Study of History*, abridged edition (London: Oxford University Press, 1947). The concept of a "time of troubles" as the creative stage in the development of every great civilization is a central thesis in this important book.

2. I have reference here to the type of schizophrenia which is usually labeled "catatonic". A more extended consideration of schizophrenic thinking will be found in my *Exploration of the Inner World* (New York: Harper, 1936), ch. I; and in my articles, "The Form and Content of Schizophrenic Thinking", in *Psychiatry*, May, 1942, pp. 23–33, and "Onset in Acute Schizophrenia", in *Psychiatry*, May, 1947, pp. 159–166. See also H. S. Sullivan, "Conceptions of Modern Psychiatry", in *Psychiatry*, February, 1940, pp. 1–117, especially Lecture IV.

3. *Human Nature and Its Remaking* (New Haven: Yale University Press, 1923), ch. 42.

4. August Hoch, *Benign Stupors* (New York: The Macmillan Company, 1921).

5. Boisen, "The Form and Content of Schizophrenic Thinking", *Psychiatry*, May, 1942, pp. 23–33.

6. The term "mystical", as used in this book, denotes an experience interpreted as direct contact with the superhuman.

14

COMING TO TERMS
WITH DEATH*

David Bakan

*Not every personality will encounter the crises considered in the previous
two chapters, but no one will escape death; and the problem of death
poses the most difficult and most serious crisis which religion has often
been expected to resolve. While man has achieved extraordinary
mastery over natural and cultural forces through the accumulation of
knowledge and the development of technology, his impotence in the face
of death causes him greater anguish than ever; when religion fails to
help man come to terms with death, his anguish is further increased. A
common reaction to death is the attempt to conceal it under elaborate
and expensive funeral procedures. Men such as Freud, Fromm, and
Menninger have stressed that we must face the fact of death; furthermore, we must recognize powerful destructive tendencies within us that
can lead us to inflict death upon ourselves and others. These psychoanalysts have labored to increase our awareness of our own death impulses so that we might strengthen our will to live and combat with
intelligence and vigor the wish to die. Some have rediscovered religion
to be an ally in this battle for greater life.*

*In examining the roots of personality and religion the psychologist
David Bakan has suggested that there are two fundamental modes of
human existence. One is agency, which represents the self-asserting
existence of an individual organism; the other is communion, which
represents the participation of the individual in a mutual, interpersonal*

* An edited version, used with permission of both the author and the publishers, from David Bakan, *The Duality of Human Existence* (Chicago: Rand
McNally & Co., 1966), pp. 197–236.

reality. In view of the duality of existence he finds a fruitful way to interpret some of man's crucial problems, including his own death. As man in Western culture has greatly developed the agentic mode he has made great strides in improving his situation, but he also has encountered new needs, problems, and dimensions of conflict. Bakan reexamines the Jewish and Christian traditions as sources of some of modern man's problems; more important, however, he looks to them as providing insights into the nature of man's fear of death and his awareness of death impulses along with productive attempts to overcome them. The scientific study of religion and personality thus comes full circle. While religion has turned to the personality sciences to learn something about its meaning, the personality sciences return to religion to gain insights pertinent to the resolution of a crucial existential problem.

Some questions for discussion: What were the most significant aspects of the Jewish development of a patrocentric religious ideology? How does the latter differ from a filiocentric religious ideology, especially with respect to the death impulse? How did it resolve infanticide impulses? What is the significance of infanticide impulses in view of the duality of existence? What does Bakan recommend as the most adequate way to combat death? How do his views compare with those of Fromm? How are his views related to those of Erikson with respect to resolving an identity crisis?

For further reading one may wish to consult Bakan's Sigmund Freud and the Mystical Tradition, *published by Van Nostrand Co. (New York, 1958) and* Disease, Pain, and Sacrifice: Toward a Psychology of Suffering (*University of Chicago Press, 1968*). *Also relevant is the volume edited by Herman Feifel,* The Meaning of Death, *published by McGraw-Hill (New York, 1959*).

IN *The Future of an Illusion,* Freud said that the gods that man creates have a

. . . threefold task: they must exorcise the terrors of nature, they must reconcile one to the cruelty of fate, particularly as shown in death, and they must make amends for the sufferings and privations that the communal life of culture has imposed on man.[1]

In the previous discussion, I have indicated that by the gross separation of the agency and communion features of the psyche, we have been brought to the point where man's dominion over nature has essentially been won; we have succeeded in exorcising the terrors of nature, and found many ways by which to reduce "sufferings and privations", Freud's first and third points. Man himself has largely taken over these functions, which he had in the past ascribed to God.

But it is with respect to the second problem, that of coming to terms with death, that an anthropocentric view appears to be of relatively little value. We are presented with a paradox. Whereas it is clear that the exaggeration of agency at the expense of communion has worked to exorcise the terrors of nature and to reduce suffering and privation, death is also associated with agency unmitigated by communion.

The material on cancer which I have presented may be read as a kind of modern parable. Cancer appears to be a disease associated with the psychological feature which has been critical in our victory over the material world. This victory has given us greater longevity and has spared us from various causes of death, leaving us to die, at last, from something which is "immanent in the organism itself".

Even if we were to find, on the basis of further research, that the seeming relationship between agency and cancer is spurious, it still remains true that man is mortal. He was indeed a genius who put together the inexorability of logic with the inexorability of death in the famous syllogism of Socrates' mortality. It is a certainty that "I will die". Doubt concerning mortality applies only to the question of *when*, not *whether*, and even the when runs between very narrow limits.

In purely biological terms, there is only a scrap of immortality. This is, as Weismann was aware, and was so cited by Freud, the immortality of the germ plasm. However, there is characteristically little comfort to be derived from this, because the germ plasm, while still part of the body, tends to be removed from the ego. Even if the ego is foremost a body ego, as Freud said, the germ plasm is a part of the body which is hardly central to it. The semen in the male is characteristically as remote from the ego as urine and feces. In the formation of the ego, such products of the body are the original "other". But here we must note again the factor of sex differences. It may be that in some sense menstruation in the female, which indicates that she is not pregnant, is a "weeping of the uterus". But there is little reason to believe that the male weeps for the semen which has not fertilized an egg cell. It is the "I" that dies, the ego. But that which has not been included within the ego may possibly be immortal. Freud and Jung speculated on the possibility of a transgenerational existence of the unconscious. Freud wrote that: "Our unconscious, then, does not believe in its own death; it behaves as if it were immortal."[2] His psychological Lamarckianism must have involved taking the unconscious at its word, as it were. On the other hand, the ego, which is consciously aware of death, and which contains within it the mute death instinct, does die. Immortality of the germ plasm as a part of the ego is further compromised in that, in order to live, it must fuse with the germ plasm of another, an "other" who is, at least at first, alien to the ego.

Up to this point, I have leaned very heavily on the thought of Freud, although with qualifications. And here I must qualify again. I do not share his deep pessimism and gloom. These I attribute to his deficiency in mitigating agency with communion, although he appreciated the latter in a way which has been rare. I cannot share his psychological Lamarckianism; his case for the latter is remarkably lacking in cogency. He was insufficiently aware of the possibility of our urban industrial society working to reduce the suffering and privation resulting from want of material things. But, most importantly, in his various writings on religion *he tended to focus on the filiocentric rather than the patrocentric character of religion.*

In the remainder of this essay, I attempt to elaborate on the meaning of this sentence. My effort is to follow the injunction of Bultmann and attempt to read out of the Judeo-Christian heritage to which we are heir the significant meanings which are relevant for us. The considerations of the last chapter brought us up sharply to the problem of death. Religion in the past has been helpful in coming to terms with death. Contemporary intellectuality has entailed the rejection of religion, but it has largely failed to come to terms with death. The question I pose is whether there is not something in the religious tradition which can be helpful in coming to terms with death and which also is compatible with contemporary intellectual canons.

PATROCENTRISM AND FILIOCENTRISM

Man, in the course of life, passes from a stage in which his dominant role is that of a child to his parents to one in which he is independent of his parents and becomes an adult himself. In his adulthood, he may exist in an independent state or shift into the position of being a parent. There is the stage of early childhood, the intermediate stage in which he is less a son and not yet a father, and the stage of fatherhood. In the first and third stages, the communion feature is a very significant part of his role. In the intermediate stage, he is largely given to the exercise of the agentic. I would suggest that the substance of religion is much more relevant to the first and the third stages than it is to the intermediate stage. I would also suggest that mankind at the present time is largely in the intermediate stage, and that this is reflected in the ideology and in the kind of rejection of religion which is characteristic in the modern world.

One of the fundamental notions of psychoanalysis is that man projects himself in the images he creates, although the nature of projection is such as to endow his projections with phenomenological "otherness". This was, for example, the critical insight which enabled Freud to comprehend the nature of dreams; the dreams a person dreamed are not "other", but are of the person's psyche itself. It is remarkable and interesting that Freud should have failed to avail himself of this fundamental insight in his discussion of religion. He interpreted the notion of God as the projection of the *father*. In all of his interpretations, he took it that this was based on the person's real father projected upon the heavenly father. God was then the father and man the son. *What Freud failed to see was that the projection of fatherhood on God must also be interpreted as mankind projecting its own fatherhood.* In this instance, he failed to realize what he had seen so clearly in other instances, that phenomenological "otherness" must be circumvented to appreciate the meaning of man's images. Freud's analysis of the psychology of sonhood, especially as contained in his various discussions of the Oedipus complex, was eminently profound. Yet he failed to give much recognition to that part of the Oedipus story in which the infant Oedipus is *first* put out to die by his father, Laius. His concern was principally with that which is associated with moving from sonhood into the intermediate stage between sonhood and fatherhood. His attitude toward religion indicates that the integration was incomplete, reflected in his difficulty in coming to terms with death. Thus, there may have been deep relationships in Freud among his *Todesangst*, his views on religion, and, finally, his cancer – although, as I have indicated, his very thought in connection with these things may have had a "therapeutic" significance.

GOD AS FATHER

I take it, then, that the notion of God as father is a projection of a characteristic of man. I shall attempt to read the Bible as a "psychological document" in which important problems of ultimate concern are reflected. My thesis is that the Old Testament expressed what we may consider to be the "motherization" of man, including the conflicts and the crises associated with this process. Alluding back to our earlier discussion of the nature of projection, in which I said that projection occurs partly because the individual would make of that part of himself something "other" than himself, it would then appear that the projection of fatherhood onto God is already indicative of man's difficulties in conceiving of himself as father. And I would also allude back to Bultmann's notion that the separation of man from God is already the beginning of the sinful state. My task is then based on the psychoanalytical injunction to circumvent the "otherness" of projection, to discover the kerygma entailed in the projection of God as father.

One of the pervasive themes that runs through the Bible is that there is *a biological role for the male in conception*. We may presume that there was a time in history prior to biblical times in which this was not known. It is certainly not "obvious". Sexual intercourse can take place without conception. The interval between conception and either the signs of pregnancy or the birth of a child is considerable. And whether a particular woman has had intercourse or not often remains her "secret". If we consider a two-way table with pregnancy–no pregnancy on one axis and intercourse–no intercourse on the other, observation would show that there are instances of pregnancy and no pregnancy with intercourse; and definitive data in the no intercourse cells are hard to come by. We can presume that there was an early "scientist" who made the discovery of the relationship between sexuality and pregnancy. Furthermore, as I have already indicated, the natural development of the male ego does not usually encompass the ejaculated semen; and we might presume that there may have been a good deal of resistance to the acceptance of the validity of this "scientific discovery". In contrast, there was probably no time in human history in which the biological connectedness of the mother to the child was ever in question, the act of childbearing being too prominent a part of experience. In the same way that more recent scientific discoveries have shocked mankind with their implications, so must there have been a time in history when mankind was similarly shocked by this particular "scientific discovery", and its implications. I take it that the Bible is a document which expresses man's efforts to come to grips with the problems presented by the fact that the male has a biological role in conception.

The Bible expresses man's effort to extend the boundary of his ego to include his "seed". This particular metaphor for semen is interesting in that it not only suggests property and food, but also tends to make the male even more important than the female, as seed is the determining factor of the nature of the plant, with the soil, water, and sun playing only enabling roles. The very conception of semen as "seed" which is deposited in the ground is suggestive that the ego has moved to include the semen.

The major personages of the Old Testament are presented principally in their role as fathers to their children. This is particularly

evident in the patriarchs Abraham, Isaac, and Jacob. Even the son-
hoods which are represented are transitionary to fatherhood. The
very name "Abraham" means father. Jacob has two names, Jacob,
largely for his sonhood, and Israel, characteristically used to designate his fatherhood. In these figures, there is evident not only the
extension of the ego to their "seed" but to the children themselves.
Their principal preoccupations are with their children. As I have
indicated, we can interpret the image of the father as presented in the
Bible as a kind of "motherization" of the male. These are males who
provide for their children. Yet this provision, too, takes place
through the agentic. The biblical patriarchs are affluent; they have
flocks and servants and position. It is through their property that
they can provide for children; and the economic conditions of their
lives are such that by the increase of their children they themselves
increase in wealth and power. Thus, we can perhaps speculate that
conditions of the patriarchate were such that the motherization of
the male served the agentic in him.

Let us consider Abraham. The biblical account essentially begins
when he is seventy-five years old, with the Lord telling Abram (his
name later to be changed to Abraham) to separate himself from his
"kindred", that the Lord will make of him a "great nation", which
will inherit the land of Canaan (Genesis 12 : 1-2). In Egypt, where
Abram goes to avoid famine, he passes off his wife, who is also the
daughter of his father but not of his mother, as his sister; she is taken
by Pharaoh to be his "wife". Following this, Abram's bounty increases greatly. The Bible makes repeated references to the Lord's
promise with respect to his "seed". The Lord tells him that "out of
thine own bowels shall be thine heir" (Genesis 15 : 4). The Lord enjoins him to circumcise himself, all the males in his household, and
all subsequent males on the eighth day after birth. Here is an aged
man, without children, relatively rich but tenuously so because he
owns no land, concerned with food and famine.

He is a man in whom the boundary of the ego has come to encompass his "bowels" from which the "seed" emerges. He has a
deep wish for children, a further extension of this ego boundary. He
envisages a God who promises him not only children, but a land
for them to live on. This God is one who takes care of children and
who abides in time past the time of his own mortality. He is functionally a primitive, personalized insurance policy which provides
for one's children after one's death. In Abraham and his fantasy
we see the fusion of agency and communion. The image of God is
of one who abidingly looks after children.

Freud, we know, conceived of the circumcision as a symbolic castration. If we can read Freud's notion of castration more generally as the attenuation of agency, then we can see its significance in Abraham. For in order to integrate the agency and communion features within himself, it was necessary for the agentic to be reduced to allow the repression of communion to be overcome. Furthermore, if agency is indeed related to death, and if Abraham were seeking to overcome death, it is essential that agency be mitigated.

The significance of Abraham's *mono*theism may also be noted here. The God which is projected is a motherized father, a father in whom there is an integration between the agency and the communion features of the psyche. To a certain extent, this ideal is depicted in the biblical notion of God as father. The dread of deviation from a strict monotheism is the dread of the separation of agency from communion and the repression of communion.

THE INFANTICIDAL IMPULSE

But the integration in the Bible is an uneasy one, reflecting the difficulties of making it. It is manifested in providing abiding care for children, and its failure is manifested in *infanticide*. Freud had made killing the father central in his various discussions of religion. This feature may be important in psychological development. However, I believe that close examination of the biblical text indicates that, in addition to the Old Testament being much more patrocentric than filiocentric, the killing of children as a psychological impulse is highly significant. If there was some original holocaust of the kind that Freud envisaged, it appears less likely that it was the killing of the father by the son than the killing of the children by the father.[3] The allusions to the killing of children in the Bible are numerous, and the injunction against it is repeated so often as to indicate that this was not only a psychological tendency, but one which was at least sometimes "acted out". If the characteristics attributed to God come from man himself, we may note an infanticidal tendency in the numerous references to God killing people, his children, throughout the Old Testament, as exemplified in the Flood and in his killing of the Sodomites, the Egyptians, and so on. God is tempted to kill all of the Children of Israel but is dissuaded by Moses (Exodus 32 : 9 ff.), who then goes down from the mountain and himself kills about three thousand men (Exodus 32 : 28).

The story of Abraham's move to sacrifice Isaac is indicative not only of the infanticidal impulse, but also of ambivalence about infanticide. God enjoins Abraham to sacrifice Isaac as a burnt offering. Psychologically, Abraham has projected his infanticidal tendency onto God. When he is about to slay Isaac, his arm is restrained (Genesis 22 : 1 ff.). The infanticidal impulse in Abraham is also evident in his treatment of Ishmael, whom he banishes to the wilderness with only bread and a bottle of water for himself and his mother (Genesis 21 : 14). Abraham is told, after demonstrating his readiness to kill Isaac, "because thou hast done this thing, and hast not withheld thy son, thine only son: That in blessing I will bless thee, and in multiplying I will multiply thy seed as the stars of the heaven, and as the sand which is upon the sea shore" (Genesis 22 : 16–17). This may be interpreted as a reaction to the infanticidal impulse. God of the Bible is deeply ambivalent about this tendency within him. Its "neurotic" character is indicated by his tendency to kill and then make promises not to do it again (Genesis 9 : 9 ff.). The story of Abraham and Isaac is, as has often been pointed out, a harbinger of the crucifixion of Jesus, in which the arm that would kill the son, referred to as "thine only son", is not restrained.[5]

It may be pointed out, parenthetically, that this same ambivalence has been represented by Freud in a "myth" of his own making, his analysis of the statue of Moses by Michelangelo. This strange essay by Freud, which I have discussed elsewhere,[6] projects upon the figure of Moses an impulse to kill the children of Israel, which he restrains:

In his first transport of fury, Moses decided to act, to spring up and take vengeance and forget the Tables; but he has overcome the temptation, and he will now remain seated and still, in his frozen wrath and in his pain mingled with contempt.[7]

In this essay, too, it should be pointed out, Freud took it that he was of "the mob upon whom his [Moses'] eye is turned" (p. 213), and appeared to fail to appreciate the way in which he himself was projected upon the figure of Moses, or upon God, with whom he identified Moses.

We can identify two sets of motives for the infanticidal impulse. The first is that the necessities of child care are such as to force the integration of agency and communion, so that the existence of children threatens the agentic and its separatistic tendencies. The second is that, in an early stage of the integration of agency and communion, in which the ego boundary has extended to include the semen of the male, the authenticity of paternity of children becomes very important. Doubt over this authenticity provokes the tendency to kill the child of doubtful paternity.

INFANTICIDE AS A RESISTANCE TO THE INTEGRATION OF AGENCY AND COMMUNION

In our earlier discussion of the nature of human sexuality, it was indicated that the coming together of male and female entails the integration of the agency and communion features of the human psyche both between and within individuals. The child is a reminder of the fusion of agency and communion, and his existence demands the continuation of the fusion. Killing the child is an expression of resistance to such an integration. Sexual relations without children, or sexual relations and the killing of children, allow the expression of the agentic feature of sexuality without mitigation by the communion feature and maintain its repression.

A major threat to the integration of these two features occurs when individual survival is in jeopardy or when want prevails. Under these conditions, the agency feature asserts itself to the exclusion of the communion feature; the boundary of the ego is drawn inward to become a "body ego" bent on its own survival. Our knowledge of the social conditions of Canaanite culture, which constitutes the background of the development of our religious tradition, is relatively small.[8] But we do know that often poverty prevailed and that children were sometimes sold or exposed by their parents. The Canaanites, we learn from the writing of King Rib-Addi of Byblos, were sometimes forced to sell the "wood of their houses, and their sons and daughters in order to procure food for themselves".[9] Both from the Bible and other sources, we know that child sacrifice took place in Canaanite culture. To put it most simply, the child constitutes another mouth to feed and an inhibition of the freedom to go out and find food for one's self; when there is crowding and a shortage of food the impulse to kill and even eat (II Kings 6 : 29) the child arises.

Reference to the agentic feature throws some light on the question of why the biblical writers so often saw idolatry, sexual deviation, and infanticide as essentially one and the same. Idolatry, as the splitting of the image of the divine into parts, was indicative of the splitting of the agency feature from the communion feature. Ezekiel complained, for example, "For when they had slain their children to their idols, then they came the same day into my sanctuary to profane it" (Ezekiel 23 : 39). We know that there were varieties of deviant sex practices associated with the worship of some of these idols, and we hear Isaiah charging: "Enflaming yourselves with idols under every green tree, slaying the children in the valleys under the clifts of the rocks?" (Isaiah 57 : 5). The biblical writers freely used "adultery" and "whoredom" as euphemisms for idolatry. The essential object of criticism of the prophets is agency separated from communion, which they attacked in three of its manifestations, idolatry, sexual deviation, and infanticide, all of which they saw as one.

There are inherent threats to the integration of agency and communion in the very interaction of parents with their children. On the one hand, the child is so evocative of the communion feature that it threatens the repression of communion, leading to a strong compensatory rise of the agentic. This point has been recognized in a very astute paper by Friedman and Jones, in which they indicate that the Oedipus complex is not only to be understood in terms of the reaction of the child to the parent but also of the parent to the child. They point out that capacity for intimacy by the child threatens the stability of the contra-intimacy forces in the adult, leading to the impulse to kill the child.[10] On the other hand, the later development of a strong, unmitigated agentic tendency in the child, such as arises in the anal stage and persists into the later stages, manifested particularly in disobedience, is also provocative of the agentic in the father, because it threatens the father's mastery. The integration of agency and communion in the father is always tenuous. In this integration he has managed to allow the boundary of his ego to extend to encompass the child; as long as the relationship of the child to the father is such as to serve the latter's ego, his integration can be maintained. However, when the agentic becomes prominent in the child, that extension finds it difficult to maintain itself, and the father is tempted to say, "You are not my son!" The writers of the Bible were particularly aware of this dynamic and projected it upon the image of God, who threatens to kill in response to disobedience. The emphasis on obedience in the religious tradition has its foundation in the necessity of maintaining the integration of agency and communion in the father in order that he not be tempted to lose it, to regress to a condition of unmitigated agency, and kill the child. "Honor thy father and thy mother" is followed by "that thy days may be long" (Exodus 20 : 12).

The God of Mount Sinai and the people at the foot of the mountain cannot be separated. The people of Israel are suffering from lack of food and water in the desert. We may presume that the children are a threat to the food supply, and that the Israelites are tempted to kill them, as they long for the fleshpots of Egypt. According to my interpretation, the agentic in them is aroused, and they make a golden *calf*, symbolic of the child they are tempted to kill. Attributed to God are the words, "let me alone, that my wrath may wax hot against them, and that I may consume them" (Exodus 32 : 10). Some scholars have even argued that an early form of the Jahwe religion actually entailed the sacrifice of children, and that, around the seventh century B.C., this was dissociated from the religion of the Israelites and attributed exclusively to the other Canaanite cults.[11] But whatever the validity of this, the Bible itself presents adequate information to indicate that infanticide, whether acted out or sufficiently counteracted so that it would not be acted out, was a significant psychological problem. . . .

PSYCHOLOGY OF JESUS

My analysis of the Old Testament in terms of the effort to counteract the infanticidal tendencies in man also suggests an interpretation of Christianity. The centrality of the crucifixion of the "only begotten Son" would indicate that the infanticidal impulse plays at least an equal role in Christianity. However, the New Testament contains a significant change from the Old Testament. The "Son" is much more prominent; and we may allow that, whereas the Old Testament entails the projection of man in his role as father, the New Testament also entails the projection of man in his role as son, a change from patrocentrism to filiocentrism, the psychodynamics of which I will discuss presently. It is noteworthy that Jesus was a child and a young man who died before he became a father.[12]

In this section, I venture some speculations on the psychology of Jesus, recognizing that he grew up in a culture in which the thought patterns associated with the Old Testament were dominant. I accept his historicity and the general facts of his life as indicated in the Gospels. . . .

Jesus seems to have been aware of the profound "resistance" in the mind of man to facing the infanticidal impulse, a "resistance" which, interestingly enough, was also commented on by Freud. In a paper entitled "A Child Is Being Beaten" Freud expressed surprise at the frequency with which his patients fantasied the beating of children. He noted that this fantasy was told to him only with hesitation, and that its analysis was met with great resistance. He commented that the shame and guilt connected with this fantasy were even greater than the shame and guilt connected with sexual matters. This fantasy, he wrote, "Very probably . . . [is] still more frequent among those who have not become patients".[13] It would seem that at the Last Supper, the Passover celebration, which became the basis for the Pauline eucharist, Jesus came close to the repressed wish by forcing his disciples to "eat and drink" him, in much the same way that Moses forced the defectors from the Law to consume the Golden Calf (Exodus 32 : 20), as an ironic demonstration of what they were so deeply involved in. Jesus gave the disciples bread to eat and said, "Take, eat; this is my body", and wine to drink and said, "For this is my blood of the new testament" (Matthew 26 : 26, 28). In John (6 : 61), when he enjoins his disciples to eat his body and drink his blood, they "murmured at it", and he said, "Doth this offend you?" sensing that he had come very close to the quick, the repressed infanticidal wish including the eating of the child. Reacting to the confrontation, "From that time many of his disciples went back, and walked no more with him" (John 6 : 66), as a patient might do when confronted too quickly by the psychoanalyst's interpretation of his unconscious wishes. We might say that Jesus was attempting to do what, according to Freud, the psychoanalyst tries to do, to bring the repressed wish to consciousness.

CHRISTIANITY

We may interpret the Christianity of Jesus as an "insight" into the nature of a repressed wish. It involved a release from various of the defense mechanisms associated with the maintenance of repression. It took the repressed wish out of the deep unconscious and made it at least partially conscious, providing also a kind of fantasy satisfaction of this repressed wish in the image of the crucifixion of Jesus and the Pauline eucharist. The "vail" that Paul spoke of in connection with Moses may be interpreted as repression:

And not as Moses, which put a vail over his face, that the children of Israel could not stedfastly look to the end of that which is abolished: But their minds were blinded: for until this day remaineth the same vail untaken away in the reading of the old testament; which vail is done away in Christ. But even unto this day, when Moses is read, the vail is upon their heart. Nevertheless when it shall turn to the Lord, the vail shall be taken away (II Corinthians 3 : 13–16).

The "newness of life" (Romans 6 : 4) may be identified with the release from the defenses against the repressed wish which comes with insight. It is the integration of agency and communion made possible by beholding what was denied. Paul no longer found it necessary to follow the Law of Moses. "Christ hath redeemed us from the curse of the law" (Galatians 3 : 13), he said. The kerygma in Christianity may be identified with the corresponding "good news" of psychoanalysis, a moral imperative to bring to consciousness the deepest repressed wishes, out of which can emerge a "newness of life".

It in no sense entails an imperative to "act out" this repressed wish.

On the contrary. When the wish is unconscious, it acts in such a way as to bypass the conscious moral sense. Making it conscious places the person in a position to control it sensibly in the light of more mature perception.

In my interpretation, one of the most significant features of the Christian doctrine is that it tended to lift the infanticidal impulse closer to consciousness. In so doing it universalized the crucifixion of Jesus. . . .

The Christian tradition which followed Jesus could *not quite* come to cognize fully the message "revealed . . . unto babes", that men have infanticidal impulses, however. It partially elevated the revelation from the unconscious, but at the same time aroused forces of resistance to it. A major psychodynamic mechanism of this resistance is expressed in the development of an ego identity principally on the basis of the "Sonhood" of Jesus, keeping men from fully becoming fathers psychologically. With the development of Christianity, there was an intensification of the "otherness" of God, the Father. Facilitated by the notion of the Son, Jesus, being God incarnate, there was an intensification of man conceiving of himself as a son. By making the priests a separate class, clearly distinguished from other men, the Fatherhood was projected upon them as "other" as well. If God, the Father, was repeatedly envisaged as expressing his infanticidal tendencies, then, by remaining a son, one is spared the dangers, conflicts, and temptations of fatherhood. God, the Father, engaged in infanticide; but man, the son, did not. It is partly through this mechanism that the filiocentric emphasis of religion comes about. Needless to say, the religion of society is not something which is created by children. It is rather the creation of the adult members of the society, principally the men. The need for an adult male to be a son inheres in his reluctance to enter into and bear the conflicts which are associated with civilized fatherhood.

I might comment parenthetically on Freud again. Freud's position on religion, as I have indicated, was essentially filiocentric. His notion that God was the projection of one's own father can be regarded as an example of what Bultmann has referred to as "shallow enlightenment".[14] It is interesting that Freud, who was so well able to uncover unconscious material within himself, still participated in this same mechanism whereby one keeps one's self from entering into and managing the conflicts of fatherhood, indicative of his relative failure to integrate agency and communion. He clung tenaciously to the centrality of the Oedipus complex and his filiocentric interpretation of the Oedipus myth, his version of the Christian identification of himself as son. Indeed, it makes equal, if not better, sense to think of the father as being threatened by the birth of a child and wanting to kill the child as did Oedipus' father, Laius. We might speculate that the Oedipus complex is a secondary process in response to the father's tendencies toward the child.

In the same way that the Christian tradition removes the "vail" by making almost literal the infanticidal tendency, so does it remove the "vail" of the father's sexuality. It does this by suggesting that Jesus was "begotten" of God, and that the angel Gabriel "came in unto" Mary,[15] a biblical expression for sexual relations. The New Testament would appear to fill out the characteristics of God by adding biological paternity.

At the same time that it alludes to sexuality in God, however, the New Testament attempts to remove it from man. This is seen in the idealization of Mary, who has a child without sexual intercourse with man, and in the image of Jesus, in whom there does not appear to be the slightest hint of sexual desire. Paul's injunctions concerning marriage are interesting in that he conceived of sexuality almost completely in terms of its agentic feature, and paid little attention to the relationship between sexuality and the having of children. Drawing back from "commandment" about marriage (I Corinthians 7 : 6), he nevertheless saw the unmarried state as better than the married state. "He that is unmarried careth for the things that belong to the Lord. . . . But he that is married careth for the things that are of the world" (I Corinthians 7 : 32–33). Sexual relations in marriage are to keep Satan from tempting one (I Corinthians 7 : 5), and "it is better to marry than to burn" (I Corinthians 7 : 9). He was at best tolerant of sexuality. Whereas, in the Old Testament, deviant sex practices were forbidden, and sexuality in marriage was conceived of largely in terms of the having of children and the significance of having children, Paul was against all forms of sexuality and only tolerated it in marriage to prevent "burning". The father as the progenitor and caretaker of children was essentially bypassed. Thus, what we have in Christianity is a splitting of agency from communion, with agency attributed largely to God. The aversion to the agentic is so great that even its role in procreation appears to be given at best a secondary place. Psychodynamically, the reaction to the infanticidal impulse is so great that the occasion for the expression of the impulse would be avoided by not having children. The role of the male in procreation is conceived of as sin in the Christian tradition, as Augustine put it in his discussion of his son, ". . . for I had no part in that boy, but the sin".[16]

That the problem is still very real is indicated by the combination of the encouragement of celibacy, on the one hand, and the aversion to contraception and abortion, on the other hand, on the part of the Roman Catholic Church. For celibacy keeps one from the situation in which one is tempted to commit infanticide; and, in the profound aversion to infanticide, contraception becomes a kind of infanticide as well. Of course, infanticide has other forms. Besides the actual beating and murder of children, we can recognize the infanticidal impulse in child neglect and undereducation, the poverty associated with the too rapid multiplication of people, and total war, which does not separate children from adults. In our times, the absence of contraception is conducive to these other forms of infanticide.

THE JUDEO-CHRISTIAN TRADITION AS COMING TO TERMS WITH DEATH

The most primitive form of coming to terms with death is in its denial. This is expressed in such notions as a literal resurrection, an afterlife, or some form of salvation in "Heaven", an "other" place or at an "other" time. This type of "solution" needs to be rejected on two sets of grounds. The first is simply that it cannot be maintained on the basis of contemporary intellectual canons. The second ground is actually the more important one: it projects onto the afterlife the individualistic existence, the egotism, the commitment to the agentic, which is at root the "sting" of death, to use Paul's word (I Corinthians 15 : 55).

One of the profoundest features of the Christian message is the way in which it would distinguish between actual literal death in the sense of the cessation of the vital functions and the kind of "death" which can prevail throughout life. Christianity recognized the fundamental identity of the two by using the same term for them, taking note of the despair which is associated with the agentic, as well as the difference between them. Christianity saw that the agency which served to keep the individual alive was at the same time related to its death. Thus, we can understand such a paradoxical statement as, "Whosoever shall seek to save his life shall lose it; and whosoever shall lose his life shall preserve it" (Luke 17 : 33). Agency seeks to preserve life, but in this preservation it can, if unmitigated, bring onto the whole of life the condition of its termination. Paul's invocation, "And deliver them who through fear of death were all their lifetime subject to bondage" (Hebrews 2 : 15), becomes equally clear. Death, in the literal sense of the termination of the vital functions – Unamuno's cry that he wants an immortality of flesh and blood can certainly not avail[17] – is not to be avoided. It is the intrinsic counterpart of the agentic split of one being from another in being born and growing into a separate being. Being conceived and born is, in this sense, "original sin". And when we recall the relative number of males who die by spontaneous abortions, it seems that even *in utero* the wages of agency are death. But it is to the possibility of mitigating agency in other aspects of existence that the religious tradition directs itself, that the life prior to its termination should not also be a "death".

One of the most prevalent forms of such "death" prevails in certain segments of our intellectual community. William James, who was admired by Freud because of his evident readiness to face the termination of his life (Freud having been with him when he had an angina attack), saw this very clearly. There is, wrote James, a "sadness [which] lies at the heart of every merely positivistic, agnostic, or naturalistic scheme of philosophy. . . . Place round them . . . the curdling cold and gloom and absence of all permanent meaning which for pure naturalism and the popular science evolutionism of our time are all that is visible ultimately, and the thrill stops short, or turns rather to an anxious trembling."[18] Paradoxical as it may seem, there is a fundamental identity between that religious primitivism which creates for itself an afterlife for the existence of the individual and the kind of positivistic philosophy to which James was referring. Both work to prevent the mitigation of agency by communion in that part of life which precedes its termination. Both essentially deny the reality of death and conceive of the processes before and after death in the same agentic terms.

The essential task of the religious enterprise is to face the actual termination of individual existence, on the one hand, and to create a transindividual ego identification, on the other. The recognition of the inexorable death of the individual need not demand anticipatory deference to it. And we can recognize that in the time before the inexorable death one can avoid that other death by allowing communion to function together with agency.

The religious tradition has worked toward the creation of a transindividual ego identification. There is the extension of the ego to include the children, as in the case of Abraham; the deflection of the infanticidal tendencies toward the education of children, including especially the art of integrating agency and communion. The greatest threat to the integration of agency and communion is the condition of want which mobilizes agency and represses communion. But if our total life condition is such that want will be less of a problem in the centuries to come, it is now possible for us to devote ourselves to the care and education of children to an extent which has rarely been possible before in the history of mankind. The musculature, called by Freud the organ of the death instinct, which has been so significant in the creation of material goods, is rapidly being supplanted by machinery. We can turn from singlemindedly "making a living" to the care and education of the young. We are in a position to "suffer little children" (Matthew 19 : 14; Mark 10 : 14; Luke 18 : 16) in ways far more extensive than ever before. The kerygma of the Messianic tradition is that our salvation inheres in those who are yet to be born. This is true both in the Jewish Messianic tradition and in the Christian tradition that looks to the "second coming".

The ecumenical tradition of Christianity and the emphasis on charity of both Judaism and Christianity have attempted to bring communion to bear upon agency throughout the centuries. This attempt has been strained sorely when the interests of one group have conflicted with the interests of another. But this world upon whose threshold we now stand is pledged simultaneously to two major commitments, the commitment of mankind to manage its own affairs and the commitment of human beings the world over to live with each other. On an everyday level, the foreign aid program of the United States, say, is based not only on simple "charity" but on the recognition of the world-wide mutual dependence of people on each other. It is no longer a strain between charity, on the one hand, and self-interest, on the other. We have rather a situation in which there is a coalescence between charity and self-interest, between communion and agency. The crucifixion is a reminder of the fact that there is only one real death, the termination of the vital processes, for each of us. That "Christ died for us" and was resurrected does not mean that we will be spared termination as individuals. What it does mean is that we need not submit to the forces of unmitigated agency while we are yet alive. It is the destiny of all of us that our individual existences will be terminated, and we are "all in this together". But in so far as we are, we can be spared the sense of ultimate despair by not separating ourselves from each other. . . .

What, then, is a "proper" way to die? It is the agentic within us that brings us to death. That petulant arousal of the body in asexual reproduction which we call cancer is certainly not a desirable termination of the vital functions. Our thought is brought back to the musculature, the organ of the death instinct. There is a model for a proper way of dying in that daily suspension of the agentic we engage in which we call sleep and rest. The proper way of dying is from fatigue after a life of trying to mitigate agency with communion.

NOTES

1. *The Future of an Illusion*, p. 27.

2. *The Standard Edition of the Complete Psychological Works of Sigmund Freud*, Vol. XIV (London: The Hogarth Press, 1957), p. 296.

3. After I completed this study, a book came to my attention (E. Wellisch, *Isaac and Oedipus* [London: Routledge & Kegan Paul, 1954 and New York: Humanities Press, 1955]) which expounds on the significance of infanticide and is very relevant in this connection.

4. Leviticus 18 : 21; 20 : 1 ff.; Deuteronomy 12 : 31; 18 : 10; Judges 11 : 3–40; I Kings 11 : 7; II Kings 3 : 27; 16 : 3; 17 : 17; 17 : 31; 21 : 6; 23 : 10; Psalms 106 : 37–38; Isaiah 57 : 5; Jeremiah 7 : 31; 19 : 3 ff.; 32 : 35; Ezekiel 16 : 20–21; 20 : 26; 23 : 37; 23 : 39.

5. See, for example, John 3 : 16: "that he gave his only begotten Son".

6. *Sigmund Freud and the Jewish Mystical Tradition* (New York: Van Nostrand, 1959), pp. 121–131.

7. *The Standard Edition of the Complete Psychological Works of Sigmund Freud*, Vol. XIII (London: The Hogarth Press, 1955), p. 229.

8. Wayne E. Barr, "A Comparison and Contrast of the Canaanite World View and the Old Testament World View", unpublished doctoral dissertation, University of Chicago Divinity School, 1963.

9. *The Interpreter's Dictionary of the Bible* (New York: Abingdon Press, 1962), I, 497.

10. Neil Friedman and Richard M. Jones, "On the Mutuality of the Oedipus Complex: Notes on the Hamlet Case", *The American Imago*, XX (1963), 107–131.

11. Otto Eissfeldt, *Molk als Opferbegriff im Punischen und Hebräischen und das Ende des Gottes Moloch* (Halle [Saale]: Max Niemeyer Verlag, 1935); W. Robertson Smith, *Lectures on the Religion of the Semites* (New York: D. Appleton and Company, 1889), pp. 352–353.

12. Thomas Jefferson once suggested that it was regrettable that Jesus died before his ideas could fully mature.

13. *The Standard Edition of the Complete Psychological Works of Sigmund Freud*, Vol. XVII (London: The Hogarth Press, 1955), p. 179.

14. "New Testament and Mythology", *Kerygma and Myth*, Vol. I, ed. H. W. Bartsch (London: S.P.C.K., 1953 and New York: The Macmillan Company, 1954), p. 3.

15. Luke 1 : 28. In the Greek this is καὶ εἰσελθὼν ... πρὸς αὐτήν (literally, and entering to her). That this expression may be used to designate sexual intercourse quite literally in the Greek is indicated by the fact that it is the phrase used in the *Septuagint* for the sexual relations between Judah and Tamar, when he took her to be a harlot, καὶ εἰσῆλθεν πρὸς αὐτήν (Genesis 38 : 18). I am indebted to Professor Meyer W. Isenberg for help with the Greek on this point.

16. *Confessions*, p. 158.

17. Miguel de Unamuno, *The Tragic Sense of Life, in Men and in Peoples* (London: Macmillan and Company, 1921).

18. William James, *The Varieties of Religious Experience* (London and New York: Longmans, Green, 1914), pp. 140–141.

PART FOUR: RE-EVALUATING RELIGION IN RELATION TO PERSONALITY DEVELOPMENT AND THE PERSONALITY SCIENCES

15

PARADOXES OF RELIGIOUS BELIEF*

Milton Rokeach

The scientific study of religion as a living agent operative in the formation of a personal world provides insights into some possible meanings of religion and potential dimensions of personality. However, the awareness and understanding which emerge point beyond a strictly scientific concern toward a personal re-evaluation of religion. From this perspective old categories are less applicable than they used to be; some new distinctions begin to emerge. The dichotomy between sacred and secular is not at all clear cut with respect to phenomena such as perception and motivation; as several contributors have implied, we need to learn to recognize the religious significance of experiences that from some viewpoints might be regarded as secular, just as we have learned to detect the latent psychological meanings in manifest religious experiences. It is time we recognize that the old distinction between individual and organized religion is also tenuous. Some time ago Thomas Paine advocated individual religion in contrast to organized religion, which he claimed was "no other than human inventions, set up

* This chapter was published as Appendix B in *Beliefs, Attitudes, and Values* (pp. 189–196) by Milton Rokeach. Published by Jossey-Bass, Inc., San Francisco. © 1968 and used by permission of both publisher and author.

to terrify and enslave mankind, and monopolize power and profit". Since then many supposedly enlightened people have shared that view. Yet we are well aware that all organized religion is composed of individual persons for whom that same religion has diverse meanings within their personal worlds; furthermore, although a person does not adhere to a distinct religious group, yet in so far as his values are integrated into a coherent form and are affirmatively expressed in repeated behavior patterns, then his personal value system has the equivalence of an organized religion within his personal world. In distinguishing types of religion we have found the correlation of ideology, practice, and life situation useful to personality sciences; however, rather than compare ideological content and practice within different religious systems, it has been more helpful to examine the roles religious systems have played in terms of the formation of perception, motivation, and relationships and of orienting the individual toward meanings which will enable him to resolve crises productively. From the perspective of this type of study what becomes important is not how a religion is supposed to have originated or what its claims to supernatural truth might be but what effects it has or is likely to have upon someone's personal world. One's religion may be felt to provide stability and comfort; but further examination might indicate that this same religion is also a security system which effectively prevents a person from discovering and realizing the most significant possibilities of human existence. The same might be said, however, for a person who has adamantly refused to allow religion to have any place in his personal world. In any event this kind of study should lead to some unsettling questioning about the future of one's own world and the place religion might occupy within it. St. Augustine once wrote: "I would rather find God in my uncertainty than to have missed him in my certainty." In so far as they lead persons to radical re-examination of their worlds, religion and the personality sciences would seem to have something important in common.

The chapter by Milton Rokeach brings together many of the findings encountered within this volume and leads to some provocative conclusions that will bear careful consideration and discussion. His psychological studies which often investigate religion and personality include: The Open and Closed Mind (New York: Basic Books, 1960); Three Christs of Ypsilanti (New York: Alfred A. Knopf, 1964); and Beliefs, Attitudes, and Values (San Francisco: Jossey-Bass Inc., 1968).

In view of the interest in the dialogue between science and religion, the chapter by the psychiatrist Karl Menninger provides some new and *challenging ideas about the kind of relationship which may exist between them. For further reading in this area consult the volume in this series* Science and Religion *edited by Ian G. Barbour, which, however, concentrates upon the physical sciences. For further reading in the literature by Karl Menninger consult his* Love against Hate, *first published in 1942, now in paperback by Harcourt, Brace, and World (New York);* A Psychiatrist's World: The Selected Papers of Karl Menninger *and* The Vital Balance, *both published by The Viking Press (New York), 1959 and 1963 respectively.*

ALL ORGANIZED Western religious groups teach their adherents, and those they try to convert, contradictory sets of beliefs. On the one hand, they teach mutual love and respect, the Golden Rule, the love of justice and mercy, and the equality of all men in the eyes of God. On the other hand, they teach (implicitly if not openly) that only *certain* people can be saved – those who believe as they do; that only *certain* people are chosen people; that there is only one real truth – theirs.

Throughout history man, inspired by religious motives, has indeed espoused noble and humanitarian ideals and often behaved accordingly. But he has also committed some of the most horrible crimes and wars in the holy name of religion – the massacre of St. Bartholomew, the Crusades, the Inquisition, the pogroms, and the burnings of witches and heretics.

This is the fundamental paradox of religious belief. It is not confined to history. In milder but even more personal forms it exists in our daily lives.

In 1949 Clifford Kirkpatrick, professor of sociology at Indiana University, published some findings on the relationship between religious sentiments and humanitarian attitudes. Professor Kirkpatrick investigated the oft-heard contention that religious feeling fosters humanitarianism; and, conversely, that those without religious training should therefore be less humanitarian. His conclusions were surprising – at least to the followers of organized religion. In group after group – Catholic, Jewish, and the Protestant denominations – he found little correlation at all; but what there was was negative. That is, the devout tended to be *slightly less* humanitarian and had more punitive attitudes toward criminals, delinquents, prostitutes, homosexuals, and those who might seem in need of psychological counseling or psychiatric treatment.

In my own research I have found that, on the average, those who identify themselves as belonging to a religious organization express more intolerance toward racial and ethnic groups (other than their own) than do non-believers – or even Communists. These results have been found at Michigan State University, at several New York colleges, and in England (where the Communist results were obtained). Gordon Allport, in his book *The Nature of Prejudice*, describes many of the studies that have come up with similar findings. In a recent paper he read at the Crane Theological School of Tufts University, he said:

> On the average, church goers and professedly religious people have considerably more prejudice than do non-church goers and non-believers.

Actually, this conclusion is not quite accurate. While non-believers are in fact generally less prejudiced than believers toward racial and ethnic groups, it does not follow that they are more tolerant in every respect. Non-believers often betray a bigotry and intellectual arrogance of another kind – intolerance toward those who disagree with them. Allport's conclusion is only valid if by "prejudice" we mean ethnic and religious prejudice.

Organized religion also contends that the religious have greater "peace of mind" and mental balance. We have found in our research at Michigan State University – described in my book *The Open and Closed Mind* – that people with formal religious affiliation are more anxious. Believers, compared with non-believers, complain more often of working under great tension, sleeping fitfully, and similar symptoms. On a test designed to measure manifest anxiety, believers generally scored higher than non-believers.

If religious affiliation and anxiety go together, is there also a relation between religion and serious mental disturbance? What is the relative frequency of believers and non-believers in mental hospitals, compared to the outside? Are the forms and courses of their illnesses different? I recently discussed this with the clinical director of a large mental hospital. He believes without question that religious sentiments prevail in a majority of his patients; further, that religious delusions play a major part in the illnesses of about a third of them.

It is pretty hard to conclude from such observations anything definite about the role religion plays in mental health. This area needs much research, not only within our own culture but also cross-culturally. I am thinking especially of the Soviet Union. What is the relative frequency of mental disease in the Soviet Union as compared with Western countries? To what extent could such differences be attributable to differences in religious sentiments? What is the proportion of believers and non-believers in Soviet mental hospitals? Many questions could be asked.

In a study in Lansing, Michigan, we found that when you ask a group of Catholics to rank the major Christian denominations in order of their similarity to Catholicism, you generally get the following order: Catholic first, then Episcopalian, Lutheran, Presbyterian, Methodist, and finally Baptist. Ask a group of Baptists to rank the same denominations for similarity, and you get exactly the reverse order: Baptist, Methodist, Presbyterian, Lutheran, Episcopalian, and finally Catholic. When we look at the listings of similarities they seem to make up a kind of color wheel, with each one of the six major Christian groups judging all other positions from its own standpoint along the continuum. In reality, all these continua are basically variations of the same theme, with Catholics at one end and Baptists at the other.

Apparently people build up mental maps of which religions are similar to their own, and these mental maps have an important influence on everyday behavior. If a Catholic decides to leave his church and join another, the probability is greatest that he will join the Episcopalian church – next the Lutheran church – and so on down the line. Conversely, a defecting Baptist will more probably join the Methodist church, after that the Presbyterian church, and so on. The other denominations follow the same pattern.

The probability of inter-faith marriage increases with the similarity between denominations. When a Catholic marries someone outside his faith, it is more likely to be an Episcopalian, next most likely a Lutheran, and so on.

What of the relation between marital conflicts and inter-faith marriages? In general we find that the greater the dissimilarity, the greater likelihood of conflict both before and after marriage.

We determined this by restricting our analysis to couples of whom at least one partner was always Methodist. We interviewed seven or eight all-Methodist couples; then another group in which Methodists had married Presbyterians; then Methodists and Lutherans; and on around. We not only questioned them about their marital conflicts, but also about their pre-marital conflicts. How long did they "go steady"? (The assumption is that the longer you go steady beyond a certain point, the more likely the conflict.) Did parents object to the marriage? Had they themselves had doubts about it beforehand? Had they ever broken off their engagement? For marital conflict, we asked questions about how often they quarreled, whether they had ever separated (if so, how many times), and whether they had ever contemplated divorce. From the answers we constructed an index of premarital and postmarital conflict.

These findings raise an issue of interest to us all. From the standpoint of mental health, it can be argued that inter-faith marriages are undesirable. From the standpoint of democracy, is it desirable to have a society in which everyone marries only within his own sect or denomination? This is a complicated matter and cannot be pursued here. But these findings do suggest that somehow the average person has gotten the idea that religious differences – even minor denominational distinctions within the Christian fold – do make a difference; so much difference in fact that inter-faith marriages must result in mental unhappiness.

To pull together the various findings: I have mentioned that empirical results show that religious people are on the average less humanitarian, more bigoted, more anxious; also that the greater the religious differences, the greater the likelihood of conflict in marriage. Does a common thread run through these diverse results? What lessons can we learn from them?

It seems to me that these results cannot be accounted for by assuming, as the anti-religionists do, that religion is an unqualified force for evil; nor by assuming, as the pro-religionists do, that religion is a force only for good. Instead, I believe that these results become more understandable if we assume that there exist simultaneously, within the organized religions of the West, psychologically conflicting moral forces for good and evil – teaching brotherhood with the right hand and bigotry with left, facilitating mental health in some and mental conflict, anxiety, and psychosis in others. I realize that this seems an extreme interpretation; but the research bears it out.

Gordon Allport makes a similar point:

> Brotherhood and bigotry are intertwined in all religion. Plenty of pious people are saturated with racial, ethnic, and class prejudice. But at the same time many of the most ardent advocates of racial justice are religiously motivated.

We are taught to make definite distinctions between "we" and "they", between believer and non-believer; and sometimes we are urged to act on the basis of these distinctions, for instance in marriage. The category of man that comes to mind when we hear the word "infidel" or "heretic" is essentially a religious one. It is part of our religious heritage. But it is difficult psychologically to love infidels and heretics to the same extent that we love believers. The psychological strain must be very great; and a major result must be guilt and anxiety.

This kind of dichotomy is not confined to religion. Gunnar Myrdal, in *The American Dilemma*, described the conflict between American ideals of democracy and practice of discrimination against minority groups, and the guilt, anxiety, and disorder it spawned. We are familiar in international affairs with the enormous psychological discrepancy between the humanitarian ideals of a classless society advocated by the Marxists and the anti-humanitarian methods employed by them for its achievement. No wonder there have been so many defections from the Communist cause in America and Europe! When the strain between one set of beliefs and another set of beliefs – or between belief and practice – becomes too great, one natural response is to turn away from the whole system.

I suspect that such contradictions lead often to defection from religion also. Most of the time, however, the result is psychological conflict, anxiety, and chronic discomfort arising from feelings of guilt. The contradictions in religious teachings are more subtle than those in politics and would, for the most part, be denied consciously. A conflict between ideological content and ideological structure – between *what* is taught and *how* it is taught – must be very subtle. A particular religious institution not only must disseminate a particular religious ideology; it must also perpetuate itself and defend against outside attack. It is this dual purpose of religious institutions, I hypothesize, that leads to the contradiction between the *what* and the *how*. It leads to the paradox of a church disseminating truly religious values to the extent possible, while unwittingly communicating anti-religious values to the extent necessary.

Gordon Allport, writing on the relation between religion and bigotry, has suggested two types of religious orientation. He calls them the *extrinsic* and the *intrinsic*. The extrinsic outlook on religion is utilitarian, self-centered, opportunistic, and other-directed. The intrinsic, in contrast, includes basic trust, a compassionate understanding of others so that "dogma is tempered with humility" and, with increasing maturity, "is no longer limited to single segments of self interest". Allport does not imply that everyone is purely either intrinsic or extrinsic; rather, all range somewhere along the continuum from one pole to the other.

The extent to which a particular person has an intrinsic or extrinsic outlook depends largely on the way he is able to resolve the contradictory teachings of his religious group. This in turn depends on the particular quality of his experiences with others, especially with parents in early childhood. A person is more apt to be extrinsic-ally-oriented if his early experiences included threat, anxiety, and punishment or if religion was used punitively, as a club to discipline and control him.

Good empirical evidence exists to support Allport's distinctions. W. Cody Wilson has succeeded in isolating and measuring the extrinsic religious sentiment and in showing that it is closely related to anti-Semitism. Also, one of my collaborators, Dr. C. Gratton Kemp, has isolated two kinds of religiously-minded students, all enrolled in one denominational college. One group was open-minded and toler-ant. The other group was closed-minded and highly prejudiced. Dr. Kemp studied their value orientations over a six-year period. He found that while they expressed similar values when in college, they diverged sharply six years later. Both groups ranked their religious values highest but then parted abruptly. The open-minded group put social values next and theoretical values third. The closed-minded group also ranked religious values highest, but political values were second in importance for them and economic values third. It is obvious that the total cluster of values is quite different between the two groups. These findings clearly suggest that religious people do indeed differ strongly in their orientations toward life to the extent that their religious outlook is, as Allport claims, extrinsic or intrinsic.

All the preceding leads to the following tentative conclusions: the fact that religious people are more likely to express anti-humanitarian attitudes, bigotry, and anxiety and the fact that religious similarity and dissimilarity play an important role in marital conflict may both be interpreted as the end result of the emergence of the extrinsic rather than the intrinsic orientation toward religion. They also sug-gest that, in most people, the extrinsic orientation predominates. This greater prominence of extrinsic attitudes in turn seems to arise out of the contradictory beliefs transmitted through organized re-ligion: humanitarian on one side, anti-humanitarian on the other. One constructive suggestion that might be advanced is that ministers, rabbis, and priests should better understand the differences between the *what* and the *how* of belief, and the fact that contradictions between the *what* and the *how* can lead to excessive anxiety, per-vasive guilt, and psychic conflict and, therefore, to all sorts of defensive behavior capable of alleviating guilt and conflict. Rep-resentatives of organized religion should consequently become more sophisticated about the unwitting contradictions introduced into religious teachings, and try to eliminate them – as the Catholics are doing now with belief in Jewish guilt for the crucifixion.

Parents are really the middlemen between the forces of organized religion and the child. What factors in rearing, in parental attitudes, in discipline techniques, in the quality of reward and punishment are likely to lead to what Allport has called the intrinsic orientation toward religion? What factors lead to the extrinsic? The data suggest that the more the parent encourages the formation and development of extrinsic attitudes toward religion, the more he hinders the growth of the child into a mature and healthy human being. The more he strengthens the intrinsic religious orientation, the more he helps his child grow healthy, mature, tolerant, and happy.

The conflict between the ideal and what seems to be the practical is widespread. But the current readjustment in racial relations, in which clergymen have taken so large a part, for all its upset and pain indicates that these dichotomies are neither eternal nor inevitable. Nor is the extrinsic orientation necessarily the "practical" one. Research and practice in race relations, criminology, and child-rearing have consistently shown that the non-punitive and accepting approach brings better results.

Change is underway, in the church and in the home, and brings with it, hopefully, greater emphasis on resolving the paradox between the what and the how of religious belief.

16

THE COMMON ENEMY*

Karl Menninger

SOME TIME ago a Harvard professor of psychology, Dr. David McClelland,[1] addressing audiences at Haverford and later at Princeton, declared: "Speaking publicly about religious matters presents many difficulties for a behavioral scientist today. To admit to a religious point of view, to some personal commitment, is to violate the most fundamental rule governing the behavior of a scientist – namely, to be objective. Personal bias serves only to distort the search for truth. So it is part of the professional role of the scientist, particularly if he is interested in human affairs, to keep himself free from entangling commitments, to remain in a state of suspended judgment so far as many of life's most serious issues are concerned.

"And most of my colleagues live up to their professional role with great strictness so far as religion, and in particular Christianity, is concerned. I can hardly think of a psychologist, sociologist, or anthropologist of my generation who would admit publicly or privately to a religious commitment of any kind. . . ."

This, I think, is a startling statement and one I find a little difficult to accept literally. I myself know quite a number of psychiatrists and psychologists who "admit" both privately and publicly to religious commitments. Doctor McClelland implies that scientists are intimidated in regard to acknowledging their beliefs which he contrasts with the case of men in politics: "I have known men," he says, "whose interest in religion seemed to begin the moment they assumed public office."

* Reprinted with permission of the author and the Menninger Foundation from *The Bulletin of the Menninger Clinic*, 25 (1961), 277–289.

With the morals of using religion politically I am not so much concerned. I think people soon detect how religious a public figure really is. But I think it is deplorable that scientists who are committed to the search for truth should today feel obliged to conceal their religious beliefs lest they be professionally defrocked. A part of this no doubt is in reaction to that opposite state of affairs which once prevailed, when a scientist who would remain in good standing did well to proclaim his religious orthodoxy. Today some scientists feel obliged to make a noisy proclamation of their atheism or agnosticism.

This is really the dilemma; Christians have always been enjoined to publicly confess their faith despite ridicule and persecution, and some do so. Some are reluctant to make public declarations out of a sense of dignity and good taste, or even from a disinclination to appear to be advertising or exploiting one's religious convictions. They believe that one's religious convictions should appear in one's way of life.

But silence in this instance does not give consent; it may equally well indicate disbelief, or weak convictions. The public may conclude quite logically that such silence is dictated by fear and this is precisely what Professor McClelland has concluded, a conclusion buttressed by the sophomoric bumptiousness with which some otherwise cogent scientists make proclamations of their agnosticism.

It might seem, therefore, to be the duty of some of us who are perhaps a bit less vulnerable than younger scientists, or perhaps just more battle-scarred and toughened, to declare our position. To do so might encourage the fainthearted. But, more important, it would, as the politicians like to say, "put the record straight" regarding the compatibility of religion and psychiatry.

In the beginning one might well inquire "Just what is the question?" What is the issue between our religious life, or our religious convictions and theories, and our scientific work? What is the quarrel between those who concentrate their study and thought upon the former and those who concentrate study and thought on the latter? I have no doubt that the most pious theologian makes use of electric lights and penicillin, just as the most zealous empiricist recognizes the existence of behavior properly called religious. These things exist, they co-exist, they are common knowledge. We all participate in benefits accruing to society from both sources. Again, then, what is the question?

Surely most psychiatrists and theologians are too sophisticated for such popular conundrums as: Which is more important – religion or science? Do you believe in God? Do you believe in heaven? Do you believe in the atom? Do you believe the observer affects the phenomena observed? Can a psychiatrist be a Presbyterian? Can a Catholic be a psychoanalyst? I call these conundrums because while the answers to them seem obvious, strictly speaking the answer given will depend in each case on how the words are defined or interpreted. Nor are we likely to find interest in a rehashing of the various mis-interpretations of Freud's views on religion. The afore-mentioned Doctor McClelland, using studies made by Bakan, has shown how much psychoanalysis owes to Hassidism and religious mysticism. Tillich, Hiltner, Pike, and many others have shown how great a dis-guised ally of theology Freud was. Curiously enough, some scientists of extreme positivistic and Cartesian leanings would confirm the idea that Freud was an ally of theology; psychiatry and psycho-analysis, they say, properly belong to religion, rather than to science.

But it is true that some psychoanalysts and psychiatrists and scientists in other fields are staunchly loyal to the dogma[2] of their own field of knowledge and investigation, but strongly reject any-thing labeled "religious". The latter is apt to be described as "neur-otic". The late Heinrich Racker, a distinguished psychoanalytic teacher and writer, has well commented that "hostility to religion and lack of faith are not infrequently as much an expression of neurosis as is religiosity. The violence with which certain unbelievers jump at anything smacking of religion points to the paranoid anxieties it touches off in them. . . . With atheism there may be con-nected disillusions the child has suffered from his parents. But these disillusions may also be of a neurotic nature. We know the patho-logical advantages of viewing the parents (or either of them) as devalued."[3]

A distinguished biologist, Seymour S. Kety, Chief of the Labora-tory of Clinical Science for the National Institute of Mental Health, has illustrated the intensity of this exclusionism in science by a clever conceit.[4] Doctor Kety develops a theme about an imaginary society, like our own in every respect except that they have never seen a book. One day books appear, an event which is immediately studied by a commission in which each researcher uses the techniques and con-cepts of his discipline.

The anatomists conclude that these objects are "roughly rectangu-lar blocks of material, covered ventrally and dorsally with two fibrous encapsulated laminae . . . between which lie several hundred white lamellae". And so forth and so on.

Chemists get hold of the book, burn it, compute the energy re-leased per gram, and analyze the elementary composition and report traces of elementary carbon – the ink!

The biochemists slice the book, mince it, and homogenize it "because on the slices . . . they can still see those black contaminants" which can be centrifuged out, permitting them to work with a "Pure System".

The molecular biologists polish up their bright and expensive equipment and "having hung a sign over the door reading 'No twisted book without a twisted molecule', proceed to search for the molecule . . . by extraction, centrifugation, electrophoresis, hydrolysis, and repolymerization".

The physiologists, having read the report from the anatomists, speculate on how and why the lamellae are attached on one side only. "They study the movement of the pages as the book is riffled and derive complex equations to describe it."

The biophysicists stick electrodes into the book and the cyberneticists get into the act and bring a computer which describes a tremendously complex repetitive pattern ultimately discovered to be an arrangement of carbon molecules in the form of "THE". The behavioral scientists come along, some of them counting the number of letters, some of them analyzing content in other ways.

By now the moral is obvious: "I merely wanted to point out," says the author, "that we do not always get close to the truth as we slice and homogenize and isolate. . . . A truer picture of the nervous system and behavior will emerge only from study by a variety of disciplines and techniques, each with its own virtues and its own peculiar limitations."

And so, again, what is the question? And were I to try to answer the question, would I be expected to answer as a physician, as a psychiatrist, as a Presbyterian, as a psychoanalyst, or as a philosopher (an amateur one, indeed, but then philosophy, like religion, is something which we can all make some pretensions to)? I attended a scientific seminar one evening when some question about religion came up, and a colleague who is both an authoritative psychoanalyst and a Protestant communicant directed a question at the speaker: "Are you a believer?" he asked. The speaker began to quibble. "Oh, I believe some things," he said. "I believe this and that and so forth." But my friend interrupted him and pointed out that he was not expressing beliefs, but only the acceptance of established facts. He was asked again: "Are you a believer? Do you tend to believe things you cannot prove, or do you tend to doubt them?"

This indeed is one of the crucial issues. The worst thing that the Crusaders could call a Turk was "unbeliever". But when the scientific awakening directed attention to the psychological subtleties of believing, the development of radical positivism made believing almost a sin and the scientist stepped forth proudly proclaiming his universal skepticism.

It was Max Born[5] who said, "There are two objectionable types of believers: those who believe the incredible and those who believe that 'belief' must be discarded and replaced by 'the scientific method'. . . ." Born, himself, believed in continuous creation and flatly disputed the metaphysical principle that everything must have a cause. It is inevitable, he said, that a monistic concept of experience has to be abandoned. "If quantum theory has any philosophical importance at all, it lies in the fact that it demonstrates . . . the necessity of dual aspects and complementary considerations." Let there be no more loose talk about the holy principle of psychological determinism. "Nature is ruled by laws of cause and laws of chance in a certain mixture."

We all know from the practical experiences of daily life that there is more or less belief and more or less skepticism in each of us. But to simplify matters let us say that some are chiefly or predominantly believers, some chiefly doubters. They both do great things (and some petty things). The believers dream dreams; they form ideals and set goals; they build castles in the air and schemes on paper. Meanwhile, the skeptics, who work alongside them and share their meals and their taxes and their pleasures and their sufferings, quarrel with them only in theory. For the skeptics work away in their laboratories proving theories or disproving them. A theory proved no longer requires belief; if disproved, it no longer deserves belief.

It takes both believers and skeptics to make a civilization. For while they work together and need each other, they do not get along very well in theory. The believers are optimistic in a way which the skeptics sometimes consider fatuous. The skeptics tend to be pessimistic. Skeptics are practical and tough-minded, as William James put it; believers are more idealistic and tender-minded. The believers regard the skeptics as materialistic and shortsighted; the skeptics regard the believers as naïve and a bit balmy.

It is easy, of course, to identify belief and skepticism with religion and science respectively. But that would be a false polarity. Actually, both religion and psychiatry depend upon belief. But scientists are busy trying to prove or disprove what they believe; indeed, they almost make a religion of doing so, whereas in religion there is no compulsion to prove anything. In fact, this disinclination to ask proof seems more than a little remiss to the scientists, who put belief to a different purpose. But belief the scientists do have.

All other themes in human history, said Goethe, are subordinate in importance to the conflict of skepticism and faith. About love there seems to be no argument; in hope there seems to be relatively little interest at the moment. But faith – faith in the unseen, acceptance of the unprovable and the undemonstrated, belief in such tangibles as purpose, meaning, value – this faith is a mystic substance, indeed – one which is "unto the Jews a stumbling block, and unto the Greeks, foolishness", unto philosophers an enigma, unto scientists a sin.

Time was when I would have agreed with this statement of Goethe's, but as I have grown older, I am less inclined to distinguish sharply between skeptics and believers. It is an idea as old as Heraclitus and Empedocles in the general philosophical idea – that out of conflict comes concretion. Actually believers and skeptics should be the best of friends, and indeed – like Freud and Pfister – often are. They need each other. The believers, to keep their thinking straight, need the skeptics, and the skeptics, to keep up their spirits, need the believers. For even the most skeptical man has to fight down recurrent wisps of wistful belief, just as the staunchest believer must quell his occasional gnawing doubts.

No, I think the apparent conflict between belief and skepticism, between scientists and theologians, between clergymen and psychiatrists, is a pseudo conflict; these people are all on the same side. They are all united against a common enemy. They are people of minds, people of hearts, people who are trying to understand themselves and their fellow men and the world in which they all live. The real opposition to believers and skeptics – the common enemy, if you please – is something else. It derives from neither doubt nor belief. It is neither optimism nor pessimism. It is the most dreadful thing in the world.

The common enemy in opposition to believers and empiricists alike is the great, stolid, frivolous mass of public indifference and public ignorance. It is the complacency, the apathy, the hardness of heart which troubles neither to believe nor to doubt[6] – it simply does not care. The enemy is not some materialist, it is not some starry-eyed idealist – not even, as Norman Cousins[7] says, some powerful nation, or totalitarian power controlling world ideology. It is rather "the man whose only concern about the world is that it stay in one piece during his own lifetime . . . up to his hips in success . . . [who] not only believes in his own helplessness, but actually worships it [assuming] that there are mammoth forces at work which the individual cannot comprehend much less alter or direct".

Cardinal Stritch[8] once said, "For God's sake don't ever become complacent. The complacency of good people has been the cause of most of the troubles we have had throughout history whether between nations or within nations." But twenty-five hundred years before Cardinal Stritch said this, indifference of the masses was publicly deplored by Zoroaster; a little later Pericles and Socrates and Plato deplored it; the Hebrew prophets deplored it ("I will take away the stony heart out of your flesh"–Ezekiel 36 : 26); still later Jesus and John deplored it ("And he looked around at them with anger, grieved at their hardness of heart" – Mark 3 : 5a), and since then thousands more. Everyone who thinks, everyone who has any concern for human life, everyone who makes any observation of human suffering – and who can avoid them? – has been puzzled by this "certain blindness in human beings". It is not the presence or absence of belief, but the presence or absence of a moving concern for mankind – this is the issue.

Writes an American seer, "To feel emotion is at least to feel. The crime against life, the worst of all crimes, is not to feel. And there was never, perhaps, a civilization in which that crime, the crime of torpor, of lethargy, of apathy, the snake-like sin of coldness-at-the-heart, was commoner than in our technological civilization in which the emotionless emotions of adolescent boys are mass produced on television screens to do our feeling for us, and a woman's longing for her life is twisted, by singing commercials, into a longing for a new detergent, family size, which will keep her hands as innocent as though she had never lived. It is the modern painless death, this commercialized atrophy of the heart. None of us is safe from it."[9]

It is difficult to know just how to designate our common enemy for rhetorical purposes of a presentation such as this. Evil goes by one name in a course on philosophy, by another name in the chemical laboratory, or the law court, or the church lobby, or the seminar on ego psychology in the psychoanalytic institute. Evil is one thing in France and another thing in the Congo – or is it? Maybe the best word, after all, is "The Devil".

It is a curious thing that some people get around to believing in God by way of first discovering the Devil. Faced with the undeniable existence of the latter, they go on to find his adversary. Professor Cyril Joad[10] put it well for many of us when he declared, "For most of my life I have been a Rationalist . . . my name appearing regularly with that of Bertrand Russell as a derider of religion. . . . All things, I held, are theoretically discoverable by reason, and when the universe had ceased to be mysterious, God would go to the scrapheap of man's discarded superstitions. . . . Then came the war, and the existence of evil made its impact upon me as a positive and obtrusive fact. All my life it has been staring me in the face; now it hit me. . . .

"I am not seeking to pretend that this belated recognition of evil constituted . . . an argument." He goes on to say that he had been taught to believe that the evil in man was due to economic circumstances or other such explanations, that if certain things were only removed, good would prevail and virtue reign. "I have come flatly to disbelieve all this," he said. "I see now that evil is endemic in man, and the Christian doctrine of original sin expresses a deep and essential insight into human nature.

"Reject it and you fall victim, as so many of us whose minds have developed in an atmosphere of left-wing politics and rationalist philosophy have fallen victim, to a shallow optimism in regard to human nature which causes you to think that the millennium is just around the corner waiting to be introduced by a society of adequately psychoanalyzed, prosperous Communists. . . ."

Joad is correct; earlier Freudian tenets did permit facile and shallow meliorism: "There are no bad children – just bad parents." "Adult misbehavior only reflects the frustrations of childhood", etc. I myself have indulged in some of these pious evasions, and with a good deal of concurrence at the time. For they are not untruths, but half-truths. They emphasize, and properly, the redemptive possibilities, the saving grace of the "life-force", the power of love, the constructive and creative instinct. (I use these as synonyms.) But they neglect the intrinsic, endemic, destructive urge that cannot be successfully controlled so long as its very existence is denied.

A colleague, Dr. Bruno Bettelheim,[11] in a provocative article entitled "Ignored Lesson of Anne Frank", begins by raising the question of why so many millions of people let themselves be systematically executed in large masses without more uprising. The Frank family, he says, could have escaped and probably all members could have been saved. He reminds us that the play based on her diary ends by Anne implying her belief in the good in all men. He attacks this one-sided emphasis. "If all men are basically good," he says, "and if just going along with intimate family life means everything, then indeed we can all go along as usual and forget Auschwitz." "Anne Frank died," says Bettelheim, "because she couldn't get her family to believe in Auschwitz."

There are even some psychiatrists who still do not believe in Auschwitz – the Auschwitz element in every human being. They repeat sweetness-and-light platitudes and denounce belief in the innate destructive trend of mankind as superstitious, or as "an unnecessary postulate".

It is possible that Bettelheim leaves out one consideration, namely, intercommunication. One wonders why the millions of hounded, whipped Negroes in South Africa do not feel some common vibration and unite their efforts in revolt, regardless of the initial sacrifice. Think of the great herds of buffalo: at any moment – had some message gotten around – the buffalo could have turned and trampled their persecutors to death in minutes. Instead, the buffalo, not the hunters, were exterminated. But what impairs proper communication in adult human beings? Surely there are enough media. But sometimes these media need to become converted, or perhaps just convinced. Once this happens, once they lay the facts before the public in a sufficiently vivid and persistent way, some of the apparent public apathy vanishes. It was the press and radio, particularly two or three individuals working in these professions, who put in action the state hospital revolution in Kansas. They put before their readers and listeners the facts of neglect, abuse, and futile extravagance which went on behind the stone curtains of the state hospitals, until from the public there arose a saving remnant, a very large saving remnant indeed, which demanded that these things be changed.

We all heave a sigh of relief thinking that the original Auschwitz has disappeared; but there remain many others. I do not intend to catalog all the activities of the Devil. I realize that devil-seeking can be distorted into a defense for such horrible things as the Spanish Inquisition, the burning of witches, the destruction of the beautiful churches in England by the Cromwellians, and even the unspeakable campaigns of Hitler. I can understand how some people take refuge in the other extreme of "Hear no evil, see no evil, think no evil". But these latter people, who shake their heads over the zealots and the fanatics and the cynics, can be equally destructive with their Pollyannaism – as Bettelheim suggests.

Strangely, even some self-styled psychoanalysts, or former psychoanalysts, have tended to identify themselves with the sweetness-and-light position. They consider Freud "too biologically oriented", "too pessimistic", "too blind to human potentialities", "too independent of culture". Some of these exponents of renovated Freudianism have been almost savage in their attack upon the man who founded the very technique of personology inquiry which they exploit in the word "psychoanalysis". Within the ranks of the professionals, this has made a bitter and sad schism, and I am not sure how many non-professionals may have accepted some of the watered-down and distorted concepts of psychoanalysis under the impression that they were philosophically identical with those which the majority of us hold.

Some of Freud's followers, said Tillich,[12] ". . . have rejected the profound insight of Freud about existential libido and the death instinct, and in so doing they have reduced and cut off from Freud what made him and still makes him the most profound of all the depth psychologists . . ." (including Jung). And Robert Elliott[13] has added, "Religious people have been tempted to play footie with Jung because he makes *religious* noises, while Freud makes *atheist* noises. But I am convinced that Jung presents a viewpoint profoundly antithetical to a Biblical and Christian anthropology, in contrast to which Freud is practically an Old Testament man in the flesh."

The members of each generation find the world in a somewhat different stage of conflict. At one moment the good seems to be triumphant, and we are about to say that the world has grown much better, when our eye is caught by the threat of imminent self-destruction toward which the nations seem to be headed. Social improvement in one part of the world encourages us only so long as we keep our eyes away from South Africa, or the American prison system, or the arms race.

I do not mean by this to imply that the recognition of evil and good, or even the acceptance of our own responsibility for combating evil, is the beginning and end-all of religious sentiment. Nor would I agree that Einstein's thoughtful and humble admiration of the "illimitable superior spirit who reveals himself in the slight details we are able to see with our frail and feeble minds" quite fulfills it. Einstein[14] went on to say, "That deeply emotional conviction of the presence of a superior reasoning power, which is revealed in the incomprehensible universe, forms my idea of God."

Max Planck[15] went a little further: "Thus, we see ourselves governed all through life by a higher power, whose nature we shall never be able to define from the viewpoint of exact science. Yet, no one who thinks can ignore it. . . . The individual has no alternative but to fight bravely in the battle of life, and to bow in silent surrender to the will of a higher power which rules over him. For no man is born with a legal claim to happiness, success, and prosperity in life. We must, therefore, accept every favorable decision of providence, each single hour of happiness, as an unearned gift, one that imposes an obligation. The only thing that we may claim for our own with absolute assurance, the greatest good that no power in the world can take from us, and one that can give us more permanent happiness than anything else, is integrity of soul, which manifests itself in a conscientious performance of one's duty. And he whom good fortune has permitted to cooperate in the erection of the edifice of exact science will find his satisfaction and inner happiness, with our great German poet, in the knowledge that he has explored the explorable and quietly venerates the inexplorable."

These men I have quoted are not psychiatrists, but they are outstanding scientists trying to describe what they feel in the clumsy, inadequate terms of our common speech – feelings of humility and reverence before the facts of the universe. All scientists are occupied in the systematic scrutiny of small fragments of this universe, and unless they are devoid of any perspective, they are pervaded with a sense of its mystery and magnificence.

Some scientists experience such emotions upon certain occasions, recurrent but always effective. Perhaps these differ for each individual. For some saintly souls like Francis of Assisi, every incident of life provokes it. The starry heavens had this effect on the psalmist and upon the philosopher Kant and upon many others of us. Sitting by or talking with a dying patient always evokes it in me, and I think in most physicians, but no less the tears of joy in the eyes of a recovered patient and his relatives, and the experience of receiving so much undeserved gratitude.

This reverence for mystery, for vastness, for beauty, for inscrutable intelligence, for order and power – this is one component of the sentiment called religious. Some describe it as "the sensuous experience of God". There is more to the religious sentiment than reverence, even when reverence becomes actively expressed in worship. There is the matter of believing, of accepting the unprovable thing, the unlikely thing, the impossible thing – the miracle. Life itself is such a miracle. Perhaps evil, too, is a miracle – an unwanted one, but there, all the same.

And so, likewise, is the persistent determination to combat evil a miracle, the urge to allay suffering, to help others, to improve our world, to seek for the highest good for all living, to plan benefits for generations we shall never see, to reach out toward the unmanifest – and to note our mistakes, to repent our sins, and to try again. And, whether or not they declare belief in it, scientists as well as saints share this miracle, stiff-necked skeptics as well as worshippers. Both are impelled and sustained by it in their unending warfare against the common enemy.

NOTES

1. David McClelland, *Psychoanalysts and Religious Mysticism* (Wallingford, Pa.: Pendle Hill, 1959).

2. Whitehead reminds us that every science has its particular dogma. In terms of Webster's unabridged dictionary, dogma is "that which is held as an established opinion, especially a definite and authoritative tenet. Also . . . formulation of such tenets. . . ."

3. Heinrich Racker, "On Freud's Position Towards Religion", *American Imago*, 13 (1956), 12–121.

4. Seymour S Kety, "A Biologist Examines the Mind and Behavior", *Science*, 132 (December 3, 1960), 1861–1870.

5. Max Born, *Natural Philosophy of Cause and Chance* (Oxford: Oxford University Press, 1949).

6. E. B. Cherbonnier, in his beautiful long essay, *Hardness of Heart* (New York: Doubleday, 1955), lists the hidden gods of cynicism, the forms of idolatry which occupy the hardhearted. He includes nationalism, humanism, communism, phallicism, promiscuity, the glorification of money, and the various euphemisms such as frugality, shrewdness, and sound economy. Cherbonnier even lists existentialist despair, iconoclasm, and a so-called state of "adjustment" and "relatedness" toward which some psychiatrists are believed to steer their patients.

7. Norman Cousins, *In Place of Folly* (New York: Harper and Row, 1961).

8. Samuel Alphonsus Stritch, quoted by Gervase Brinkman in "Corrections Today, Problems and Prospects", Presidential Address to the 90th Congress of the American Correctional Association, Denver, Colo., 1960.

9. Archibald MacLeish, *Saturday Review*, 44 (Aug. 12, 1961), 24.

10. Cyril E. M. Joad, in *The Faith of Great Scientists*, a collection of "My Faith" articles from *The American Weekly* (New York: Hearst, 1950).

11. Bruno Bettelheim, "Ignored Lesson of Anne Frank", *Harper's*, 221 (November 1960), 45–50.

12. Paul Tillich, *Theology of Culture*, ed. R. C. Kimball (Oxford and New York: Oxford University Press, 1959).

13. Robert Elliott, *The Perkins School of Theology Journal*, 14 (Winter, 1960), 47.

14. Albert Einstein, in *The Universe and Dr. Einstein* by L. K. Barnett (New York: Sloan, 1948).

15. Max Planck, "The Meaning and Limits of Exact Science", *Science*, 110 (September 30, 1949), 319–327.

70 71 72 73 10 9 8 7 6 5 4 3 2 1